Contents

Preface *vii*

1 **Introduction to research**   1

Older methods of obtaining knowledge   2
The modern method of research   6
The role of theory   10
Construct and model   12
Distinction between the social sciences
and the natural sciences   14
What is research?   16
Types of research   18

2 **Educational research**   22

The nature of educational research   23
Definitions   26
Operational strategies in educational research   28
Problems in educational research   30
Evaluation of educational research   33
Classification of educational research   35

3 **Educational research: past and present**   41

Historical development of educational research   42
Modern educational research   47
The present position   51

4 Methods of educational research   53

Historical method of research   54
Descriptive method of research   57
Experimental method of research   67
A concluding statement   84

5 Tools of research in education   85

Tools and techniques in collecting data   86
Psychological tests   93

6 Some key statistical concepts in educational research   115

Normal distribution and the normal curve   117
Testing populations and large samples   124
Sampling from a population   127
Some other theoretical distributions   133
Non-parametric distributions and tests   140
Correlation regression   146

7 Educational research and the teacher   152

Research and the teacher   156
The role of the educator/researcher   159

8 Examples of some educational research   164

Glossary of educational research terms   178

Bibliography   192

Index   203

Preface

Since we started being involved in educational research, lecturing to educators and others connected with education and supervising research many years ago, we have become increasingly aware of a great gulf between educational research and practice, and between theory and practice. Very often the educational researcher and practitioner seem to exist in two completely different and somewhat antagonistic worlds, although they share a mutual common interest — education.

The gap between theory and practice seems, to some extent, to be based on the inability of both the practitioner and the researcher to put educational theory based on research findings into practice. For instance, the practitioner (i.e. the teacher) often complains that educational theory and research are either totally irrelevant to his/her work or completely incomprehensible. In other words, teachers are not often convinced of the functional value of research to the practice of their profession. This implies that they lack knowledge of research technology. On the other hand, the researcher frequently feels frustrated by the apparent lack of interest shown by teachers in the educational theories and research findings; and often reacts strongly to the suggestion that he/she is unaware of what goes on in the battlefield of the classroom.

In view of this antagonism between educational theory and practice, between the theoretician (the researcher) and the practitioner (the teacher) we have designed this book in an attempt to minimise this conflict. We believe that to some extent the gulf between the findings of educational research and the classroom pay off is more the result of misunderstanding in terms of linguistic communication than the result of working at cross-purposes. The language of many research reports tends to be a real barrier in the communicative process. A glance through the literature clearly shows that there are very few useful materials available to teachers which provide them with the framework needed to understand educational research, and place it in context.

Much of contemporary research does not require considerable knowledge of statistical terms, yet the practitioner is often unable to cope with this since his background/training is lacking in essential statistical technology and research methodology. Statistics, to many people, seems like another language — yet when one gets down to the bones of the research and its applicability to the teaching situation, a comprehensive knowledge of sophisticated and complex statistical techniques does not seem necessary. In much published research, statistical terms tend to unnecessarily camouflage useful work. Keeping this fact in mind we have structured this volume specially for teachers, teacher-in-training, undergraduate and postgraduate students in the social sciences (particularly education). The book is intended to help these audiences discern the relevant amongst the camouflage. It is important that readers and consumers of research data understand the terminology, the methodology and the strategy of systematic research, and be able to evaluate the published research reports that are found in professional publications. We append a glossary of educational research terms.

Teachers have long hoped that research would provide them with tools to solve classroom problems. No simple techniques have emerged so far, nor are likely to emerge because of the nature and process of the educative method. However, research can provide general principles and techniques that will help the teacher to deal effectively with many classroom problems.

Innovations in teaching methods, materials and curriculum have made educators, researchers and administrators acutely aware of the need for careful investigation to evaluate the new procedures and tools. The materials in this volume are expected to help them to examine more critically research reports and articles in order to judge their strengths and weaknesses.

In writing this book our intention is also to encourage practitioners (teachers) to view their role not merely in terms of consumers of research but also in terms of producers of research. This would entail being constantly evaluative of one's role and progress as educators, and attempting to advance the frontiers of educational research by being actively involved in it. An important message of this book is that research has an important role to play in the learning-teaching situation.

In designing the book we have also kept in mind the viewpoint and orientation of those who are entering the field of educational research for the first time. The book can serve as a primer for students of education who plan to conduct their own research. Thus, we hope that the materials will give teachers and students confidence and impetus to undertake modest research and to broaden and deepen their knowledge in this field.

The discussion emphasises understanding research and flexibility in conducting research. Experimental research has been given extensive treatment because of its wide use in the field of education. The importance of the theoretical framework has also been stressed.

Finally, we would like to express our thanks to our friends, who have read all or part of the manuscript and have made comments. They are not, of course, responsible for any faults which the reader may discover.

Gajendra K. Verma
Ruth M. Beard

1 Introduction to research

There is no universally accepted, inflexible meaning of research. In one instance, research may appear to be a simple exercise, while in another an extremely complex activity. It may take place in archives, laboratories or educational institutions; it may be the effort of a single individual or a group of researchers; it may contribute to human knowledge considerably or simply extend the frontiers of knowledge a little. But under whatever conditions research occurs, there is one element that seems common to most research activities; that element is contained in what has been described in the literature by the term *systematic study*. In this simple description the concept of research is ingrained as we will see in a moment.

The present day nature of research is much more difficult to describe because of the technological advancement. However, research as a human endeavour is characterised by its persistent and deliberate effort to extend our understanding about the world in which we live. We may, perhaps, call research a quest for knowledge. Research workers attempt to provide us with information that is reliable and that will be meaningful. For most of us the discovery of the means for curing cancer would be a meaningful extension of our existing knowledge. Thus, the impact that research can have upon human life cannot be over-estimated. Before discussing the nature and characteristics of research, its methodology and the types of research, let us briefly examine various approaches and methods which man has evolved in his search for knowledge in order to improve his pattern of life and thus to make it more comfortable and secure.

Older methods of obtaining knowledge

Historically, the emergence of research activities has been quite interesting and well defined. Throughout the period of written history, man has tried to obtain more knowledge about himself and his environment in order to improve the quality of human life. Even as early as Aristotle, research findings and empirical knowledge were used in the physical and biological sciences (Rummel, 1964). Research in the social sciences, which includes education, developed much more slowly, partly because the social sciences deal with those ideas and concepts which are less amenable to controlled evaluation, and partly because problems in the social sciences often involve the personal interests, values and emotions of researchers which tend to make investigations more complex (see chapter 2). However, an examination of the literature suggests that man's efforts to collect information, to analyse it, to put it together and to evaluate it have given great impetus to the development of research in all fields of human life.

The methods of obtaining plausible explanations to man's problems or queries have undergone considerable changes across the centuries. A consideration of the older methods of acquiring knowledge is necessary in understanding the gradual development of current research methods used in most disciplines. History tells us that when man's habitual method of dealing with problems failed to produce satisfactory results, he adopted crude trial and error methods in an effort to solve his problems. In this process of trying one thing after another, he was able to refine his knowledge seeking devices. Simple trial and error method may be regarded as the first method that man used in an effort to gain knowledge or find an acceptable solution to some of his problems.

In earlier centuries seeking help and advice from the medicine man, the priest or the king was quite a common and well established method of solving problems. Perhaps this reflects man's natural tendency to rely on the judgement of authorities when confronted with day-to-day problems. Even today, opinions of experts or those recognised as authorities in their disciplines are often sought and practised. For example, a teacher may turn to an educational psychologist to find the probable cause of pupils' truant behaviour. We also quote 'experts' of the past whether we accept their views or not. There are many practical situations in which one tends to seek the advice of someone who has had previous experience of a particular problem. A probationary teacher, for example, may take seriously the views of an experienced or knowledgeable colleague about classroom practice. It should be borne in mind that such advice from experts or authorities is sought on personal trust.

Generally speaking, experts are better informed in their field than other people because of their ability, training and experience. But there is also evidence that many expert opinions have been proved partly or completely wrong, particularly in the social sciences. Therefore, one should not accept, without a proper appraisal, a particular viewpoint for all time. In the Middle Ages an uncritical acceptance of authority was characteristic of the problem solving methods. There is no denying that authorities or experts are useful sources of gaining knowledge; however, opinion should not be accepted without critical evaluation. Sometimes two experts disagree about a particular issue (e.g. recent controversy about the determinants of intelligence, the nature-nurture issue); under these circumstances a more careful evaluation of both the arguments and evidence is necessary before placing any confidence in either proposition. Indeed, this kind of disagreement is more common in the social sciences, including education, than in the natural sciences because of the complexity of social phenomena.

In some societies certain traditions and customs are so predominant that people accept elements of their culture without questioning. It may be argued that such acceptance of approved modes of behaviour is often necessary because life is too short to question *all* things. Quite often people follow the traditions of their culture in order to answer many social, political and educational questions. For example, many educational practices have a long history, and teachers seem to accept them without critical scrutiny. But it should not be assumed that traditions and opinions of authorities are free from error and bias. Perhaps it can be said that the use of established practices is necessary as a guide for future actions, since it will be impossible to verify all the propositions of the past.

In spite of the weaknesses of authority and tradition as a source of reliable information, complete rejection of such a source of gleaning knowledge is imprudent. It is virtually impossible for each individual, each social group or each generation to start from scratch in order to generate ideas or verify existing knowledge. On the other hand, an uncritical acceptance of authoritative opinion, as prevalent in the earlier centuries, can also hinder social, educational and personal progress. In the *Structure of Scientific Revolutions*, Kuhn has pointed out the ways in which scientific knowledge is acquired and the process by which an older theory is replaced by an incompatible new one. According to the analysis of Kuhn, scientists are involved in 'normal science' which is research based upon past scientific achievements and that provides the foundations for its further practice.

Personal experience is another source of seeking solutions to one's problems. In the earliest civilisations, man gradually began to feel that the operations of the forces of Nature were not as capricious as he had been led to believe by those in authority. He also began to perceive an orderliness in nature and certain cause-effect relationships. But his observations lacked any logical explanations for all of the observed relationships in the environment. Nevertheless, reliance on personal experience to understand the operations of natural forces challenged the sanction of vested authority, and this represented an important step in the direction of 'scientific' enquiry.

In our everyday life we tend to utilise our personal experience to find solutions to many of our problems. A great deal of information which is passed from one generation to another is the outcome of man's experience. A teacher may recall his experience to ascertain the most effective way of motivating his pupils to learn. Most of us would agree that the ability to gain from past experience is an important element of an individual's adaptation to his present situation which helps him to make progress in society.

Reliance upon personal experience as a means of acquiring knowledge also has its limitations. If one uses personal experience uncritically it may lead to incorrect conclusions. Another pitfall of experience as a source of information is that the investigator may over-generalise on the basis of incomplete evidence. He may even ignore complex factors operating at the time of his observations or allow his feelings and prejudices to influence both his observations and conclusions. Psychological research has shown that we tend to distort evidence in order to support our beliefs, values and attitudes. For example, two observers studying the same situation at the same time could make different portrayals.

Some of the dangers in appealing to personal experience have been summarised by Van Dalen (1966): A researcher may,

> (i) omit evidence that does not agree with his opinion, (ii) use measuring instruments that require many subjective estimates, (iii) establish a belief on insufficient evidence, (iv) fail to observe significant factors relating to a specific situation, or (v) draw improper conclusions or inferences owing to personal prejudices.

Although reliance on personal experience as a source of knowledge has obvious limitations, its usefulness in decision making cannot be denied. However, great care must be exercised when turning to experience in the search for reliable knowledge.

It was only when man began to think systematically in his search for reliable knowledge that the era of logic began. The first systematic approach to reasoning, attributed to Aristotle and his followers, was the deductive method. This method of acquiring knowledge involves a thinking process in which one proceeds from broad assumption to specific statements using prescribed rules of logic. In other words,

4

it is a system in which one first starts with a recognition of a universal law and applies it to the interpretation of particular phenomena. The process operates through a series of statements called *syllogism* which attempts to establish a logical relationship between a major premise, a minor premise and a conclusion. An example of syllogistic reasoning is:

Human beings cannot survive without oxygen (major premise)
Eskimos are human beings (minor premise)
Therefore, Eskimos cannot survive without oxygen (conclusion)

As can be seen from the above example, the major premise is a self-evident assumption which is a universal truth; the minor premise is a particular case related to the major premise. Having established a logical relationship between the two premises one can draw a conclusion which is also true.

Although the deductive reasoning method has made a significant contribution to the development of modern research methods, it has a number of weaknesses. The acceptance of false major premises based on unreliable evidence can lead to error. Therefore, one must begin with those premises which are universally true. Another limitation of this method is that the universal truth of many statements dealing with scientific phenomena cannot be established. The third shortcoming is that deductive methods can show new relationships on the basis of facts which are already established, but may not provide knowledge as a source of new truth.

In spite of its limitations, the method of deductive reasoning has survived so far as a valuable tool in the research process. It is used in everyday life to solve a number of problems. An educational psychologist uses this method when searching among evidence and symptoms to find out the precise cause of a pupil's truant behaviour. He selects the materials which seemed to be fragmented at first, and then he puts the pieces of evidence together in such a way that they logically yield a conclusion. In the learning-teaching situation this method has made some contribution in bridging the gap between educational theory and educational practice.

As the weaknesses of the classic deductive method became evident to scientists, particularly its inability to verify the truth of the major premise, new methods of acquiring knowledge were sought. Francis Bacon (1561–1626) advocated a new approach which came to be known as the inductive method. This process required the application of direct observation of phenomena, arriving at a conclusion through evidence by observing many cases. This approach of direct observations eliminated some of the flaws in deductive thinking. Bacon suggested that one should personally observe the phenomena carefully

5

without any preconceived ideas, collect the facts and use these as a basis for making generalisations.

Unfortunately the inductive method did not provide a completely satisfactory system for the solution of many problems. It is almost impossible to observe all the cases of a given phenomenon according to the Baconian system. In order to be absolutely certain of an induction conclusion, the investigator must observe all the examples of a given class of objects or events. This is known as perfect induction. In real life situations it would not be feasible because of the time and effort involved. For example, it would not be possible for a researcher to observe the behaviour of all the secondary school pupils in Britain who are left-handed. In practice, a researcher can observe only a small group of pupils, and then he has to draw conclusions concerning all left-handed children attending secondary schools in Britain. This is an example of imperfect induction. It is important to remember that the size of the samples selected for observation and the extent to which they are representative of the entire group limits the degree to which the conclusions are trustworthy (see the section on 'sampling' in chapter 5). The conclusion drawn on the basis of imperfect induction does not necessarily provide an absolute truth; it can provide useful and reliable information (in varying degrees of probability) upon which decisions for action can be made. In social sciences the inductive method can rarely lead to generalisations and theories.

The modern method of research

The exclusive use of inductive reasoning generated a series of unrelated and isolated bits of information which lacked a specific orientation. Because of the lack of unity in the collection of facts it did little to advance the boundaries of knowledge. It was also recognised by scientists that many problems could not be solved by the induction technique alone. It was natural, therefore, that they would try to integrate the relevant aspects of the inductive and deductive methods into a more useful method of acquiring reliable and significant knowledge. Darwin's theory of evolution is a product of the application of the inductive-deductive method which is now frequently used in scientific research. His observations of animal life failed to give him a satisfactory answer about man's development. His reading of Thomas Malthus' *Essay on Population* about the concept of the struggle for existence led him to assume that natural selection explains the origin of the different species of animals. This hypothesis provided him with the necessary orientation to pursue his investigations. He proceeded to test this

6

hypothesis by making deductions from it. He collected the facts which confirmed the hypothesis that biological change in the process of natural selection, in which unfavourable variations were destroyed and favourable variations survived resulted in the evolution of new species. This synthesis of both inductive and deductive reasoning has provided scientists with a method which is now recognised as an example of 'the scientific' approach in research.

We have described the inductive-deductive method under the heading 'The modern method of research' which is often called 'The scientific method'. The reason for using the term 'the modern method of research' is that the scientific method has several meanings, and it includes the elements of an inductive-deductive process which are applied to both the natural sciences and the social sciences. It is often defined as 'the systematic and refined use of specialised tools and procedures to obtain a more adequate solution to a problem than would be possible by less discriminating means' (Rummel, 1964). This method frequently implies hypothesis, data, testing, conclusion, application or some such process. It sometimes refers to the method of controlled experiment, and as far as possible it stresses a quantitative approach. Thus, measurement forms an important element of scientific research. 'Whatever exists at all exists in some amount', (p.16) as put forward forcefully by Thorndike (1918), implies that the application of this method is valid for the social sciences as well as chemistry, physics and biology. It is true that what has been broadly called the scientific method has proved valuable in the study of natural sciences, and has also helped social scientists to gain insight into many of the problems. However, the quantitative is not the only knowledge of reality, and all things do not exist in quantity. There are other research techniques to explore reality such as Piaget's (1926; 1932) investigation of the beginnings of a child's concepts. Further, there are many behaviours and events that cannot be measured — appreciation of music, an imitative gesture, and so on. In view of the above observations, we have deliberately called this section 'The modern method of research'.

Research methods do not seem to be isolated; they overlap. The investigator needs to reflect on his own thinking when using any systematic research method for obtaining reliable knowledge or getting at the 'truth'. Dewey (1933) gave the so-called scientific method an impetus of major importance in modern times. He described the five main stages that thought passes through when man attempts to acquire new knowledge by this means:

1 Recognition and definition of the problem which needs to be solved;
2 Observations, collection and classification of data which is considered to be relevant to the problem;

3 Formulation of a tentative hypothesis concerning these observations or the phenomena;
4 Verification of this hypothesis against all the obtained facts — this may involve the collection of additional/new data and the modification of the original hypothesis;
5 Formulation of a conclusion/conclusions in terms of general principles concerning the problem or the phenomena.

While the above pattern seems to be a useful guide in the development and implementation of some methods of research, the researcher does not always follow these steps in a rigid way. In a practical situation, his thinking frequently moves to and fro across these basic steps. The exact formulation of research strategy varies from investigator to investigator and according to the nature of research. Thus, the modern method of acquiring knowledge is more flexible than the older methods described earlier in this chapter. Briefly, the modern method of obtaining sound information (knowledge) is simply a systematic way of reasoning, whereby observations or experiments are done, hypotheses are put forward and tested, and if necessary amendments are made to the original hypothesis or hypotheses in the light of evidence obtained, and then conclusions are drawn. As pointed out earlier, not many researchers follow these steps rigidly in the conduct of their research which merely suggests that the modern method has become closely bound up with the values, attitudes and perceptions of the researcher. Scientific knowledge exists within a particular framework of expectation; the work of Kuhn challenged the existing belief that science is a rational and objective enquiry (Kuhn, 1970). Another point to remember is that there are many questions, particularly in the social sciences, which cannot be answered by the scientific method. Some people even suggest that each discipline requires a different method of investigation. Other scholars are of the opinion that the scientific method is simply a general method which gets modified in various ways to suit the purposes of different disciplines. Although controversy exists with regard to the nature and use of 'the scientific' method, it is important to keep in mind that this method represents one way of describing and studying the world around us and that there are various other legitimate approaches which can be adopted.

There are other points which must be made here. Sometimes the planning of a research programme may include a great deal of exploratory work which is often intuitive or speculative, and at times fragmented. Although the investigator has to define the problem in a precise manner at some stage, his concepts and ideas might initially be vague and ill-defined. He may observe and study the situations

8

and even collect some preliminary data in order to establish the relevance of his vaguely conceived ideas. At this point in the research process his intuition, speculation, hunch or intelligent guess becomes necessary for the formulation of a clearly defined problem. It should be emphasised that problem recognition is one of the most difficult as well as crucial parts of the research process.

A clearly defined problem may generate one or several hypotheses. The hypothesis must be stated clearly in order to test its logical or empirical consequences. The use of hypothesis may help an investigation from becoming too broad in scope or disorderly in construction. Since an hypothesis is a kind of anticipated solution to the problem being sought by research it must be adequate and take in all the requirements of the situation. Writing about the need for carefully formulated hypotheses Van Dalen (1966) states that 'No scientific undertaking can proceed effectively without well-conceived hypotheses . . . Without hypotheses, research is unfocused, haphazard and accidental' (p.457). Hypotheses are important because they tell the researcher what should be done to get an answer, and how it should be done. Thus, the focussing of research towards testing specific hypotheses guides the researcher to arrive at valid conclusions.

Another reason for establishing carefully formulated hypotheses is that at some stage the investigator has to examine relationships and trends between the variables stated by the hypothesis and hence he can 'test' these relationships. Kerlinger (1973) remarks, 'The scientist cannot tell positive from negative evidence unless he uses hypotheses' (p.26). Hypotheses are the core of research activity and therefore they should not be based upon wild speculation.

It should be noted that many hypotheses, particularly in behavioural research, cannot be tested directly because they may deal with abstractions. The investigator must choose a sample of behaviour that can be tested or observed directly. This sample of observable behaviours may then be evaluated in terms of its consistency or inconsistency with the formulated hypothesis. On the basis of obtained evidence the researcher may deduce the logical consequences of the hypothesis. For example, a research worker might formulate a hypothesis that mixed ability teaching provides greater intellectual stimulation for less able children than if taught in a streamed class. Two classes can be carefully selected − one containing mixed ability pupils and the other with less able pupils. A test of scholastic achievement can be administered at the end of the school academic year to both the groups. If the hypothesis were true, less able children in the mixed ability group would show significantly higher achievement scores as compared with those less able children who were taught in a segregated class. Thus, the researcher draws the consequences of the hypothesis.

9

The role of theory

At this point in the discussion of 'the modern method' of research some statements about the role of theory in research would be appropriate. As we have seen, the researcher collects many facts to test his hypotheses. In order to put the facts into some kind of coherent and meaningful pattern he must organise and classify the data. It is also necessary to identify and explain relevant relationships between the facts. In other words, the researcher must produce a concept or build a theoretical structure that can explain facts and the relationships between them. Thus, the theory is one of the fundamental concepts in systematic modern research, although theories can range from the very simple to the extremely complicated. In its simplest form it may mean a speculation, a hunch or an idea. For example, a teacher concerned with practical problems in the classroom has some idea about the best method of teaching humanities. A more complicated theory may be a synthesis of facts, an analysis of a set of variables to demonstrate their relationships with one another, or a plausible general principle to explain and predict certain phenomena. Examples of such theories may include studies which attempt to explain pupils' motivation, their learning patterns or means of keeping their attention, which concerns people of all ages.

The term theory has a multiplicity of meanings (Snow, 1973). In social sciences, theories usually imply a set of statements describing and explaining the relationship between human behaviour and the factors that affect or explain it. Best (1970) writes that 'a theory establishes a cause-effect relationship between variables with the purpose of explaining and predicting phenomena' (p.6). This definition would be of questionable validity in the social sciences, including education, where it is notoriously difficult to establish cause and effect relationships. However, the role of theory as a framework for research is not in dispute. The importance of theory is to help the investigator summarise previous information and guide his future course of action. Sometimes the formulation of a theory may indicate missing ideas or links and the kinds of additional data required. Thus, a theory is an essential tool of research in stimulating the advancement of knowledge still further.

Generally speaking, good theories are built upon facts or evidence and not on mere speculation. The work of most natural and social scientists can be related to the use or construction of theories of some kind. But the distinction can be made in at least two ways. Those whose work is primarily concerned with the development of theories are often called rationalists (Travers, 1978); those who focus their attention on the collection of data or facts are often referred to

10

empiricists. Skinner's (1959) work, for example, can be described as an empirically oriented approach to research. In practice, however, most scientists are both rationalists and empiricists. Another broad distinction is the work of those researchers who spend a great deal of time in the formulation of theories and may not be concerned with their practical application; and those who are primarily concerned with the application of new knowledge for the solution of everyday problems. However, even in pure research a theory, once established, may suggest many applications of practical value.

It is often said that social scientists have been less successful than natural scientists in developing theoretical ideas that can be proved to be true. Critics often state that Freud's theoretical terms or concepts such as Ego, Id and Super-ego are as theoretical and abstract today as they were when he first proposed their use. There is no denying that many aspects of human behaviour cannot be observed directly. But it is important to remember that theoretical terms such as attitudes, beliefs, interests, creativity and many others have been constructed to explain why an individual behaves in a particular way. The explanation of *why* usually precipitates the use of theoretical constructs. Also, in behavioural sciences a combination of different theoretical constructs can be used to explain the particular behaviour. For example, the concept of social class is often defined in such a way that it embraces aspects of social interaction, norms and values. The phenomena of reality do not belong to any particular discipline. A study of human behaviour is not only the concern of the psychologist, but also of the philosopher, the sociologist, the physician and the political scientist. Although there is some disagreement about the methods for theory development, there seems to be a general acceptance with regard to the practical value of theory in extending the existing body of knowledge.

As mentioned earlier, theories consist of a number of statements about variables and about the relationships between variables. Those statements or propositions which are supported by a good deal of scientific evidence are referred to as laws. In social sciences, laws are rarely formulated, although even laws need to be modified if new evidence is not consistent with the law. In other words, in spite of the practical value of a good theory in research, the investigator must be prepared to amend or abandon it if and when new evidence is obtained which is not consistent with the original theory.

Sometimes the formulation of a theory may suggest whether additional facts are required and further research is needed. For example, a theory concerning inter-ethnic perception amongst urban school pupils can be relevant, but the facts may also indicate that the theory has not been tested to hold true for rural school pupils. The researcher

11

must then decide whether to collect additional data and if so what kinds of questions may require further attention.

Many teachers are often suspicious of theories developed by educational researchers. They seek practical 'advice' and 'guidance' for the solution of classroom problems. Teachers want to know *why* a child is poorly motivated rather than *what* the relations are among various types of behaviour. They, also, have their views, ideas or 'theories' that are based on many years of experience or observation. Their main concern, however, is with practicalities, that is, with techniques for solving specific current problems in the context of things as they are, not as they might be if certain changes were made. However, the basic difference between the theory of the scientist and that of the teacher is in the methods of deriving or implying theoretical terms. The scientist constructs his theory involving a combination of inductive and deductive reasoning described earlier in this chapter. Such research usually involves well defined questions and hypotheses. The researcher tries to establish relationships between isolated facts by supplying missing information, and to keep manipulating ideas until he is able to develop a theoretical framework that can explain facts and inter-relationships among them in a meaningful and precise way. Thus, the product of all research in the social sciences is a set of conclusions that indicate or imply theoretical terms. The teacher, on the other hand, develops his theories primarily from his observations which are often unsystematic. Such 'theories' are not based upon rigorous analysis of the inter-relationships between the fragmented facts. One of the advantages of the teacher's theories however, is that they are easily communicated to other professional colleagues in layman's terminology. It is true to say that many educational practices and policies are based on teachers' judgements. There is the need to analyse the gap between the teacher's 'theories' and the researcher's contribution to the solution of educational problems. Given this reasonable aspiration educational theories would acquire scientific status before long.

Construct and model

The term 'construct' is often used in the social sciences. At times, many unobservable internal processes may be of interest to the social scientist. Such processes as 'anxiety' or 'creativity' cannot be directly observed, although their effects can be manifested in an individual's behaviour. These unobservable internal processes are referred to as hypothetical constructs. This implies that the term 'construct' is a construction of the social scientist's imagination which helps him to understand the underlying mechanisms of an individual's thought and behaviour. For example, many theories of learning refer to a motivational factor in human behaviour. Motivation is not directly observable — it is a theoretical term — and hence social scientists prefer to say that the term motivation refers to a construct. Thus, constructs are used to provide a plausible explanation of the consistency of human behaviour. It should be mentioned that hypothetical constructs are used both by natural scientists and social scientists.

The question can be raised whether anything useful is gained by including the construct to an understanding of human behaviour. The use of constructs help the researcher to explain a large number of different human behaviours at various ages in a variety of situations, and therefore, its utility is not of questionable validity by many social scientists.

Another term frequently used by both natural and social scientists is *model*. This means a close representation of certain aspects of complex phenomena used in order to gain insights into the phenomena that scientists wish to explain. It has been pointed out that models are essentially analogies (Chapanis, 1961). For example, a teacher can help his pupils to conceptualise the earth by showing them a globe with countries, continents, mountains and oceans marked on it in different colours. Thus, the globe is a convenient model representing the important features of the earth in a way that can be easily understood by pupils. A replica model looks like the real object, or thing e.g. miniature plastic toys. Models may also be symbolic. An example of a symbolic model is an engineer's plan for a house construction. The model representing the building quite accurately helps the contractor to produce the house from the plans. In the field of education Piaget's model of the intellect would seem to be a good example.

Simulation, one of the procedures used by behavioural scientists for the development of ideas within the context of discovery, is based on the idea of a 'model'. The use of models is quite common in the teaching-learning situation. Models may consist of words, mathematical symbols, pictures or physical objects, and can be very useful in thinking about complex phenomena. A model can provide a very simple representation of quite complex events and make them more intelligible.

A model may contain certain facts which are not in accordance with reality. On the other hand, a theory is developed to describe the facts and relationships among them, and any facts that are inconsistent with the theory invalidate the theory. Another distinction between models and theories is that models are evaluated in terms of their usefulness, and theories in terms of their testability and capacity to explain and predict. Models are simply tools that are used in the construction of theories.

Distinction between the social sciences and the natural sciences

Research in the social sciences is becoming an important activity in most societies. The fundamental goal of research seems to be to attain accurate explanations and predictions of human behaviour. Some people believe that it will be impossible to achieve this goal. Although the social sciences have not attained the same 'scientific' status as the natural sciences (in terms of explanation, control and prediction) a great deal of progress has been made in the systematic study of human behaviour since the beginning of this century. Such knowledge of human behaviour has provided the basis for a variety of social technologies. Few would deny that the need for such knowledge is increasing as societies are becoming more complex. It would seem that the importance of research in the social sciences such as education, anthropology, economics and social psychology cannot easily be overestimated.

Most people would agree that the greatest obstacle to progress in the social sciences is the extreme complexity of human behaviour. It is much more difficult to develop sound theories of human behaviour than it is to develop theories that predict events in the physical sciences. Similarly, in the field of psychology, it is far more difficult to understand and explain the development of an individual's personality or the processes involved in human thought and problem solving than the forces operating in physics and chemistry. In the natural sciences, rigorous controls of systematic observation and analysis are often applied, whereas such control is almost impossible with human subjects.

One of the beliefs surrounding social scientists is that they have a set approach to research, whether it is an experiment, a survey, or an in-depth interview with a few cases. Their conviction that a particular method is superior to all others for most problems hardly seems to be based on rational grounds. Such a strategy may lead to the use of methods inappropriate to a given problem.

Despite the difficulties outlined above, the social sciences have made a significant contribution to our understanding of the society in which we live. Let us now briefly examine the crucial differences between the two groups of sciences.

1 In social sciences, many researchers deal with events or occurrences which are not repeatable. Historical and many descriptive

studies (see chapter 4) for example, are concerned with unique and non-repeatable matter. Also, there are many social phenomena or events which cannot be observed directly. For example, an individual's past experience cannot be observed directly; the researcher has to rely upon written information or a person's recall of past events. It may be possible to assess a child's reading level and vocabulary but it will be difficult to determine his motives or the intensity of his feelings objectively. On the other hand a pathologist can objectively test a blood sample, and his findings can easily be reproduced by other pathologists.

2 In social sciences, it is impossible to control the factor or factors being studied. Because of this difficulty laws are rarely formulated in the social sciences. For example, in a classroom situation there are a very few factors which can be identified and controlled (e.g. age, sex and height of pupils), others can be identified but not controlled (e.g. hobbies), and many other significant factors can neither be identified nor controlled. The natural scientist is rarely confronted with the same kind of problem.

3 In most cases, the natural scientist has to deal with a limited number of variables that are amenable to manipulation and precise measurements. The social scientist, on the other hand, may have to deal with a large number of variables simultaneously in order to explain phenomena satisfactorily. Another difficulty for the social scientist is the complex nature of variables such as temperament, attitude, motivational and personality characteristics which are not only difficult to assess but they interact in subtle ways.

4 In social sciences it is difficult to make wide generalisations, because no two individuals are exactly alike in feelings, drives or emotions. What may be a reasonable explanation for one may be irrelevant for another. Furthermore, no one person is normally consistent from one situation to another because of the experience gained. For example, if a student took psychological tests for the second time his behaviour would not be quite the same as one who had not taken the tests previously. His response is likely to be influenced by the interaction with various elements in his environment. In the natural sciences it is often possible to repeat the situation, without prejudicing the outcome.

5 The behaviour of an individual is influenced by the research process itself. The knowledge of being involved in an investigation makes an individual conscious that his behaviour is being observed or studied, and this can affect his response to the situation. The natural scientist does not need to consider the motives or feelings of planets etc.

6 In social sciences the researcher's interests, background, ability, prejudices, attitudes and values are likely to determine what he observes and the way he interprets his observations. In the natural sciences, however, this situation is less likely to occur.

7 In natural sciences complex constructs are defined in operational terms whereas the social sciences have been limited by a lack of adequate definitions. Many human characteristics (e.g. anxiety, hostility, motivation) are not directly observable. As constructs they can only be postulated, and since they cannot be seen or felt they can only be inferred on the basis of test scores. Furthermore, there is poverty of tools or instruments for measurement in the social sciences which makes it more difficult to describe many of the constructs. It has already been mentioned earlier that an understanding of human behaviour is complicated by the large number of variables acting independently and interacting in a complex way.

Although there are difficulties in formulating theories of human behaviour, the problems may not be insoluble. It must be stressed, however, that the researcher working in the field of social sciences must exercise great caution in making generalisations from his studies. There is a need to adopt a research strategy incorporating qualitative judgements and quantitative measurements. (For a detailed discussion see chapters 5 and 6). By using a variety of techniques or tools the social scientist may be able to generate sound theories to explain human behaviour.

Despite the limitations, there has been a great deal of advancement in the social research technology. Still, there are many crucial social, educational and political questions which can only be answered by further development and refinement of research methods.

What is research?

At this stage it seems appropriate to ask the question, 'what is research?'. As pointed out at the outset of this chapter, the word research does not have the same meaning in all academic disciplines because of its diverse and pervasive activities. There is some agreement, however, about the general nature of research. A few randomly selected definitions from the literature might provide an answer to what is meant by research.

Encyclopaedia of the Social Sciences (1934) offers the following definition:

16

. . . manipulation of things, concepts or symbols for the purpose of generalising and to extend, correct or verify knowledge, whether that knowledge aids in the construction of a theory or in the practice of an art. The mechanic or physician is a research worker only when he attempts to generalise about all automobiles or all patients in a given class.
(pp.330–4)

It suggests that research is an intensive activity which involves the discovery of new information or relationships with a view to generalising the outcome of analyses.

In considering a distinction between the terms scientific method and research, Best (1970) states:

Research is a more systematic activity directed toward discovery and the development of an organised body of knowledge. It is based on critical analysis of hypothetical propositions for the purpose of establishing cause-effect relationships, which must be tested against objective reality.
(p.9)

Given the above dimensions to the definition of research one becomes aware of the rigorous standards required in carrying out research.

A broader definition of research has been proposed by Wise, Nordberg and Reitz (1967):

. . . it is characteristically and inevitably a systematic inquiry for verified knowledge. In that simple description is implied the whole syntax of research.

This perspective implies that systematic enquiry constitutes the essential nature of research. The question can be raised whether this systematic enquiry is the only requirement of research in the sense in which the term is used in both the natural and social sciences. If so, could we give the name research to an enquiry into the number of hours per week that a certain class spends in reading? The answer would normally be in the negative since this kind of information can easily be ascertained. Research is an organised activity which requires the investigator to go deeper into existing knowledge. Furthermore, an investigation must involve the scientific approach that has been described in the earlier section under the heading 'modern method of research' to be designated as research. Although research may take place in different settings (e.g. laboratory, classroom, archives), at different levels (e.g. local, national, international) and may utilise different methods (e.g. experiments, tests, observations, interviews), research is universally a thorough and systematic search for trustworthy and meaningful knowledge.

Some people who have a superficial concept of research describe it as activities that involve 'review of the literature' or 'compilations of existing knowledge'. There are others who regard only the experimental design as scientific research. Some writers on this topic have highlighted one or more characteristics of research while others have minimised the focus on them. Thus, opinions seem to differ regarding the meaning of research.

It would seem useful to briefly mention some of the characteristics of research in order to clarify its methodology. Research is an organised and deliberate effort to collect new information or utilise existing information for a specific and new purpose. It is directed towards seeking answers to worthwhile, fairly important and fundamental questions through the application of sound and acceptable methods. The researcher may use diverse methods for the collection of data (see chapter 5) in order to answer the question. Research is logical and objective, using every possible test to validate the methods employed, the data collected and the conclusions reached. Although absolute objectivity is impossible, the researcher must try to eliminate personal feeling and bias in the analysis of data. The final outcome of research contributes in some meaningful way to the gaining of new knowledge and a better appreciation of the issues concerned.

Before concluding this section it must be mentioned that research has greatly expanded the scope of its activities since the beginning of this century. Today it would be difficult to identify any aspect of human life which has not been affected by research technology. Sometimes information obtained from research may be somewhat unsystematic and vague which does not help in reducing man's areas of ignorance. However, research has attained a great degree of respectability amongst educators, politicians, and business men who often turn to researchers seeking reliable information for making decisions. In fact, we live in a research oriented world.

Types of research

Research has been classified in various ways, e.g. by method (see chapter 4), by area of academic discipline (sociological, psychological, statistical among others), by the type of data collection procedure (see chapter 5) or by purpose. There has been considerable controversy among scientists as to which type of research is of most value. However, if we define science in a broad sense it is possible to produce a taxonomy of types of research. From the various combinations available in the literature the following four classifications have been identified, although these labels do not represent discrete categories. It should also be pointed out that classification of educational research activities (see chapter 2) produces a similar framework although there are certain variations:

1 Pure or basic research
2 Applied or field research
3 Action research
4 Evaluation research

The typology has the advantage of highlighting certain crucial differences between research that is oriented to the development of theory and research designed to solve practical problems. It also points out the degree to which each type emphasises precision and control as compared to reality.

Pure or basic research

This type of research is typically oriented towards the development of theories by discovering broad generalisations or principles. It has drawn its pattern and initiative from the physical sciences emphasising a rigorous, structured type of analysis. The main purpose of 'pure' or 'basic' research is to discover facts which are fundamental and important in the sense that their discovery will extend the boundaries of human knowledge. It is not necessarily immediately useful to an individual or group. This kind of research is usually carried out in a laboratory or controlled situation which implies that control and precision are maintained at the cost of reality. Many studies use animal subjects because they are more concerned with fundamental principles of behaviour than with the application of the findings to human problems. This type of research has been primarily the activity of psychologists. In recent years most learning theories have been questioned on the grounds that studies were conducted in a controlled situation with animals as subjects and therefore the findings cannot be directly applied to human problems. However, the findings of many basic psychological research studies have been applied to educational problems. It is true to say that the findings from such work may take some time before they are brought into prominence or become part of the general stock of knowledge.

Applied or field research

This type of research is concerned primarily with the application of new knowledge for the solution of day-to-day problems. Although applied or field research has some of the characteristics of pure research (e.g. the use of sampling techniques, inferences about the target population) its purpose is to improve a process by testing theoretical constructs in actual situations. Most educational research is applied research, for it aims at establishing generalisations about teaching-learning situations (see chapter 2). As one would expect, control is often sacrificed in field research in order to conduct the enquiry in a setting similar to that in which the findings are applied.

It should be mentioned that applied research also utilises experimental techniques, and hence it is difficult to make a clear distinction between basic and applied research. However, applied research needs to be conducted in order to determine how various theories operate in the actual situation. The Schools Council's Humanities Curriculum Project (Schools Council, 1970) in Britain is a good example of applied research. Although the Project's aim was founded on psychological principles of learning, it was not concerned primarily with the development and testing of learning theories, but with the development and testing of specific methods and materials for teaching humanities. The emphasis in this study was upon direct application of the research findings to classroom situations (Verma, 1980).

Action research

The term 'action research' was first introduced in the fields of social psychology and education. It is a type of applied social research differing from other types in the immediacy of the researcher's involvement in the action process.

Action research is more concerned with the immediate application rather than the development of theory. It focusses on a specific problem in a particular setting. In other words, its findings are usually judged in terms of their applicability in a specific situation. Action research is similar to applied research in many ways but the fundamental difference is that applied research allows generalisations of its results. Furthermore, applied research usually involves a large number of cases for studies whereas action research can be conducted in a modest way by using a very small sample (e.g. a single classroom).

In recent years action research has generated a great deal of interest in the field of education. Corey (1953) believes that limiting educational research to professional researchers alone is to take a narrow view of the educator's role. He asserts that classroom teachers can be better decision makers and effective practitioners if they are encouraged to conduct action research. (See chapter 2 for further discussion.) For example, if it is proposed to alter the organisation of a school and its curriculum, it is most useful to have on the staff one or more researchers who can monitor the effects of the changes.

In concluding this section it should be pointed out that action research also uses 'scientific' methods to real life problems that are obviously far better than relying on personal experience which often guides decisions in the field of education.

Evaluation research

The term 'evaluation research' is often used to refer to the systematic procedures which are adopted to collect and process data concerning the effectiveness of a particular programme. For example, a teaching programme can be evaluated at several stages. If evaluation is carried out at intermediate stages to implement changes in the programme, it is called process or formative evaluation. Evaluation at the completion of the planned programme is known as summative evaluation.

Evaluation research has been widely performed in the last two decades. Many social action programmes (such as educational disadvantage, teaching about race relations, ethnic discrimination) and curriculum innovations have adopted this type of research in order to monitor the effectiveness of such programmes. Evaluation research highlights the symbols of measurement and scientific neutrality but attempts to minimise the influence of the behavioural science prospective. Evaluation research of the summative type is often used to assess change programmes.

In concluding this discussion it is important to mention that there are several ways in which the term 'research' is currently used. It may be conducted at various levels of complexity. Meaningful and acceptable research may even be of the simple descriptive fact finding type. But under whatever conditions research is undertaken, it is essentially an intellectual and creative activity.

21

2 Educational research

In the preceding chapter very little has been said specifically about educational research, although in the discussion of research in general examples from the educational field were cited wherever it was appropriate. Many contemporary writers hold the view that there are essential differences between educational research and research in such disciplines as psychology and sociology (Taylor, 1966; Simon, 1978). But according to Cronbach (1962) 'most educational research, though not all, is psychological.' Taylor (1966), making the distinction clear, states that 'it is the centrality of practical judgements which distinguish educational research from other kinds of research which use similar methods.' There are some, like Travers (1978), who assume that educational research is similar to research in natural sciences seeking generalisations, and there are others (e.g. Gowin, 1972) who are critical of such generalisations when dealing with human behaviour. According to Gowin (1972) the search for generalisation in educational research is bound to prove fruitless because human behaviour is context dependent. In chapter 1 we have briefly described some of the differences between the natural and the social sciences. This chapter attempts to discuss certain aspects of educational research which will enable the reader to have a better perspective of the domain of educational research.

The nature of educational research

The nature of educational research is much more difficult to describe than many educators would seem to appreciate. One of the problems is the diversity of techniques and approaches that are employed in the study of educational phenomena. Another issue stems from the methodological problems in educational research. While reading studies related to education, one becomes aware of the diversion of opinion regarding the nature of educational research. Some researchers seem to be convinced that the experimental technique is the most powerful research method to deal with educational problems. The opponents to this method assert that only the non-experimental approach can discover the 'reality' which is inaccessible to this quasi-scientific educational research. Thus, the distinction is often drawn between experimental and non-experimental approaches to the study of educational phenomena. In spite of this diversity of opinion there is a fairly clear description in the literature of what educational researchers have in recent years achieved. Yet, many practitioners (teachers, educational psychologists) conceive of research in a narrow framework.

During the early part of this century research was primarily concerned with the collection of descriptive data concerning educational phenomena, and with the development of test instruments (see chapter 3). By the middle of the 1930s leaders in the field began to question the quality of research data since much of the work was repetitive, biased and fragmented in design and methodology (Van Dalen, 1966). Such studies made little contribution, if any, to the knowledge concerning education.

From about 1940 research workers began to make close examinations of the shortcomings that existed in educational research designs and tools of research, and of the gaps that existed in the overall production of research findings (see chapter 3 for a discussion of 'modern educational research'). Furthermore, in an attempt to expand the frontiers of educational knowledge psychologists raised questions about the nature of learning and the processes by which children learn. Upon becoming familiar with the various theoretical explanations of learning educators began to appreciate that learning was a more complex process than they had thought (Van Dalen, 1966).

The work of Tyler (1949) represents another research related trend that challenged some existing school practices. He introduced into the learning-teaching situation the idea that objectives of education should be specified in precise terms, a doctrine that has continued to have an impact on school systems, particularly in the United States. Although Tyler has made some contribution to curriculum construction, his main thesis of defining educational objectives with precision did not lead to any significant advances either in education or in the thoughts behind it. His attempt to reduce the complexity of educational phenomena to simple behavioural components did not prove to be a useful way of describing human intellectual performance, and did not seem to generate any provocative educational research.

The emphasis of much educational research in recent times has been on the solution of educational problems through various research methods. As a result of this emphasis many methodological advances have been made in the domain of educational research. Page (1975) points out that the period between 1965 and 1975 has been the period of great achievement 'for concept after concept has been sharpened and tested, and myth after myth has been exposed'. Tremendous impetus has been given to educational researchers over the last two decades by providing them with generous financial support. In Britain attempts were made to promote the development of educational research from the earliest part of this century. But in fact substantial financial support for educational research is a product of the last twenty-five years. For example, Douglas's (1964, 1968) longitudinal study, Pidgeon and Yates's (1957) work on secondary school selection had made some impact on the educational climate of the country. Because of the time, effort and money which have been expended in the past three decades, both the quality and quantity of research in education have increased (see Ward, Hall and Schramm, 1975).

Another significant change which has taken place in the character of educational research is the involvement of many disciplines. Since the beginning of this century researchers from many disciplines have, from time to time, turned their attention to the school as the locus of historical, psychological, philosophical and sociological problems. As a result of this, much of modern educational technology seems to represent an attempt to bring a multi-discipline approach to the solution of educational problems.

The expanding boundary of educational research reflects, in part, that society has placed enormous responsibilities on and faith in the educational enterprise. This may, in turn, imply that the central problems of education are concerned with the issues that are related to the values society holds. Bloom (1966) rightly remarks that 'Education is looked to for solutions to problems of poverty, racial discord, crime and delinquency, urban living, peace, and even for problems arising from affluence.' It seems, however, that for many social problems, decision makers turn to education for their solution. In the last few decades research workers have become more aware of the need for evaluating critically the varied and conflicting explanations of educational phenomena, and to test them in a wide variety of situations.

In recent years some researchers have introduced the notion of 'paradigm' into the language of educational research (see Parlett and Hamilton, 1977; Esland, 1972); the term 'paradigm' was originally developed by Kuhn (1970). In a brilliant article McNamara (1979) has argued that 'the introduction of the term "paradigm" into educational research is based upon a misunderstanding or inaccurate representation of Kuhn's work and that it can lead to muddled and unclear thinking among educationists, especially those involved with curriculum evaluation.' This shows the way in which research workers in the field of education operate. Researchers from different 'discipline' backgrounds adopt individual techniques and approach in a somewhat eclectic way (McNamara, 1979), the point mentioned earlier in this section. A glance through the literature suggests that there is a body of opinion doubtful about the use of 'positivist' paradigm in educational research. An alternative approach, claimed to be more flexible and more holistic, has been advocated in the field of education (Elliot and Adelman, 1978), curriculum development (Wheeler, 1967; Verma, 1980) and organisational change (Clarke, 1972).

In spite of the complex nature of educational research, most producers and consumers of research data hold the idea that its main function is to provide meaningful and trustworthy information (knowledge). It is also emphasised that research knowledge must lend itself to practical application in the solution of educational problems. In other words, the results of research should be obtained and then used by educators who convert the findings of the research worker into practical applications. As pointed out by Eggleston (1979) 'philosophers and educational researchers who have reflected on the nature of the educational research enterprise have frequently emphasised the centrality of practical concerns' (p.5). Thouless (1969) agrees with this rationale of educational research. According to him education is an applied science, which implies that educational research should be conducted in response to questions arising from the educational context, and that success can only be achieved when the findings are applied to current educational practices. Some educationists view this perspective as restricting the domain of educational research as we will see in a moment.

However, the application of research findings is a difficult task. Therefore, practising teachers ought to have understanding of research terminology and methodology in order to make intelligent educational decisions. The critical evaluation of research reports by teachers will keep them informed of educational developments, and might reduce the gap between research findings and their applications. The current resurgence and reorientation of research efforts show a growing awareness amongst educators that research is a slow but effective tool for educational progress. As a result, schools have come under the focus of interest of professional researchers in recent years. This increasing interest is reflected in the number of educational research projects accomplished over the last two decades. At this point of discussion it may be pertinent to examine some definitions of educational research.

Definitions

As pointed out earlier, it is extremely difficult to give a definition of the term 'educational research' which would be acceptable to all those concerned with educational decisions and practices. Lovell and Lawson (1970) neatly summarise the situation by saying that 'it is virtually impossible to give a definition of the term . . . which would command universal acceptance, as there are innumerable meanings that can be given to the word "education".' Traxler (1954), holding a similar view, states that the overlapping of educational research with research in the other social sciences is inevitable because of the nature of the process of education itself.[1] However, definitions are a valuable aid in understanding a concept or an idea and not a means of forming inflexible categories.

During the 1930s educational researchers adopted the idea that all terms should be defined in operational terms (Travers, 1978). This strategy has not proved useful in eliminating the vagueness of educational language. For example, many psychologists have defined the concept of intelligence through intelligence tests, but the tests have proved far less valuable than test designers had hoped for. Some terms in research are intuitively understood (e.g. the work of Piaget).

Watson (1953) asserts that 'In education we would do well to stop mimicking the physical sciences. Educational research is ultimately concerned with people. It is best shared as lay and professional educators are involved.' Such a perspective would obviously appeal to many classroom teachers who have come to see research as the private concern of a particular group of people — as something accomplished for its own sake, and not necessarily as an exercise which will contribute directly to their own professional interests. Corey (1953), one of the pioneers in action research, agrees with the previous author that limiting educational research to professional researchers alone is to take too limited a view of the educator's function.

The research literature related to education indicates that many writers have conceptualised educational research in a broad sense. Travers (1978) for example, has defined it as 'an activity directed toward the development of an organised body of scientific knowledge about the events with which educators are concerned.' According to him, the goal of educational research is to discover laws or generalisations about behaviour that can be utilised to make predictions and control events within the educational context. Not all of those engaged in educational research would feel sympathetic to this idea of using research as a means of achieving this end. Ary, Jacobs and Razavieh (1972) state that 'When the scientific method is applied to the study of educational problems, educational research is the result.' In this simple description of research is implied that educational research has the same general goals as other research.

Peters and White (1969), expanding the boundaries and questioning the assumption in much of the literature that most educational research is psychological or social scientific (e.g. emphasised by Cronbach, 1962), define research as 'systematic and sustained enquiry carried out by people well-versed in some form of thinking in order to answer some specific type of question.' The authors have attempted to enlarge the dimension of research in order to include all those disciplines which are engaged in 'the more reflective side of scientific work'.

Recent British contributors to the discussion of the nature and scope of educational research seem to have the narrower perspective. Thouless (1969) in the preface to his book, *Map of Educational Research* offers the following definition: '. . . educational research was to be understood as embracing empirical and experimental researches, but not historical and comparative studies in education.' A similar definition is suggested by Nisbet and Entwistle (1970), restricting it to 'areas which involve quantitative or scientific methods of investigation', and pointing out that 'there are other important forms of research in education, such as historical or philosophical enquiry'.

Despite the differing conceptions of the goal of educational research, the common element passing through most of the ideas is the application of systematic methods to the study of educational problems. Given this dimension to the definition, the search for meaningful and trustworthy knowledge becomes central in the whole process. It should also be remembered that research in education has been greatly influenced by research in other disciplines such as psychology, anthropology and sociology. Nevertheless, it has made progress since the beginning of this century, and many educational decisions have been implemented through the processes of research. Before concluding this section it should be emphasised that there is no universal recipe for conducting educational research. All research studies are characterised by some general format which is consistent with the basic procedure of the modern method of research described in chapter 1.

Operational strategies in educational research

In chapter 1 a number of investigative methods were described as a broad framework in the execution of systematic research. These are: the selection of the problem; development of the hypothesis; collection and analysis of data; and drawing appropriate conclusions. Generally speaking, educational research follows the similar pattern except that it is limited in scope to those issues which are broadly defined as educational. Sometimes it becomes difficult to make a clear cut distinction between educational and non-educational issues. However, the tendency in educational research is to try and focus upon the unique characteristics of educational phenomena.

All research activities, regardless of type or discipline, are characterised by some general format. Although the methods developed in the natural sciences gave impetus to the development of research in education, the differences between the two sciences are recognised (see chapter 1).

1   The first and foremost task of the educational researcher is to establish the purpose of research in a clear concise way. The problem must be recognised as worthy and capable of investigation. A clearly stated problem provides the most essential element in constructing a frame of reference that can give direction to the study. Too wide and too general a purpose such as 'to investigate teaching styles' may prove too complex and diffused.

2   When a problem has been identified, the next phase requires a systematic and critical analysis of the research problem. This analysis involves the search of available information specific to the area of study, and definition of the problem in a logical way. For example, an educational researcher might begin with a thorough study of the previous literature that has a direct or indirect bearing on the research problem. This helps in defining the research topic satisfactorily. Many educational terms have several meanings, e.g. 'sociability', 'maladjustment', 'intelligence'. A study of text books and journals would help to do further analysis of these terms and concepts. Sometimes a review of the literature raises more questions rather than providing clues to the solution of the problem. It might even suggest that the original research problem needs to be modified, and if so, what would be the form and nature of the revised hypothesis/question. This activity provides insight into the work of other investigators who explored a similar area. At this stage of research the investigator is likely to crystallise the meanings of various concepts and ideas related to his investigation.

3   Although the formulation of hypotheses is not always essential in educational research, their use provides a direction in deciding upon the research methodology to be adopted. However, the research worker might decide to formulate questions rather than hypotheses. The key to hypothesising is careful preparation and analysis of available information (see chapter 1).

4   Depending upon the nature of the problem and the resources available, the researcher decides whether to use experimental design (e.g. psychometric approach) or non-experimental design (e.g. case study, interviews, observations). Choice of research design often dictates the kinds of tools and procedures which are to be utilised in order to study the variables/factors. Sometimes appropriate tools may not be available or may be inappropriate in a particular cultural setting. Some insight into the problems of measurement is necessary to be able to select the correct instruments or tools (Verma, 1979). A number of standard designs and types of research exist (see chapter 4), but many modifications to them are possible.

In educational research, the discussion should not be centred around the best methodology, but rather the consideration should be given to the most appropriate methods or techniques which can be employed in a given situation. Most research projects require the use of more than one method or technique. Researchers, therefore, need to keep abreast of a wide range of research designs and methods, and be confident of making appropriate selection from them.

5   The next step involves actual data collection and analysis. This also includes administration of instruments (if used), interviews, observations, case studies or any such method or combination of methods. The need to understand the procedures of analysis cannot be overestimated. In educational research the investigator often deals with a large number of variables which would require the help of a mathematical process, i.e. statistics. Depending upon the research design, statistics can play an important role from the planning stage right through to the evaluation of the results. Many professional researchers would argue that some knowledge of statistical techniques is essential for both producers and consumers of educational studies.

6   The final stage of research is perhaps the most delicate and complex one. This is concerned with discussion and the presentation of research findings. The investigator needs to draw the conclusions in an intelligent form in order to communicate his findings to a large audience. It is also essential that the conclusions of the study are kept within the boundaries set out initially by the definition of the problem. This part of the research report should also contain implications and

limitations on the extent to which the findings can be generalised. The major drawback in many research reports is the tendency to make incorrect/invalid generalisations. This stems from a failure to appreciate the complexity of factors. For example, in a classroom situation there are a very few variables which can be identified and controlled, and there are many which can neither be identified nor controlled. The research worker is often forced to use common sense or intuition in identifying and interpreting the uncontrolled or floating variables. The researcher's personality is another factor which is likely to influence the way conclusions are drawn. In view of the above mentioned factors, the researcher must exercise extreme caution in making generalisations of the findings.

A word about the reporting of research findings ought to be mentioned. People have different abilities and experiences which can influence the way they receive and use research reports. Technical or statistical information may not be meaningful or comprehensive to some people. One of the reasons often cited for the slow advancement of educational research is that there is a wide gap between professional researchers and classroom teachers (consumers). In recent years, the present authors in the course of their research projects, were able to confirm this proposition from a large number of teachers in British schools. Very few seemed to have any knowledge of the research evidence which appears at the end of the projects. The researcher must make the findings available in a simple and intelligent way, using the minimum of jargon so as to be easily understood by both decision makers and consumers.

Before concluding this section it must be emphasised that the operational strategies described in the preceding paragraphs should not be adopted as a rigid framework. These strategies overlap considerably, and depending upon the nature and design of the research one may need to move back and forth from one step to another. For example, systematic reading of the literature may suggest redefining the problem and amending the enquiry accordingly.

Problems in educational research

Education is a more complex field to research than the biological and physical sciences. In spite of the many useful contributions research has made to education (e.g. in the areas of learning, transfer of training, motivation, classroom dynamics and assessment techniques) it has not provided all the answers educators seek about educational phenomena. There seem to be many reasons for falling short of their expectations.

An educational researcher has to deal with many variables simultaneously, and some of them may not be controlled or quantified. Furthermore, research is complicated by factors such as the interaction between the investigator and his human subjects of study, and this can influence the way conclusions are drawn. Such an interaction may even produce changes in human behaviour (subjects of the study) which might not have occurred otherwise. However, in practical terms it is extremely difficult for the researcher to dissociate himself from the phenomena under study.

In the classic division between the researcher and his field of study a number of principles seem to have wide acceptance. These include such propositions as; a) the researcher must maintain an 'objective' position in relation to what he studies, and avoid, to the best of his ability, intervening in ways which might influence or distort the data under scrutiny; b) the search for objectivity is at the centre of all that the investigator tries to achieve, and it helps if events can be reproduced in experimentally contrived conditions (i.e. in the laboratory). Although objectivity in research is widely accepted as an essential element, its accomplishment is more difficult in the social sciences than in the natural sciences. Nevertheless, the scientific method attempts to deal with events whose occurrence, in principle, can be agreed upon by anyone. But the researcher's personality, attitudes, beliefs and values might influence his observations of phenomena and assessment of the findings, and consequently can affect generalisations of the results; c) statistical principles are applied where possible to ensure accuracy and precision in measurement and analysis of data. In the classic experimental design, quantification is seen as a major goal to be pursued.

In educational research the application of the above mentioned principles and methods have often given rise to large-scale social surveys. In these, the major research effort has been to produce effective instruments of enquiry, and once this has been accomplished, to analyse the data which they have yielded. This is usually undertaken by statistical methods, and computerisation has greatly facilitated this process.

In recent years a substantial body of social scientists (including educational researchers) have rejected this positivistic approach, and the physical sciences' model on which it is drawn. They have argued that these principles have little to offer in terms of relevance in the study of complex social situations and human behaviour. Some of them have highlighted the need for qualitative research and analysis of interpersonal structures, and their approaches have been based on a quite different set of assumptions. It should be mentioned that the qualitative approach is also not free from weaknesses.

Turning to problems in educational research, there are other issues involved such as ethical considerations which need to be adhered to by professional researchers. Until recently, researchers did not have to confront these issues. For example, Dennis (1941) investigated the role of social stimulation on child development by raising a pair of twins in virtual seclusion for a year. Today, the situation has changed, and ever increasing attention is being given to the ethical considerations of research with human subjects. The research procedures may produce undesirable psychological side effects. Additionally, human beings have the right to refuse participation in research, the right to remain anonymous, and the right to ask the researcher to treat the data confidentially. When conducting classroom research, the investigator often obtains personal information about the pupil, sometimes by means of deceptive methods. These practices raise both ethical and legal questions concerning the rights of research subjects. The human subject should not be viewed as an ingredient in the research laboratory. These ethical issues obviously make educational researchers re-think their strategies of research.

Another type of problem concerns the way society perceives social science research, in contrast with the natural sciences. As early as 1949, Remmers had remarked that our thinking about research is quite different in the fields of natural and social sciences. Such attitudes still seem to prevail. For example, it is hard to change public attitudes, beliefs, values and traditions in the light of new ideas and findings based on social research. However, there has been some positive shift in society's expectations from educational enterprise in recent years as mentioned earlier (Bloom, 1966), and this has resulted in increased funding of educational research.

One problem connected with education is just the opposite of the one mentioned above. Whilst many people resist change to improve their way of life as a result of social research findings, there are some who accept the findings without question. They seem to have complete faith in research data. An example of this is the reaction to the notorious study by Jensen (1973). His findings, published in the book *Educability and Group Differences* argued that black children have inherently lower intelligence than white children. Many researchers have pointed out methodological weaknesses in Jensen's work (see, for example, Bagley, 1975). However, many educators have accepted Jensen's results without examining the research critically. This can seriously affect the performance and achievement of a black pupil in two ways: first, by a teacher being openly prejudiced in his interaction with the black child, and secondly by having low expectations of the child's abilities and achievement. Both these attitudes can be found among white teachers in British schools (Giles, 1977). It must be stressed that both researchers and consumers should evaluate critically any research findings, and should avoid acceptance or rejection on emotional grounds.

A recent trend in educational research has been a greater emphasis on applied rather than basic research. Many researchers believe that this has created a vacuum in the theoretical aspects of education. Whether or not there has been little emphasis on basic research, most consumers (particularly classroom teachers) agree that there is a wide gap between research findings and practical applications. This gap can be narrowed if more and more teachers are involved in practical research, and solutions to many of the classroom problems are sought in the natural settings. That is to say, teaching and research should become co-activities. Both professional researchers and teachers can make significant contributions in bridging the gap. Researchers should conduct their studies on sound theoretical positions, should make their hypotheses explicit and should disseminate their research findings and implications in a form that teachers are able to understand. Teachers should also develop research sophistication in order to appreciate research findings and their implications.

In summary, it can be said that educational research has not accelerated the educational practice to the extent it had hoped for. In the current international economic situation it is doubtful whether sufficient funds for educational research would be made available. However, it would seem that one of the essential strategies is to spend some of the resources and time available at the disposal of educational researchers to improve the training of both producers and consumers of research. Educational practitioners have a vital role to play in implementing educational change in any society. Hopefully, one day many classroom problems can be effectively studied by the teacher when research becomes a natural consequence of teaching. Stenhouse (1975) rightly remarks in the chapter on 'The Teacher as Researcher' that '. . . it is difficult to see how teaching can be improved or how curricular proposals can be evaluated without self-monitoring on the part of teachers. A research tradition which is accessible to teachers and which feeds teaching must be created if education is to be significantly improved.' (p.165).

Evaluation of educational research

In order to critically evaluate research findings educators ought to ask themselves a few questions when they read a particular research report. Since there is no universally accepted yardstick (as mentioned earlier) for judging research reports, the following format might provide a useful guide to those who wish to embark on research activities of their own or to teachers who are anxious to improve their educational practices in the light of research findings. Briefly, the questions should be concerned with the theoretical aspect of the study, the significance of the problem, the appropriateness of the hypotheses or the goals, the research methodology, meaningfulness and trustworthiness of the techniques (if tests are used, then their reliability and validity), the representativeness and adequacy of the sample, the conclusions and implications of the study. These concepts are elaborated below:

1   Does the title of the study explicitly indicate the problem area?

2   Does the problem have a precise theoretical position or a theoretical assumption? Has it been stated clearly and accurately? Is the problem significant and worthy of investigation?

3   Has the previous literature been thoroughly reviewed covering the relevant variables under study?

4   Has the evaluation of previous studies helped the investigator to generate hypotheses or to formulate questions?

5   Has the researcher stated the hypotheses, null hypotheses or questions in a clear, concise way? If the hypotheses are developed to collect facts and to examine the relationships between variables, has it been made clear? Are the stated hypotheses testable? If so, are the assumptions or inferences on which they are predicted made clear?

6   Has the investigator provided any operational definitions? Have the relevant terms and concepts concerning the research been defined and analysed clearly?

7   Are the techniques, procedures and materials used to attain the goal of the research reliable? Have they been adequately described?

8   Has the sample been adequately described including the criteria for selection?

9   Has the investigator pointed out any probable source of error in the data that might have influenced the results of the study?

10 Have any statistical techniques been used for the analysis of data? If so, were they appropriate in view of research objectives?

11 Has the data been analysed objectively, clearly and accurately?

12 Are the results presented intelligibly and free of all ambiguity? Has the researcher mentioned the limitations of the study? Can the findings and their implications be understood by many educators?

13 Have the conclusions been clearly stated showing their support from the data obtained? Have the findings been over-generalised?

14 Has the researcher suggested further investigation in the area highlighting the gaps?

The questions are suggested in order to make a reader of research reports critical. It should be mentioned that sometimes research reports do not use specific headings (e.g. the problem, hypotheses) which is not crucial. What is important, however, is that these aspects are dealt with in the research report. It should also be emphasised that one of the essential characteristics of research is the degree of flexibility when seeking the solution of problems or the answer to questions.

It must also be recognised that the techniques required by the educational researcher, particularly in quantitative research, include some knowledge of statistics. This is necessary even in comparing the difference between test scores of an experimental and a control group. The investigator needs to ascertain whether the difference between the two groups on any characteristics under study is 'significant'. For many research purposes it is also essential to be able to calculate a correlation coefficient (see chapter 5 for a discussion of statistical concepts). However, those who read the research findings of others need perhaps less knowledge of statistical techniques than those who contribute to research. Nevertheless, it would seem essential that both researchers and readers of research reports should grasp the general principles of research methodology and of the determination of significance.

Classification of educational research

Any attempt to classify educational research under categories poses a difficult problem. A glance through the literature indicates that research in education has been classified from many points of view: according to discipline (e.g. psychological, philosophical, sociological, etc.); according to the type of data collection procedures (e.g. interviews, observations, testing, etc.); according to the methods employed (i.e. historical, descriptive and experimental, see chapter 4). A simple dichotomy frequently used in social science and educational research is that between quantitative and qualitative or psychometric and reflective/illuminative. The advancement of computer technology and the improvements in statistical methods have resulted in a rapid increase in quantitative studies during the last two decades. However, these labels do not represent discrete categories or clusters, but are merely endpoints of a continuum scale. Sometimes a piece of research may fall into more than one of these categories. Some writers have classified research methodology in a general way such as library, life and physical science, social and technological research (Rummel, 1964). This categorisation seems less clear, and does not appear to make a significant contribution to our understanding of research methods. In view of methodological advances it would be difficult to devise a single categorisation scheme to include all the possible combinations of methods used in educational research.

Another useful way to classify or categorise educational research is by purpose which lies along a continuum from the most basic to the most applied. That is to say, is the research designed to add knowledge to the field of study which may or may not be of any immediate value (basic), or is it designed to be of immediate practical application? In the educational context, problems studied in basic research can range from learning, and the transfer of training (materials to be learned) to the development of systematic knowledge (e.g. how children think, studies of interaction in various types of classroom groupings). The findings of basic research tend to push forward the boundaries of some new or established knowledge, and may be very strictly controlled. This type of research may or may not have any immediate practical relevance. It is argued, however, that findings of basic research may provide vital knowledge as a link in a practical situation at a later time.

Applied research is often designed to solve specific problems or to provide information that is of immediate use. Most contemporary educational research would seem primarily to be of the applied type. It covers a wide range of possibilities, but often takes the form of a survey of some kind. This type of research tends to be carried out by experienced researchers and may include participant observation or unobtrusive measures. In this the researcher observes the situation but does not interfere. Examples of applied research include the transfer of new teaching methods, teaching approaches or strategies from experimental schools to a representative group of schools, where teachers may be trained to use them. It should be remembered that the dimension of pure versus applied research (i.e. from theory development to implementation) is based primarily upon the purpose of research.

The above description of research category clearly shows that basic and applied research are difficult to distinguish in many studies. In many ways pure and applied research have a great deal in common.

According to Van Dalen (1962) the purpose of investigation may be different in 'pure' and 'applied' research, but the techniques used in each case may be almost indistinguishable. Hilgard (1954) pointed out that the distinction is really a continuum rather than a dichotomy. Travers (1978) differentiating between the two terms writes that:

> Basic research is designed to add to an organised body of scientific knowledge and does not necessarily produce results of immediate practical value. Applied research is undertaken to solve an immediate practical problem and the goal of adding to scientific knowledge is secondary.

The recent trend in the educational field shows that much of the research accomplished has been concerned with the immediate application of its findings. This would obviously be favoured by most classroom teachers who would argue for more applied research that can produce simply practical and immediately useful information. For example, teachers would like to contribute to applied research for the development of a machine to teach maladjusted or ESN pupils rather than a fundamental contribution to the knowledge of learning-teaching situations.

Many of the earlier psychological studies were conducted with a view to expand the frontiers of knowledge. But a large proportion of modern research in the field of testing and measurement is applied research. There has been considerable debate among educators with regard to which type of research is of more value. Cronbach (1966), like many social scientists, argues for more basic research:

> Educational improvements that really make an impact on the ignorance rate will not grow out of minor variations of teaching content and process. Effective educational designs, worth careful development and field trial, can emerge only from a deep understanding of learning and motivation.

Similarly, other social scientists believe that basic research is of more importance than applied research with regard to its impact on education (Kerlinger, 1977; Travers, 1978). Such views imply that the findings of basic research seek to make fundamental contributions to the knowledge of education whether this new knowledge has any immediate or practical application at the time.

In basic research knowledge of more than one discipline is often involved in the search for new facts, elaboration of new theories or the re-appraisal of old ones. The investigator deals with any problem which he regards as important, and this decision does not need to be hampered by considerations of practical use to which his results will be put. Basic research is not very popular among many educationalists because it demands skilled researchers, and is time consuming and expensive. However, its value at some later stage cannot be denied; it requires creativity and imagination, and often leads to further research of a utilitarian nature.

In addition to the basic and applied research dimension other terms have also been used in the consideration of educational research. Rowan (1976) has offered an outline of eleven kinds of research which, according to him, broadly cover the range used in social research and educational research: pure basic; basic objective; evaluation; applied; action; intervention; existential; experiential; phenomenological; ethnomethodological and dialectical. Rowan believes that the first four of these approaches tend to be alienated types of research, which treat people as objects to be described externally. He is also critical of these types of research on the grounds that the true purpose of the study is often concealed from those who provide research data. According to Rowan, the last seven types of research tend to be much more 'genuine' because people are not deceived. The belief that for most problems one particular approach to research is superior to all others rarely seems to be based on rational grounds. Such a conviction may lead to the use of methods inappropriate to a given problem. The appropriateness of any type of research strategy should be dictated by the nature of the problem, the goal of research, the kind of data required, and the time and resources available. For example, the broad objective of research may be oriented towards the clarification of a theoretical concept or to the solution of a practical and immediate problem. However, the eleven kinds of research outlined by Rowan (1976) do seem to overlap, and do not form a logically consistent pattern; they are not mutually exclusive.

The aspects of educational research which have received a great deal of attention from educationalists in recent years are evaluative research, action research and consumer oriented research.

The term evaluative research is often used to refer to the systematic methods used to collect and analyse data regarding the effectiveness of an educational experience. This type of research has become an essential ingredient in the field of curriculum studies (see Verma, 1977; 1980). Much of the thinking attempts to view evaluation studies as a part of a decision making process. Cronbach (1963) defines the concept of evaluation as 'the collection and use of information to make decisions about an educational programme'. He has pointed out that evaluation is almost inevitably concerned with decision making, and has discussed three types of decision where evaluation may be involved: course improvement, decisions about individuals and administrative regulation. The movement of evaluation studies has attracted a new generation of research workers, and has developed its own vocabulary and also a large amount of theoretical literature.

Important terms that came to be used in connection with evaluation research are developmental, formative and summative. One can evaluate in some way the process that goes into the design of a curriculum or a programme (developmental); when the programme is put into use one can evaluate the learning of pupils at various levels of proficiency and also determine the effects of changing various components of the programme (formative or process evaluation); then comes the evaluation of the final and total effect of the programme (summative evaluation). Summative evaluation is supposed to provide a final judgement on the value or worth of the programme.

Evaluation research is the dominant type of research in the relationships of exchange between researchers and professional practitioners. But there are many who express doubts about the utility of evaluation research, and may not even want to label evaluation as research (Guga, 1969). However, most social action programmes and curriculum innovations should be systematically evaluated both during the programme, to facilitate improvements, and at the end, to obtain the outcome, i.e. summative evaluation. The product of such research activity almost always comes out as some kind of evaluative judgement on the course of action. Thus, evaluation research is often a decision oriented activity. Many evaluative research programmes in Britain have been sponsored by the Nuffield Foundation and the Schools Council in recent years.

Action research, according to Corey (1953), is undertaken by professional practitioners in order to improve their practices. It is a type of applied research, but in this process the researcher is the same person as the practitioner. In other words, the researcher is the person who will be affected by the results. The thesis behind this dual role is that the strategy to change the behaviour of practitioners is to get them involved in conducting research on problems which concern them (Helmstadter, 1970). Corey (1953), the originator of the term, argues that teachers can become better decision makers and effective practitioners if they can conduct action research. It is suggested that this type of research can guide, correct and evaluate decisions and actions, and can provide solutions to immediate problems in the school. Thus, action research implies broad involvement of the researcher and assumes that action will be taken towards a solution to the problem under study.

Consumer oriented research seems to be preferred by many educators today. It is concerned with the kind of data which is of value to the consumer. Teachers, other researchers, employers, and parents would seem to be the main consumers of the results of educational research. Cronbach and Suppes (1969) use the terms conclusion oriented and decision oriented enquiry as synonymous with consumer oriented or audience oriented research. The audience oriented terminology, however, has come into frequent use in the discussion of educational research. Jack Wrigley (1976) drawing a distinction between various kinds of research, listed five possible audiences: 'Other researchers in the field; teachers in the classroom; policy-makers at local and national level; the general public interested in educational matters; the press.'

However, there seems to be little doubt expressed in the literature that teachers need to be consumers of the results of educational research (see chapter 7).

In summary, it is apparent that educational research can take many forms; a variety of dimensions, perspectives and rationale have been presented in this chapter. The most important point to be remembered is that the focus of educational research must be *education*, and that the foremost function is to assist teachers, administrators and all concerned in the field, with the aim of improving the quality of the educational process, and thus enhancing the quality of life.

Notes

1 For a discussion of the notion of a discipline of education, see Walton J. and Kuetha J.L. (eds), 1963, *The Discipline of Education*; Bruner J.S., 1962, *The Process of Education*.

3 Educational research: past and present

The problem of defining the term 'educational research' has been dealt with in chapter 2. As we have seen, the term does not mean the same thing to everyone within the field of education, and no single definition is universally acceptable. This may be due to innumerable meanings that are given to the word 'education'. This chapter briefly describes the emergence of research activities in the field of education, and outlines the work of a few individuals which seems to have exerted an influence on the development of educational research.

Although interest in solving educational problems through research began to stimulate educators' minds in the late nineteenth century, it was only at the turn of the century, when the social sciences established their identity, that researchers in many fields started turning their attention to the school as the locus of historical, psychological, philosophical and sociological problems. As a result of sparks of their interest educational research attempted to embrace elements of many disciplines and utilise a wide range of strategies and tactics to acquire information in the total scheme of educational thought. The current practice of research methodologies vastly differs from that of the early part of the century. Contemporary social scientists do not follow any simple routine in research programmes that can be written and communicated to others. They attempt to synthesise a complex set of techniques and approaches to acquire knowledge about educational problems. Because of the sophisticated research designs and statistical analysis, researchers are now able to tackle many of the complex and fundamental educational problems that once had to be ignored. During the last forty or fifty years research has greatly expanded the scope of its activities, and has gradually exerted influence on the practices in most areas of education (e.g. psychology, curriculum, administration, teaching methods and evaluation). Today, educational research is accepted as a necessary element in the diverse activities of any advanced society.

Historical development of educational research

At this stage it would seem appropriate to present an overview of some of the significant events which provided a background for the educational research movement.

Although educational research is a fairly recent development, it is difficult to pinpoint its formal beginning. One might say that seeds of the research movement sprung up at Leipzig in 1879 when W. Wundt established the first psychological laboratory. In England, about the same time, Galton and Pearson were working on their statistical methods which were to be used in educational research. However, most writers in this field seem to agree that at the turn of the century the science of education made a positive approach to the solution of educational problems. Realising that simple improvements in the efficiency of education could be produced through systematic studies of pupils and teachers, some educators tried to establish more efficient and objective methods to achieve this. Another significant feature of this era was an emphasis on measurement and testing. In fact, psychometric measurement formed the cornerstone of the research movement, as reflected in the following statement:

> For there cannot be a science without fairly precise quantific-ation: not that science is measurement, but those traits which are devoid of any reasonably definite quality simply do not have the required specificity for entering into the careful thinking essential to science. When quantities are disregarded almost any generalisation is true.
> (Scates, 1947, pp.253–4)

It seems that this kind of perspective was inculcated in the mind of many research workers of the pioneer period who were influenced by Thorndike's (1918) famous slogan: 'Whatever exists at all exists in some amount' (p.16). Thorndike inspired many educators who began to employ quantitative methods to obtain 'scientific' and precise information about various aspects of human behaviour.

Other influential people whose work on measurement and testing

42

made a significant contribution to the development of educational research were Darwin, Huxley, Spencer and Galton. Some people believe that Joseph M. Rice was the forerunner in the educational research movement. His two articles (Rice, 1897) published in the same year were concerned with the spelling achievement of school children in the United States. This work is regarded as the turning point in the contemporary movement for an objective study of educational problems. The findings of Rice's investigation pointed out the weaknesses in the existing methods of teaching spelling, and suggested that teaching methods in terms of how well children could spell should be evaluated. This point of view clearly implied that teachers should assess the strengths and weaknesses of their work in the classroom.

Galton, often called the 'father of mental testing', was extremely interested in the study of individual differences. His famous book *Hereditary Genius* was published in 1869 and had a tremendous bearing upon educational philosophy. By 1886 Galton had established his famous anthropometric laboratory devoted to the measurement of physical and sensori-motor characteristics of human beings. He was the first person who had worked out the concept of statistical correlations, and had applied the techniques in the analysis and understanding of individual differences (although Karl Pearson worked out the actual product-moment correlation formula). However, Galton's statistical methods were employed by Pearson, Spearman, Burt and Thompson in England and by Kelly, Thurstone and Guilford in the United States. The use of statistical inference and other quantitative concepts has become an essential element of today's development and application of measurement and evaluation in educational research.

Turning to the first quarter of the century, we find that Thorndike's work through research made a strong impact on the educational scene. His interest and many years of studies questioned the existing beliefs concerning the concept of human learning within an educational context. His early work, *Elimination of Pupils from School* (published in 1907) seemed to have inspired many educational leaders of his time. Thorndike's other major work *Introduction to the Theory of Mental and Social Measurements* (published in 1904), introduced statistical methods in educational research. Thereafter, Thorndike and his students constructed a number of tests and scales for measuring the academic achievement of children. The Stone Arithmetic Test appeared in 1908 and the Thorndike Handwriting Scale in 1910. An evaluation of his work seems to suggest that he was one of the earliest scientists whose influence on the research movement created a whole new line of research strategy that is still being practised today by many psychologists. Thorndike, like some of his contemporaries, endeavoured to change educational philosophy and educational practices through research.

One of the major criticisms levelled at Thorndike's research is that he pursued the traditional role of a laboratory scientist, having had no contact with schools and teachers. His critics say that he was divorced from reality. Thorndike himself believed that a scientist should spend most of his time in the laboratory, doing research that would have implications for educational practice. This kind of approach is not uncommon in the present educational world. Many theorists, particularly in the United States, ask their graduate students to collect data from schools, while working themselves on theoretical aspects of research. These researchers are likely to be unaware of the practical problems faced at the data collection stage. In the social sciences it is misleading to suggest that researchers work in the order set out earlier or finish with facts that are unquestionable. Educational research is not a mechanical but a creative activity, and the actual process of research may not follow a logical pattern (as discussed in chapter 2).

One of the contributions of Thorndike's laboratory research to education which has survived so far was the emphasis it placed on providing the learner with knowledge of how he was doing. Thorndike called this 'rewards' and later psychologists described this process as 'reinforcement'. A related concept, which Thorndike referred to as the 'law of effect' was subsequently given the name of the 'law of reinforcement' by Skinner. Thorndike's emphasis on the law of effect had impact because previously children in schools were given very little information about their performance and whether they were doing right or wrong (Travers, 1978). The relevance of the 'law of effect' in the learning-teaching situation is recognised by many practising teachers today.

Thorndike's research has been attacked quite often because of his superficial contact with the classroom situation. However, some of his ideas derived from laboratory research and embodied in school experience had widespread impact. For example, one of his findings was that what a pupil learned in one situation was difficult to generalise to other situations. Thorndike's well known research on transfer of training was interpreted by educators to mean that one could not generally expect much transfer, and that it would be more sound educationally if the material was learned directly. Thus, according to this theory, learning Latin would not help the child to learn English vocabulary. This conclusion produced radical changes in the school curriculum, because his research showed that no school subjects had any special powers for training the mind.

The work of Thorndike on army testing during World War I contributed to the development of measures of intelligence, although this did not have marked impact as his research in other areas of education.

In addition to the emphasis on measurement and testing in the pioneer period of educational research, another theme emerged which generated some enthusiasm amongst educational leaders. The school survey idea came into being in the early 1900s which is still one of the popular types of educational research in America. This kind of research design involves a description and evaluation of one or more aspects of a school environment. The school survey became almost part of the educational research movement with the result that standardised tests began to be employed on a large scale. Since there was already some scepticism about the use of psychological tests, and with the increased emphasis on achievement and intelligence testing in school surveys, a great controversy about the validity and accuracy of obtaining such data started. Opponents of objective measurement enquired into the 'propriety' of test data, and leaders of the research movement of the day defended the psychometric measurement (Barnes, 1960). Thorndike put the axe to the debate when he stated: 'If a thing exists, it exists in some amount; and if it exists in some amount, it can be measured' (Thorndike, 1914).

Despite the arguments for and against educational measurement the National Association of Directors of Educational Research was created at a meeting in 1915, which became the American Educational Research Association (AERA) in 1930. One of the objectives of this Association was 'the promotion of the practical use of educational measures in all educational research' which acted as a motivating force for the growth of the educational research movement. Consequently researchers felt encouraged to utilise psychometric measures in their study of various aspects of education.

During the Thorndike era Terman's (1931) logitudinal studies of gifted children was another classic work which made an impact on education. Contrary to the general belief held by teachers, his findings indicated that there was nothing 'abnormal' in gifted children, and that they could adjust well in any social situation. Of course not all of his contributions were on the same solid ground. His work on the English version of Binet's intelligence tests was a controversial issue. Karier (1973), examining the development of the testing movement in America, summarises the work of Terman (one of the movement leaders):

> Designing the Stanford-Binet intelligence test, Terman developed questions that were based on presumed progressive difficulty in performing tasks he believed necessary for achievement in ascending the hierarchical occupational structure. He then proceeded to find that, according to the results of his test, the intelligence of different occupational classes fit his ascending hier-

archy. Little wonder the intelligence quotient reflected social-class bias. It was based on the social-class order.

Nevertheless, the age of Thorndike did produce some useful ideas for educational research, although the emphasis was placed on the use of tests. For example, the publications of J. M. Cattell's 'Mental Tests and Measurements' in 1890, the development of an intelligence scale by Binet and Simon in 1905, and the development of the handwriting scale by Thorndike in 1910 were some of the contributions made in the development of techniques for educational research. In recent years these techniques and tools have been questioned by many social scientists on psychological, social and ethical grounds. Still, these early studies should be treated as potential indicators of new methods.

The next period in the development of educational research, between 1920 and 1945, was regarded as the 'publications' era. During this period well known leaders of the research movement started educational organisations and publications with a view to disseminating their findings and advancing their work. The number of psychological tests increased tremendously, and most of these became commercially available. Buros began publication of the Mental Measurements Year Book containing critical reviews of the available standardised psychological tests. A number of educational journals and periodicals appeared during this period of expansion. The Review of Educational Research published by AERA (American Education Research Association) started in 1931. A number of original books were also written during this time (Buckingham, 1926), some of which are still regarded as useful literature for the purposes of educational research.

Britain has not lagged behind in the educational research movement. Many scholars have made significant contributions to the development of educational research from the early part of this century. Cyril Burt, who started as a school psychologist in 1913, has been recognised as one of the leading educational researchers of this century, although he has come under increased attack in recent years because of fraudulent misrepresentation of data. The studies of Susan Isaac in child development, of Lindsey on educational opportunity, of Cyril Burt on the assessment of abilities, of Hartog and Rhodes on the marks of examiners, had influenced the educational research climate of the 1930s and 1940s in Britain (Taylor, 1973). Another proponent in British educational research was Rusk (1912) who strongly argued for more experimental work in education. Further impetus to the organisation and development of educational research came from the creation of the Scottish Council for Research in Education in 1928, and the Education section of the British Psychological Society in 1919. In a review of 'British Research in Education' Brehaut (1973) has shown that research in education has a longer and more complex history than some people suggest. However, the fact that Britain has been one of the pioneers of educational research is not in question.

Modern educational research

Since about 1945 social scientists have been engaged to re-evaluate educational research in the light of improvements that research has brought about in the educative process. Research methodologies in education have undergone extensive refinement in order to obtain more reliable and valid information. With the advancement of computer science more sophisticated statistical techniques have been developed for analysis of data. New terms and meanings have been introduced in the literature in order to communicate the knowledge to a large audience (see chapter 2). This reappraisal of educational research can be attributed to a new generation of educational leaders who followed Thorndike, Terman and others and include names such as Sidney Pressey, F. Skinner, R. Tyler, Jean Piaget to mention but a few. This generation has provided ideas through research which have had an impact on education.

Pressey first introduced the idea of mechanical devices for teaching. These devices were designed to have a dual function − to test as well as to teach, and to provide immediate feedback about the correctness of students' responses. Pressey promoted this machine as a good way of self teaching, particularly when students are required to learn some routine types of material. He was one of the first to publish a textbook on educational psychology which showed the relevance of psychological research in solving educational problems.

The work of Skinner has been of great significance for classroom teachers. He, unlike Thorndike, visited classrooms, observed the learning-teaching situation, and on the basis of this experience concluded that positive and frequent reinforcement was essential for effective learning. He avoided the problems that Thorndike's law of effect had by defining reinforcement as anything that increases the probability of a response. Skinner and his followers still hold the same view with regard to this issue of learning. These ideas not only revolutionised thinking about learning and reinforcement, but eliminated the possibility of measuring habit strength indirectly by keeping track of the number of reinforced responses. The work of Skinner, though based on behaviourist assumptions, is pragmatic rather than theoretical. He did not predict about what should be reinforcing and why, but concentrated on showing the effects of reinforcement on learning. Most of his work was carried out on hungry animals, but according to him the underlying principles seem to work for well fed humans too. Many teachers are critical of his approach on moral grounds, but changing behaviour by reinforcement need not necessarily be immoral. Teachers are well aware that, in a wider sense, any curriculum is an attempt to change the behaviour of pupils, whether it is explicitly stated or not.

Skinner's contribution to education through research is often associated with programmed learning and the teaching machine. He first developed the teaching materials to be used with the teaching machine, but later on the programmed text made it possible to use materials of the same format, without the use of the machine. The use of the programmed text and the teaching machine has not gained popularity as part of the school curriculum.

In the 1930s Ralph Tyler started a movement to change the educational process through curriculum research. His work played a part in encouraging schools to depart from some of their traditional practices. He introduced into education the idea that educational objectives should be defined in terms of specific behaviours or learning outcomes, a theme that has continued to have an impact ever since it was advocated. Tyler's model for curriculum construction was first articulated in 1934, and received favourable support from many educators. Undoubtedly, the Tylerian doctrine has exerted a powerful influence in curriculum research on both sides of the Atlantic during the last three decades.

As a result of Tyler's behavioural specification of objectives, sometimes called the 'Engineering Model', investigators both in Britain and the United States made efforts to define the desired course outcomes with great precision. Sometimes educational objectives were defined in enormous detail. However, it has for some the substantial merit of simplicity, rationality, utility and practicality. Although this kind of educational thought did not make much advance in understanding the complexity of learning-teaching situations, it encouraged psychologists to make greater use of psychometric measurement. Another weakness of this model is that it has not proved to be a useful way of describing human intellectual performance. Consequently, his idea of prespecifying the behavioural outcomes of any educational programme has come under severe attack in recent years. Nevertheless, his contribution to curriculum construction has made a significant impact on education.

The impact of Piaget's research on education[1] has been rather slow, partly because of the style of his writing which draws heavily from logic and biology, and partly because his theory of the nature of the human intellect is complex. The main thesis of both Skinner's and Tyler's work has been to reduce complex educational objectives to simple behavioural components, whereas Piaget's basic premise is that the complex forms of human behaviour can be reduced to simple components. According to Piaget complex phenomena should be studied in all their complexity, since laws of complex forms of behaviour operate differently from laws of simple forms of behaviour.

Piaget's studies of the intellectual development of the infant have had an enormous impact on subsequent research activities in the area. His model of intellectual development, and a description of the conditions that would improve this development has been recognised by many educators. The Piagetian model has been widely used as a basis for designing school teaching materials, particularly in the area of Mathematics and Science. For example, the Nuffield Science and Nuffield Mathematics Projects designed the teaching materials on the Piagetian lines. These programmes are widely used in British and North American schools. In Britain, in the Science 5 − 13 Curriculum Project (Schools Council, 1973) a rigorous objective type of approach was adopted which was claimed to be essentially 'child-centred'. The project was set out with a clear statement of broad aims followed by a precise classification of nine sets of objectives, illustrated with possible examples at each of three Piagetian stages. Although criticisms of the Piaget model are often made on the grounds of vagueness (Ennis, 1975), his programmes of research have undoubtedly made a significant contribution to the classroom practice. The greatest strength of Piaget's work is in the mapping out of children's mental operations which has obvious implications for educational practices.

The contribution of Bruner's work has some bearing on learning situations, and consequently on education. In fact Piaget's work provided a framework for Bruner's research. His research about the idea of translating the key concepts of knowledge into materials that can be understood by children has interesting implications for the curriculum. He first worked out this hypothesis with mathematics and then applied it to the social sciences in his *Man : a course of study* (MACOS) Curriculum Project. Bruner's well known statement that any subject can be taught in some intellectually honest form to any child shows the need to understand how a child is structuring his knowledge at present in order to amplify his power. The question arises whether any teacher can teach anything, given that it is possible to teach anything to any child? Although Bruner has been criticised on several grounds (Jones, 1972) his active interest in the effects of teaching and experience has made his research more relevant for classroom teachers.

In addition to the above mentioned individuals whose contributions to education through research work have been widespread, there are others who have also made an impact on many aspects of education. J.P. Guilford (1967), for example, has provided educators and researchers with an idea of the intellect which makes a distinction between divergent and convergent thinking. His model has made some contribution to the development of aptitude tests, and has put forward ideas about components of the human intellect which can be considered for training. Kohlberg's (1964, 1975) work on moral development has been verified in many different cultures in the world. His model, a typological scheme describing general structures of moral thought, has been criticised on philosophical and psychological grounds. Nevertheless, his theory has proved valuable in the field of education and has relevance for the classroom teacher. It should be mentioned that although most theories in the social sciences have been contradicted or modified by subsequent pieces of evidence, many still seem to hold their position, partly because no alternative models offering a greater degree of research credibility are available.

The work of Kurt Lewin, Carl Rogers and others should not be omitted when considering the impact of research on the educational world.

The reader should not get the impression that educational change has been brought about by psychological research alone. Philosophical, historical and sociological considerations have also played a part in educational research. The term research incorporates a wide range of activities within the field of education (see chapter 2). For example, the historian has studied the progress of education as one of the many factors in the general development of civilisation. The sociologist has attempted to find out in the school community paradigms of social behaviour. Similarly, the philosopher has from time to time been interested in applying principles of epistemology and ethics to an understanding of education. The psychologist has provided conceptual models and information assisting teachers in educational planning. The impact of psychological research on education has also been in terms of methodologies which are adapted for educational enquiry. For example, theories of learning, theories of cognitive and emotional development, group dynamics, individual differences in ability and personality, models of attitude formation and change, theories of motivation, all seem to have an obvious relevance to the planning of learning-teaching situations.

The present position

As mentioned in the earlier chapter, research workers from various disciplines have come together in recent years through an interest in studying education, and this has resulted in a broad, inter-disciplinary approach to educational research. One of the implications of a new network concerned with educational research has been the recognition of a wide variety of approaches and techniques as opposed to the narrower dimensions of the past. Other developments such as the rise of educational technology and the development of sophisticated statistical techniques have also contributed to the refinement and classification of methodological issues in educational research. Thus, research activity has been greatly expanded in its scope in the last two or three decades. Schools throughout the world have made striking changes in all aspects of the curriculum.

In spite of this critical appraisal and the broadening of methodological issues educational research is still undeveloped. Much of the work in defining educational phenomena may still be described as a 'hunting expedition'. There seems to be so many difficulties at both the conceptual and technical level concerning the methodology of research in education. For example, human behaviour − the concern of most educational researchers − is far more complex to understand and interpret than the forces operating to make up the content of the physical sciences. Educational research is a planned and deliberate intervention designed to improve the educational process which may differ from situation to situation, and from time to time in the same setting.

There are not many people outside the realm of education who understand the complexity of the problem faced by researchers. Some people may even be inclined to suggest that research has had the least impact in promoting effective learning. Such a view would lack knowledge of the educational field as a whole. There is sufficient information in the literature to suggest that the analysis of the complex dynamic processes involved in the learning-teaching situation by various scholars since the turn of the twentieth century is a continuing guide to the conduct of research and its evaluation. As discussed earlier in this chapter the work of Thorndike, Terman, Skinner, Bruner, Piaget and many others has had a substantial and significant influence on educational practices. Research has obviously influenced education in terms of teaching materials and methods, conceptions of the nature of the learner, and of the various means of solving educational problems.

The concepts of action research, applied research and evaluation research have played an important part in trying to bring educational researchers closer to practitioners (see chapter 2 for a discussion of these concepts). Most people would agree that the two partners have at least started a dialogue, although the gap between them is still wide. There is some evidence today of a greater acceptance by teachers of research findings than was the case, say, thirty years ago. Also, many educational researchers have now accepted, in principle, that research data must be made accessible to a wider audience including teachers (potential consumers) for both the improvement of educational practice and for the general benefit of society. Today, educational researchers seem to be less dogmatic, and are willing to consider both achievements and limitations of research design and methodology.

There is no denying that the progress of research in education has been slower than research in other fields. Of the many factors contributing to this lack of progress, attitudes between teachers, administrators and decision makers on the one hand and researchers on the other hand have not been favourable. But there is a growing realisation amongst all concerned that no matter how elusive the term 'educational research' may be or the activity it is meant to designate, they share a common view with regard to the objective of educational research. Research is identified with an enquiry or investigation conducted to gain an overall understanding of the educational field, and to direct towards a closer understanding of the learning-teaching process, with a view to improving it. Many people even believe that for all kinds of social problems the solution lies with education (e.g. eradication of illiteracy, reduction in inter-group hostility and conflict, racial discord, crime and delinquency). However, the value of research to education or to any other aspects of human life cannot be over-estimated.

Notes

1 For a further discussion of Piaget's research see R.M. Beard's *An Outline of Piaget's Developmental Psychology*, London : Routledge and Kegan Paul, (1969)

4 Methods of educational research

A glance through the literature seems to suggest that there is no generally accepted scheme for classifying educational research studies. However, the reason for using some forms of classification stems from the fact that the criteria for evaluating educational research becomes clearer when they are related to the specific methodological characteristics of each category. Another advantage in using some sort of classification is that it makes the analysis of research processes more intelligible and comprehensible, because modern educational research embraces elements of several related disciplines and makes use of a number of techniques. The three broad categories of research methodologies are:

1 Historical method of research
2 Descriptive method of research
3 Experimental method of research

None of these categories is intrinsically superior to the others. Each makes its own particular contribution to educational knowledge. In chapter 8 examples of various types of research studies in education are summarised. Sometimes a piece of research may fall into more than one of the categories. For example, after identifying the problem of investigation a research worker may usefully begin with an historical study to determine what has been done in the past, and then go on to collect information about the present state of affairs regarding the problem, which would constitute a descriptive or experimental study. Many research programmes in education make use of all three methods. It should be remembered however that the methods and strategies employed in a research programme should always be dictated by the nature of the problem and the kind of data sought.

Historical method of research

The researcher uses the historical method to understand the present in the light of past events and trends. It can be summarised as viewing today retrospectively. On the basis of information about the past it helps the researcher to predict the direction of future developments with some degree of confidence. The historical study of an educational institution for example, can give us a perspective in order to understand the present educational system, and this understanding may help to establish a basis for further progress and improvement.

During the 1920s and 1930s, historical educational research received a great deal of attention, and a number of books were published. In more recent times, the historical method in educational research has regained the reputation which it had lost during the 1930s because of the misuse of the method by several research projects in the USA (Barnes, 1960). Today, the focus and strategy of historical research have changed, attempting to achieve rigorous critical standards in dealing with educational problems. Thus, modern historical research may be described as the application of systematic and rigorous methods of enquiry for understanding the past; it is an interpretative synthesis of past events and records. According to Travers (1978) historical research 'involves a procedure supplementary to observation, a process by which the historian seeks to test the truthfulness of the reports of observations made by others'.

The research methodology consists of collection, organisation, verification, validation and analysis of information in accordance with a set of specific standards. All these steps in historical research provide the kind of evidence which may lead to new understanding of the past and its relevance to the present and the future.

Studies of an historical nature in educational research consist of a large and broad collection of data. They may include histories of the lives and work of leaders in educational thought and practice, and past information about educational movements and trends. The historical approach to educational issues such as school discipline, the 11+ examination system, methods of instruction and mixed ability teaching has been used in research. The problem involved in the process of historical research makes it a somewhat difficult task. Barzun and

Graff's (1970) recent work is interesting because it suggests how to deal with basic problems in treating historical information.

The essential steps in the use of the historical method in educational research are defining the problem, gathering the data, evaluating and synthesising the data and finally, presenting the findings. The data gathering process is largely a mechanical exercise. The second process of research (criticism of data) draws heavily from logic, and reporting the findings is based on facts and opinions. In data collection the researcher can turn to two kinds of sources: primary and secondary.

As the term implies, primary sources are first hand, original data related to events in the past. The sources for data are documents such as diaries of eye-witnesses, court records and statistics; artifacts, such as tools and art objects of the past; and on the spot records such as files and photographs. The major part of the data is derived from primary sources which constitutes the basic materials of historical research. If a researcher is studying the historical development of the tripartite system of education in the UK he must address himself to primary sources.

Secondary sources of information include the accounts of a person who relates the testimony of an actual witness of an event. Common examples of secondary sources are history textbooks, newspaper reports of an event not written by an eye-witness, biographies and other secondhand descriptions. This kind of evidence obviously has limited value because of the distortion of the facts which is likely to take place in transmitting the information from one person to another. Because of this limitation historical researchers tend to employ primary sources as much as possible.

It is not always useful to make a rigid classification of source materials because the same source may be either primary or secondary depending on how it is used. For example, if a research is designed to study the policies of a local education authority concerning multicultural education at a particular period of time, the local newspaper editorials on the subject during the time would be secondary sources. On the other hand, if the aim of the research was to explore editorial policy toward the local education authority on multicultural education, the editorials would be treated as primary sources. A main concern in the collection of data in historical research in education should be to locate primary sources, that is, to obtain data that are as close to the facts as possible.

Historians have developed various procedures for the evaluation of historical materials. They have given educational researchers two levels of criticism to consider — external criticism and internal criticism. External criticism attempts to distinguish between a misrepresentation and a genuine document or authentic relic, monument or any other source of data; but the genuineness of data does not always establish the accuracy of its contents. Internal criticism, on the other hand, aims at determining the validity and accuracy of actual historical data. In other words, the main concern of internal criticism is to reveal a true picture of what actually happened at a particular place and time. Thus, truthfulness becomes the guidelines to internal criticism.

Having subjected historical data to external criticism for genuineness or authenticity, and to internal criticism for trustworthiness or relevance of material, the question of synthesis and reporting becomes an important one. This is a philosophical process in which the researcher draws the threads together into a meaningful pattern, and then applies it to test the hypothesis formulated at the outset. Although hypotheses are not always explicitly stated in historical investigations, they are usually implied. This stage of research requires a great deal of imagination and resourcefulness on the part of the researcher. He must take great care to report facts as 'objectively' as possible.

Historical research is an interesting exercise which can make a significant contribution to the field of education by tracing a particular aspect of education through a particular period of time in order to identify factors that have influenced the development of the concept or idea involved. In fact the activities of the historian, when education is the field of enquiry, are no different from those working in any other fields. However, at this point, a brief examination of its strengths and limitations seems appropriate.

Since the historical researcher draws his data from the experiences and observations of others, he has to depend upon inference and logical analysis for filling in the details of his picture of the particular historical event being studied. This introduces bias of the researcher. The researcher has no control over which documents, relics, records and artifacts happen to be available, hence he has little control over the selection of the sample materials to be studied – he can only choose to reject some of what is available. Another limitation is that he has no possibility of replicating the study. Historical knowledge is invariably incomplete since it is derived from the surviving data of a limited number of events that took place in the past. Many historical studies in education not dealing with recent events make (excessive) use of secondary sources of information. Furthermore, the researcher often must interpret the meaning of a document in order to draw conclusions. This process is a difficult one since word meanings and usage tend to change over the years.

In spite of the many limitations in historical research, there is some relevant information which cannot be obtained by other means. For example, if a researcher wishes to assess the effects of student sit-ins on the subsequent policy of higher education in the UK since 1972 then only the historical research approach can shed some light in charting the evolution of the educational institution. That particular situation may not always be duplicated, and even if it were many circumstances would be different.

Another obvious advantage of the historical method in education is its unobtrusiveness. Since the researcher is removed from the events and situations he is investigating, there is no danger of contaminating the research by his proximity. In most historical studies the researcher does not need to get permission of, say, the school authority to carry out his research. Because of the uninvolved nature of the historical research it may be more acceptable to study even a controversial issue for which other types of research would be extremely difficult. Historical research by individuals may be limited to studies of specific educational problems in schools or colleges, but the combined picture of such research can give an indication of how and why the problem arose in a particular situation. However, in view of its limitations great caution should be taken in generalising the findings of historical research in education.

Descriptive method of research

While the historical method describes past events the descriptive method of research is primarily concerned with portraying the present. In actual fact the descriptive method in the educational field is not exactly a method, because many approaches of data collection are grouped together. However, each of them has one element in common — each endeavours to depict the present position of a given situation. The main difference between various types of descriptive research is in the process of description. For example, description by interview and description by testing are entirely different types of research, but both of them come under the heading of descriptive research.

Early developments in educational research (see chapter 2) have been concerned with making precise and accurate assessments of the educational problem and relationships of the phenomena that existed. Even today there are educational problems about which we need to know something of the nature of the factors which brought about the current condition before proceeding any further. For example, in order to solve problems of children's poor self-esteem some information has to be collected about the nature of the problem, educational practices, attitudes, home background, and existing level of self-esteem.

The process of descriptive research goes beyond mere collection and tabulation of factual data. It is not only a structural attempt to obtain facts and opinions about the current condition of things, but it involves elements of comparison, and of relationships of one kind or another. Descriptive research may not answer all the fundamental questions, but it provides useful data which can serve as a basis for further research using more rigorous experimental design. Thus, the discovery of meaning is the focus of the whole process. It should be mentioned that in social sciences it is notoriously difficult to establish cause and effect relationships. However, by identifying the nature of factors and interpreting the meaning or significance of 'what is', it may be possible to formulate some hypothesis for further work.

Although much progress has been made in recent years in identifying the variables and the relationships between them in order to solve educational problems, there are many areas about which very little is known. Hence there is a need to develop an understanding of the various stages in descriptive research and to be aware of its different techniques for the collection and interpretation of data.

As stated earlier, descriptive research involves a certain amount of interpretation of the meaning or significance of what is described. This process is often criticised on the grounds of bias towards the investigator's subjective judgements and superficial impressions of phenomena. Nevertheless, an examination of the many theses and dissertations submitted in the last two decades indicates that the descriptive method has been widely used. In order to mitigate the validity of the above criticisms it is necessary for research workers to adopt carefully structured plans.

1 Recognition and definition of the social or educational problem which is to be studied.
2 A decision must be made about the kind of data required, and a description of this would be necessary.
3 Formulation of hypotheses concerning the phenomena which are to be tested; these must be clearly stated pointing out the assumptions underlying the hypotheses. In case the study is of an exploratory nature, a tentative hypothesis should be stated — it may be difficult to specify definite hypotheses at the initial stage.
4 Selection and description of appropriate subjects/samples and a detailed description of the methods which are to be followed in the study.
5 Selection of the research tools, techniques or instruments which are to be used in the collection of data. If new/modified techniques or tools have been utilised, a more detailed description

including psychometric characteristics should be given.

6   Hypotheses should be tested on the basis of data collected; sometimes it becomes necessary to collect further data or amend the original hypothesis.

7   Finally, the results must be described, analysed and interpreted. It is important to remember that the results must be reported in clear precise terms.

Before leaving this section one or two points need to be emphasised. There are various means of data collection in descriptive research. It is often suggested that the investigator should be flexible in his approach. However, the decision with regard to the types of techniques, tools or instruments must be made in accordance with the nature of the problem, the hypotheses to be tested, and the resources available for carrying out the research. If the researcher finds that none of the existing instruments are appropriate for his particular needs, he should consider modifying them or even constructing new ones (see chapter 5 for a discussion on various tools of research in education). An example of how standardised, modified and new instruments were interwoven can be seen in the evaluation of the Schools Council's Humanities Curriculum Project (Verma, 1980).

Types of descriptive studies

There is no general agreement with regard to the classification of descriptive studies. For example, an interesting study under the title *Middletown in Transition* (Lynd and Lynd, 1937) has been classified as a survey by Jahoda, Deutsch and Cook (1951), and a case study by Young (1966). However, for the sake of convenience descriptive research in education can be classified into the following categories:

1   surveys
2   case studies
3   developmental studies
4   comparative studies

Surveys This is one of the most commonly used methods of descriptive research in education and the other behavioural sciences. Surveys involve the gathering of limited data from a relatively large number of cases at a particular time. This method is frequently employed to indicate prevailing conditions or particular trends. It is not concerned with characteristics of individuals as individuals, but it is concerned with providing information about population variables. Thus, surveys are broad studies of a generalised statistical nature rather than in-depth studies.

A survey involves a clear definition of the problem and requires planned collection of data, careful analysis and interpretation of the data and skilful reporting of the findings. It may be broad or narrow in scope involving several countries or be restricted to one nation, country, local authority or school. Survey data may be gathered from the entire population or from a carefully selected sample of the total population (see chapter 5 on sampling).

Surveys include topics such as population trends and movement, pupil and/or teacher opinions on various educational matters, pupil drop-out rates etc. The survey method has been widely used in educational research for many years in the British context. Data have been collected through the use of questionnaires, interviews, standardised tests and other techniques, and the results of such information have often helped to make decisions which have changed many educational practices in British schools.

An example of survey studies is that of the National Foundation for Educational Research's study (Townsend, 1971) which was funded by the Department of Education and Science. The project was designed to study the educational arrangements in schools for immigrant pupils, and was planned in three stages: a survey of administrative provisions in LEAs; a survey of organisation in a sample of primary and secondary schools; and intensive observation and attitude assessment in a smaller sample of schools.

Today long term surveys are more common than short term surveys. The school survey is usually the product of a team of researchers which explores and evaluates many aspects of the school system such as teaching staff, curriculum, teaching methods, financial support, buildings and so on. This type of survey can only be conducted by the sponsorship of such organisations as the NFER, Government departments, Schools Council and Nuffield Foundations. In Britain there is an increasing tendency for educational surveys to be carried out by the local education authorities and the findings are usually published in the journals. One of the major advantages in localised survey research is to provide regional information which can form the basis of administrative action. However, individuals also use the survey method for research but on a smaller scale.

As mentioned earlier, many types of educational phenomena can be explored by means of the survey. Broadly, these include various factors within and outside the school which affect pupil learning, together with information about teachers characteristics and educational achievement of pupils. Many surveys have also been conducted in recent years for the purpose of comparing educational attainment of pupils in different schools, cities, neighbourhoods and countries. Chall (1967) studied reading instruction by analysing research studies on reading and teaching materials, interviewing authors of reading methods and manuals and observing over three hundred classrooms in the United States and England. This was a three year study and was funded by the Carnegie Corporation. Another study (Husen, 1967) — The International Study of Achievement in Mathematics — compared achievement in mathematics in twelve countries. It was a six year survey, and tests were administered to thirteen year olds and to students in the last year of school prior to university entrance. More than 132,000 pupils, 13,000 teachers and 5,000 schools drawn from the twelve countries were involved. The two volume report of this survey research has compared the data obtained from across cultures.

The survey is a useful and widely used type of research. Although it does not seem to aspire to develop an organised body of knowledge, it does provide information for further research of an experimental nature which may lead to the establishment of some theory. The method seems to have the advantage of being an effective way of collecting data from a large number of sources, relatively cheaply and perhaps in a short time. Furthermore, the results can be analysed quickly and action can be taken if this is the objective of the study. Surveys usually make use of sampling to produce valid and reliable generalisation. There are limitations, however, in this type of descriptive research. The researcher's role is a minor one, since in most cases, he does not come into contact with people who provide the data. Another weakness is that if the problem is politically or socially sensitive, some respondents may not wish to divulge their true feelings. In surveys mailing is almost inevitable and recognised as a major factor in non-response. In spite of these limitations the survey method has proved useful in providing the researcher with a valid description of some of the variables involved in education.

Case studies The case study is essentially research in depth rather than breadth. The typical case study is an intensive analysis and evolutionary description of an individual. This method is not practical with a large sample. However, it can be employed in studying a small group of individuals.

The clinical type of case study is often carried out by social workers, psychiatrists and clinical psychologists for the purpose of diagnosing an individual's problems. In this context emphasis is upon the study of an individual's personality. The method perhaps has its origin in the Freudian approach which attempted to diagnose and treat patients with personality problems.

In education and the other behavioural sciences the method has been conducted with individual children, with all types of groups —

from a small group within a class to the school itself. Today, psychologists, sociologists and anthropologists seem to utilise the case study method with a view to supplementing the survey method. Young (1966) remarks that 'the most meaningful numerical studies in social sciences are those which are linked with exhaustive case studies describing the interrelationships of factors and of processes'. Case studies may reveal certain relevant information which is not obtained through the survey method. However, in many research programmes the two methods operate complimentary to each other.

The greatest advantage of this method is that it endeavours to understand the whole individual in relation to his environment. Koluchova's (1972) case study of severe deprivation in twins provides an illustration of the planned way in which case studies can and ought to be carried out. Since the interviewer has to probe deeply into the dynamics of an individuals personality, he must be trained in the planning and the structuring of the case study, in obtaining necessary information and in the interpretation of data.

There are certain weaknesses, however, in this method. One of the problems is that information obtained is often of a confidential nature, and therefore, it can hardly be evaluated by other research workers. An obvious shortcoming of the method is that the cases or the individuals selected for the study may not be representative or typical and hence generalisations will not be valid. Although the study of a single unit in this method may be thought to have limited value in establishing generalisations, its major advantage is in the formulation of hypotheses which can later be tested through more rigorous research. Another problem is that research based upon the study of a single case or a few cases can be very expensive in terms of time and finance.

Teachers are often engaged in studies of individual children. In order to understand the behaviour of children they obtain information on their home background, school attainment, attitudes and interests, relationships with the peer group, intellectual abilities or disabilities, personality and standardised test results. In this instance when case studies stem from attempts to learn about children in order to help them, the research aspect is of limited value.

Developmental studies Developmental studies are not only concerned with the description of the current state of affairs, and interrelationships of phenomena in a given situation, but also with the changes which take place as a result of the time factor. In this type of descriptive research, investigators describe children's development over a period of months or even years. This method is educationally important in the sense that educators are concerned with the physical,

mental and emotional development of childre
more about what children are like at differ
from one another within age levels, and h
In designing a school curriculum it is extre
consideration the relevant characteristics
in this design recorded data are utilise
what has been happening in the past, wh
and what will be likely to happen in
population of the immigrant community
over a period of time, one might say that by a certa
the population will reach a particular level. The assump
upon the possibility that the factors (such as higher fertility an
er age structure in case of immigrants) producing the growth w
continue to exert their influence in the future.

There are two commonly used methods to study children's characteristics, and the ways in which these characteristics change with growth:
the longitudinal and the cross-sectional methods. In longitudinal
research the same sample of subjects is studied at intervals (say, at
the age of nine, ten, eleven and twelve). For example, a researcher
may wish to investigate how reading comprehension patterns of a
group of children develop over a period of time. This would be possible
by measuring this concept at each successive year, and by plotting
the patterns of development for each child and for the group. The
cross-sectional method, on the other hand, attempts to study different
samples of subjects from each age level. The results are then plotted
showing the pattern of development for children from nine to twelve
years of age.

The longitudinal research has proved to be most effective in studying
children's development over a period of time since it allows for intensive studies of a large number of cases and of many variables. The
idea behind longitudinal studies as they have been employed in educational and social research is to answer questions about an individual's
development from evidence based on a large number of cases. However, studies of this type demand a great deal of time, resources and
money. Some of the longitudinal studies in America were maintained
for thirty-five years (Terman and Oden, 1959). Two of the major
longitudinal studies in Britain are of interest and relevance to education
in a broader sense. Douglas (1967) studied just over five thousand
children employing a wide variety of measures, and Newson and Newson (1965, 1970, 1978) have been engaged in a long term study of
children growing up in a representative English midland city. Because
of the economy of space the results from these studies are not given
here. However, one of the findings in both the studies has underlined
the significant impact that social class makes on an individual's develop-

longitudinal study enquiring into the development of
y was conducted by West (1969). The investigator followed
of London boys from the age of eight to eighteen in an
to trace the emergence of delinquent behaviour, and to ob-
the psychological and sociological characteristics that accompany

An evaluation of longitudinal studies would suggest that the way
n which studies are usually carried out serves two main purposes:
first, because the sample of subjects is studied at certain points in their
development a cross-sectional picture of a particular age group can
emerge; and secondly, if the sample has been carefully chosen and
is representative of all children of a particular age, this can give us
information about the number of children who have reached a certain
stage in development, the number with highly developed intellectual
skills, the number with particular educational problems, and so on.
The relationship between these measures and some relevant variables
(sex, parents' occupations, family size, etc.) can be of considerable
importance. This knowledge can be of great value, particularly where
the planning of educational and social policy is concerned.

Longitudinal studies have a number of inherent practical difficulties.
Contact with the same sample of subjects over a long period of time
can be difficult. Loss of subjects is quite common; and there is also
the problem of retaining the interest of subjects over a longer period
of time. Perhaps one could minimise the occurrence of these difficulties
as long as the subject is attending an educational institution, but the
main difficulty arises once employment has begun. If the sample
chosen turns out to be unrepresentative, there is no way to redress
it. Furthermore, once the study has reached its final stages it will
not be possible to introduce new variables for investigation. Therefore,
such projects require a careful planning and farsightedness, with a
degree of flexibility built into the design in order to make minor
changes possible at a later stage. Although the general format of contemporary longitudinal studies is the same − regular contact with a
sample of children, their homes, and their schools − the types of
measurements to be included and the process of data collection varies
from study to study. The word measurement should be taken in a
broader sense to imply some sort of classification or evaluation of
individuals or their circumstances.

Some of the practical difficulties inherent in the longitudinal method
do not appear in cross-sectional studies. The cross-sectional method
attempts to study children of various age levels at the same point in
time. Because this approach is less expensive and less time consuming
it is more commonly used in the field of education. An investigator

64

can collect and analyse the data in a relatively short time. Thus one of the main advantages of cross-sectional research is its cheapness and the speed with which the results can be obtained. The main limitation of this approach is that it cannot answer questions about the changes in and the relationships between the different aspects of the child's experience with time. A further disadvantage is that chance differences between samples may bias the results. Selection of age group samples which are representative of the total population may present difficulty, especially if the study is confined to one local education authority or one city. However, if we want to know about certain physical, intellectual and emotional characteristics of typical children at various stages, the cross-sectional approach is perhaps preferable because the chances of obtaining a large sample are higher. On the other hand, if we wish to learn about certain changes in children's characteristics, the longitudinal method is perhaps better since the researcher follows the same sample of subjects through their developmental stages. It should also be mentioned that most research students and university teachers tend to conduct cross-sectional studies because of the lack of sufficient financial support.

Comparative studies The comparative type of research forms a link between the two types of previously discussed research (case studies and surveys) and experimental method of research. Some investigators try to make comparisons of existing situations which provide a similar kind of information to that experimental studies might yield. Such studies may be described as causal-comparative. This method is sometimes referred to as *ex post facto* design.

In a laboratory situation, the experimenter attempts to control all variables except the independent variable which he deliberately manipulates to see what occurs. Because of the complexity and nature of social phenomena, an investigator cannot always manipulate or even control the factors in order to study cause and effect relationships. For example, it is impossible to control and manipulate home background, intelligence or social class. In these circumstances a study of what actually happens in a natural environment would perhaps be more relevant than in a controlled laboratory situation.

A research worker may decide to find out the factor or factors that are associated with certain types of pupils' behaviour. For example, studies of academically motivated children may compare the social and educational backgrounds of highly and lowly motivated children. The question may be asked about the factors common to the highly motivated and to lowly motivated children. Any factors common to one group, but not to the other might give us some indication as to the underlying causes of poor motivation.

Many educational researchers have utilised the comparative method of research in the analysis of educational programmes, practices and outcomes. The problems range from relatively simple designs to fairly complex studies in which some elements of the experimental method are also employed (e.g. the use of control groups). Studies in this category often employ correlational analysis to determine relationship. The 't' test is an appropriate statistical technique to determine the level of significance of differences between defined groups. Some writers call this method correlational studies.

It should be kept in mind that in addition to seeking probable causes, comparative research is often used in the educational field to ascertain differences between defined groups. Investigations comparing different racial/ethnic groups or those comparing normal with handicapped groups are not aimed primarily to explore causes, but to gain an insight into the relative characteristics of the groups compared.

The initial procedures of comparative design are basically the same as those employed in other methods of research. However, considerable emphasis is placed upon biographical data of the subject such as family relationships, peer-group relations, school records and other information.

One of the dangers of the comparative research method is that, because two variables or factors go together, some people conclude that one is the cause and the other the effect. This error of confusing merely association with cause could lead readers of research reports to deduce a false cause-effect relationship. Although the causal-comparative method has some merit, it has several limitations as well. Failure to isolate the real significant factor, failure to recognise that problems might have multiple rather than single causative factors and drawing firm conclusions on the basis of a limited number of occurrences may lead the investigator to misleading conclusions. Classifying subjects into comparable control and experimental groups also pose difficulties since social events are not alike except within broad categories. In comparative studies of natural environments, the investigator cannot apply the stringent criterion in selecting his sample of subjects. In spite of many limitations in the comparative method of research it does provide a means of dealing with many educational problems which cannot be explored in a laboratory situation. This method has attained some respectability in recent years with the advent of new techniques, tools and methods of conducting educational research.

Experimental methods of research

The experimental method is often regarded as the 'scientific' approach in research. As we have seen in the earlier sections, historical research studies of past events are conducted, primarily for the purpose of gaining a clearer understanding of the present, and in descriptive research attempts are made to determine the nature and degree of existing conditions. In the experimental research, through manipulating an experimental variable, attempts are made to determine how and why a particular condition or event occurs. This manipulation is deliberate and systematic. So, for any experimental study, there has to be an independent variable that is manipulated by the researcher under highly controlled conditions.

The experimental method has its roots in the natural sciences. Within the social sciences it has been applied chiefly by psychologists, but there are indications that its use is becoming more widespread in sociology and other disciplines. One of the early investigators who extended the experimental method into education was Thorndike (1924). One of the main functions of experimentation is to generalise the factor or the variable relationship so that they may be applied outside the laboratory to a wider population. However, in the social sciences it is not always possible to adopt the same methodologies and strategies as used in the natural sciences. One of the reasons is that conducting experimental research can be extremely costly and time consuming. Moreover, in educational research, we are concerned with human behaviour which is most difficult, and at times impossible, to control and manipulate. Critics of experimental research contend that experimental studies relating to education lack realism, and results obtained have little practical significance to the classroom setting. Admittedly, the control of the independent variable and outside factors is difficult when dealing with human behaviour. This is not to say, however, that the problems are difficult to overcome. The experimental method has been utilised with varying degrees of success in the field of education, where, within certain limits, it is sometimes possible to control significant influences to an extent.

In experimental research all variables or factors identified as relevant to the problem under study are controlled or held constant while the impact of one or more variables is deliberately manipulated (e.g. a particular teaching method) so that its effect may be assessed; in other words, it involves deliberate manipulation of certain stimuli or treatments by the experimenter, and the observation and analysis of how the behaviour of the subject is affected or changed. In its simplest form an experiment has three components: the variable which the experimenter systematically and deliberately manipulates during the course of the experiment is called the independent variable (the experimental treatment); the effect produced from the manipulation of the independent variable is called the dependent variable (the outcome or the result of the experiment); all the variables except the independent variable are held constant. An essential element of the experimental design is the development of the experimental and control situation prior to the actual experiment. We shall examine these and other concepts used in experimental research in a moment.

Experiments in education can be conducted either in a classroom situation (a natural setting) or in a laboratory. In a laboratory situation factors or variables can be controlled adequately whereas experiments in a natural setting are less susceptible to such control because of the many unknown and floating variables. It is true that educators prefer to undertake experiments in classroom settings arguing that if one wants to know how to influence pupil learning in the class, then one should conduct experiments in the classroom. The most difficult task for the researcher, however, is to apply strict experimental methods and strategies to educational problems by controlling the extraneous variables while manipulating the independent variable.

There is no single, simple formula which can be prescribed for conducting experimental research under controlled conditions. The essential ingredients of experimental research are the use of an hypothesis, rigid control, sensitive measurement/assessment techniques and those variables which can be carefully introduced to measure their effect or impact on the phenomenon under study. The first step in this process is to define and analyse the problem, followed by the formulation of an hypothesis. The experimenter then tests the hypothesis and confirms or rejects it in the light of the outcome. It should be borne in mind that the confirmation or rejection of the hypothesis is stated in terms of probability rather than certainty. Most social scientists accept this research process, but they are also aware that this methodology has only minor application to the study of many educational problems in the classroom context.

There are a number of essential steps in experimental design which require close attention by the research worker:

1   The investigator should first of all identify the problem and define it clearly. The source of the problem may be based upon personal experience, reading the literature in a particular area or discussion with other educators or social scientists. For example, the researcher may feel on the basis of his experience that students who are taught by the discussion method have a better understanding of controversial issues than students taught by the lecture method. A search of the literature relating to this problem may provide the basis for reformulating initial

ideas as well as for forming new ones. Thus definition of a problem involves the evaluation not just of the concepts to be utilised but of the propositions and theories as well.

2 The investigator should then formulate an hypothesis or hypotheses in clear and unambiguous terms. He may even wish to simply state broad questions at the initial stage. In some cases it may be necessary to state the null hypothesis. (See Glossary).

3 The experimenter should identify as many variables as possible which are likely to affect the understanding of students with regard to controversial issues, and should decide which of these he is going to manipulate. This process must be completed before the actual experiment begins. In moving from problem definition to experimental design, the implications of the general research objectives must be outlined in order to make decisions on specific procedures.

4 The next step is to make a list of all possible non-experimental variables that might contaminate the experiment. The investigator has to decide how to control them in some fashion.

5 The researcher's next task is to select an experimental design which constitutes the blueprint for the collection and analysis of the data. It is also important to keep in mind the limitations of the experimental design selected for application. The development of a research design, however, does not necessarily move the investigator toward more highly structured techniques.

6 At the same time as the researcher considers the design for the experiment he must consider the sample of subjects who will be involved in the study. Questions such as the size of the sample, their ability level, age, sex, etc. have to be decided. It will also be necessary to decide how to obtain representative samples of the chosen population, how to divide these subjects into groups who will be treated differently and then compared (e.g. experimental and control groups). In assigning subjects to groups for the experiment, the investigator must adopt a system that operates independently of his personal judgement and of the characteristics of the subjects themselves (see chapter 5 for a discussion of some of the problems in the area of sampling).

7 The next task of the investigator is to decide about the tests, techniques or measurement instruments which have to be used to evaluate the outcome of the experiment. If existing tools are not satisfactory, new tests have to be developed in accordance with the requirements of the research design. These tests must be evaluated by reference to the concepts of reliability

and validity.

8   The procedures for data collection should be outlined. In order to ascertain that the experimental methods will work it is always advisable to conduct a pilot experiment with a small group of subjects (say, 50 pupils). This trial experiment would enable the investigator to test the instruments and/or techniques as well as the research design.

9   At this point the scene is set to conduct the final experiment in a well planned way. The statistical or null hypothesis, whichever has been formulated, must be stated at this stage.

10 Finally, the data obtained should be processed and analysed in order to produce an appraisal of the effect which is assumed to exist. The application of an appropriate test of significance will be necessary to determine the confidence one can place on the results of the experiment. It should be recalled that hypotheses are confirmed or rejected in terms of probability rather than certainty.

It should be mentioned that sometimes the researcher is compelled to depart from the basic rules of experimental design because administrative conditions, limited resources etc. restrict what he can do. For example, the researcher may decide to assign fourth year secondary school pupils at random to three different groups to be exposed to three different teaching strategies. However, the school may not allow him to do this by saying that the pupils are already assigned to different classes for teaching purposes. Under these circumstances the researcher cannot conduct a 'true' experiment though he may still do a study that comes close to being an experimental research project. Such research studies are called quasi-experiments. The term, first introduced by Campbell and Stanley (1963), has been widely used in the social sciences. In quasi-experiments the conditions are taken as they are found in naturally occuring contexts. The 'true' experiment, on logical grounds necessarily yields more certain knowledge and understanding than the quasi-experiment, and whenever possible, should be carried out in preference to the quasi-experiment.

Terms used in experimental research design

In order to understand experimental research design, it is necessary to understand certain terms which are commonly used in the discussion of experimental designs.

Experimental and control groups

Experiments are designed to produce results that can be applied to groups other than those who participated in the experiment. Therefore, a crucial decision in the design of an experimental research project is the selection of those individuals who are to take part in the experiment. It is necessary that both the initial and the final discussion of any experiment should include information about the way in which subjects were chosen, and some indication of the groups to whom the findings can be reasonably applied.

An experiment involves the comparison of a particular treatment (the independent variable) with a different treatment or with no treatment. In a simple conventional experiment two groups of individuals are required; these groups are referred to as the experimental and control groups. The two groups are equated as nearly or closely as possible. The experimental group is exposed to the influence of a particular treatment; the control group is not. It should be remembered that the control group is basically similar or comparable (but not necessarily identical) to the experimental group. Observations or measurements are then made to determine what change/changes have occurred in the experimental group as compared with the control group.

Experiments are not always designed to make a treatment, non-treatment comparison. In other words, the control group, as earlier defined (a group receiving no treatment), is not an essential ingredient in the experimental method of research. There are many situations in which researchers are concerned with comparing the efficiency of two types of instructional method. For example, in an experiment exploring the relative efficiency of the lecture method as compared to the discussion method in teaching humanities to students there are really no experimental and control groups. In this example, each group is subjected to a different treatment. The treatment refers to the method of teaching — lecture versus discussion. On the other hand, if a researcher is investigating the impact of a new curriculum programme on pupils' critical thinking the control group becomes an essential element in the experimental design. In this case the hypothesis will be formulated to find out whether the new curriculum programme is superior to having no instruction. Pupils who will participate in the new programme are the experimental group whereas pupils who will not take part are treated as the control or non-experimental group. The decision of whether or not to employ a control group is not only a matter of the researcher's judgement, but is dictated by the type of hypothesis being studied.

It must be emphasised that whether an experimental design uses a control group (receiving no treatment) or two experimental groups (each receiving a different treatment) the research worker must try to make the two groups equivalent in respect of all the factors that may influence the dependent variable except for the factor/factors he chooses as the independent variable. In practice it is extremely difficult to select the two groups from the population who are equivalent or comparable in all aspects. However, various methods of equating the different groups are employed, and we shall briefly discuss some of them that are commonly used in educational research.

Randomisation   This can be achieved by a pure chance selection of subjects from a given population. Randomisation is perhaps the simplest and most economical way of assigning individuals to groups. The procedure involves assigning subjects to the experimental and control groups in such a way that the two groups are reasonably similar.

If two groups are required for the study, randomisation can be achieved by drawing random names from a hat. When more than two groups are involved, a table of random numbers can be used. The principle of randomisation is based on the assumption that differences between groups will tend to cancel each other out. This assumption is more sustainable in case of large groups than when smaller groups are used.

Randomisation attempts to provide an effective method of eliminating bias that enters into the experimental design and of minimising the influence of extraneous variables. However, it is up to the researcher to decide, depending upon the circumstances, as to when and what kind of randomisation should be used. He is the only person who is in a position to ascertain whether subjects should be selected randomly, or/and individuals should be randomly assigned to different treatments, or/and experimental treatments should be randomly assigned to selected groups.

Matching   Another procedure for equating groups is to select pairs or groups of individuals with similar characteristics and assign one of them to the experimental group and the other to the control group. Perhaps this is not the most efficient procedure of equating individuals in the experimental and control groups, or experimental and experimental groups. There are various problems associated with this method. First, matching is a complex method. In order to make groups as comparable as possible, it is necessary to match them on a number of characteristics because of the composition of human traits. The researcher should have a large number of individuals in the initial pool because the matching process usually results in some individuals being excluded if a matching subject is not available. Thus, the final group/groups may not adequately represent the population.

Another problem in this procedure is that in many studies the researcher is not sure about which characteristics are relevant, and hence about which variables need to be matched. Because of this uncertainty, research workers in the field of social sciences, particularly in education, are often faced with the problem of deciding what variables should be controlled or minimised.

A number of procedures have been utilised to match individuals or equate groups. Each seems to have certain limitations and problems associated with it. Many writers suggest that this method should be avoided unless absolutely essential. We believe, however, that it should be left to the judgement of the researcher to decide about the most practical and appropriate procedure to be used in his particular situation.

Analysis of covariance Because of the problems in randomisation or matching techniques, a statistical method known as analysis of covariance (ANCOVA) is sometimes used to equate the groups on certain relevant variables identified prior to the investigation. This method tries to eliminate initial differences on several variables between the experimental and control groups by covariance techniques. In this method pre-test mean scores are used as covariates. Analysis of covariance is often useful for educational research, especially in a classroom setting. Researchers who wish to use this method are strongly recommended to consult the references by Kerlinger (1973) and Lindquist (1965) for a complete discussion.

Repeated measures In this design, each subject takes both pre- and post-tests, and thus differences between the groups can be eliminated as a source of error. The advantage of this method is that only a few subjects are required for the study because several measures can be used for each subject. One main assumption in this design is that no differential transfer of training occurs at the post-test stage as a result of the pre-test. Therefore, differences between the experimental and control groups can be eliminated. The most difficult part of the repeated measurement design is its inability to control or eliminate the influence of such extraneous variables as instrumentation, specific events between the first and second testing, maturation and outdated instruments/tools.

Treatment

The experimental condition that is introduced in an experimental research is referred to as the treatment. A treatment is a type of independent variable which the researcher manipulates in his attempt to ascertain its relationship to observed phenomena. In the simplest type of educational study, differences between the presence or absence of a particular condition on individual behaviour are explored, and this would require a comparison between two levels (presence or absence) of a particular treatment. There may be more than one independent variable in a single study, although all are not essentially manipulated by the experimenter. Also, there are more complicated experimental designs involving a multitude of independent variables (treatment), and the researcher may be interested in studying the interaction of these treatments. For example, if the treatment is a teaching strategy using a pack of teaching materials, the researcher may like to explore not only the effect of teaching on student learning but also the effects of varying amounts of exposure to the teaching strategy and the material on the learning process. In this case, the researcher has to manipulate both the type and amount of treatment.

Independent and dependent variables

In an experimental study variables are the characteristics that are manipulated, controlled or observed by the experimenter. The variable that is deliberately and systematically manipulated (a teaching method, for example) so that its effects may be measured, assessed or observed is called the independent variable. The effect produced or the change in behaviour that results from the manipulation of the independent variable is called the dependent variable. In other words, the dependent variable is that characteristic which is affected or influenced by the treatment (the independent variable), that is, the outcome of the experiment.

In most educational research programmes the dependent variable is the measured change in pupil behaviour attributable to the influence of the independent variable. It should be mentioned that depending upon the type of experimental design there may be more than one dependent variable, just as there may be more than one independent variable.

Intervening variables

There are many types of educational research in which it is notoriously difficult to establish the relationship between the independent and dependent variables. One of the crucial reasons is that certain floating variables which cannot be controlled may have a significant influence upon the outcome. Such variables intervene between the treatment and the effect. For example, in a computer assisted learning (CAL) experiment the researcher is interested in determining the effect of immediate feedback upon student learning. He knows from his experience of other studies that there are certain factors which may affect the relationship, even though they cannot be observed directly or even identified. These intervening variables may be fatigue, boredom, hope of success, anxiety, etc. However, the research worker must not ignore the existence of such variables, and efforts should be made to minimise their influence through careful designing of the experiment.

Extraneous variables

Extraneous variables are those uncontrolled variables (e.g. subject's environment or personality characteristics) that hinder attributing all differences in the dependent variable to the independent variable. These variables are not explicitly taken into account in the research design. Many educational research findings are of questionable validity because no attempts were made to minimise the influence of extraneous variables. There is no denying the fact that it is impossible to eliminate or control the influence of all extraneous variables, particularly in educational research.

The meaning of the term extraneous can perhaps be best explained by means of an illustration. A researcher wished to study the effectiveness of three methods of teaching about race relations. In order to do this, sixty fourth-year secondary school pupils were selected. The researcher was unable to randomise or control such variables as teacher competence or enthusiasm and his prejudice. The criterion of effectiveness was attitude change, measured by scores on standardised tests. At the end of one school term attitude scores of the three groups were compared. It would seem clear that many extraneous variables (e.g. differences in teachers) in this example precluded valid conclusions about the relative effectiveness of the independent variables which were three teaching methods. Statistical methods exist that can be used to estimate the extent to which the resulting difference between the three methods of teaching about race relations can be considered to be reliable and not simply a result of differences between the teachers involved.

Internal and external validity

As mentioned earlier, in social science research (including educational research) conducted outside the laboratory many extraneous variables are present in the environment or are generated by the experimental design. Although these variables cannot be completely eliminated or controlled, the research worker must try to identify as many variables as he can so that he is able to exercise sufficient control to make the findings interpretable. Campbell and Stanley (1963) have provided researchers with an excellent treatment of experimental validity. According to them there are two types of experimental validity — internal and external.

Internal validity deals with such questions as: 'Did the treatment really make a difference in the dependent variable?' 'How can the investigator be sure that it was the experimental treatment that made a difference in the outcome between the groups?' External validity is concerned with the generalisability or representativeness of the research findings. It provides an answer to the question: 'How far can the research findings be generalised?' That is, to which populations, samples, situations, events and experimental variables can the observed, assessed or measured effect be generalised?

The questions concerning internal validity cannot be answered by the researcher with any confidence unless his design provides sufficient control of extraneous variables. He must therefore attempt to determine whether the changes in the dependent variable were not influenced by extraneous and uncontrolled factors. The extent to which this objective is achieved is a measure of the internal validity of the experiment. It must be recognised that the attainment of both maximum internal and maximum external validity is considered as the most skilful experimental design, but in practice it is extremely difficult to achieve.

Campbell (1957) has identified a number of extraneous variables that must be controlled. We shall consider some of the variables which can affect the internal validity of the experiment. The interactive effects of these factors with the treatment can affect the external validity of experimental findings. The following factors seem to pose threats to the internal validity:

History — in a conventional pre- and post-design some external event or situation beyond the control of the researcher may have a favourable or disturbing effect upon the performance of subjects. The appearance of these extra-experimental uncontrolled factors is referred to as the confounding effect upon the treatment. If this confounding effect is a specific event, action or situation it is called history.

Maturation — individuals change in many different ways over a period of time, and the possibility exists that these changes can be confused with the influence of the experimental treatment being studied. Thus, maturational effects are systematic and orderly over a period of time. It is true to say that in certain situations it is difficult to determine whether the improved performance over a period of time is due to the experimental variable or to maturation or an interaction of the independent variable with maturation.

Testing — the process of pre-testing prior to the experiment may influence the performance on the post-test. There are other problems associated with testing. Tests may make subjects more aware of hidden purposes of the researcher, and may act as a stimulus to change.

Instrumentation — in many studies unreliable and/or outdated tools or techniques are used to describe aspects of human behaviour. This presents a threat to the validity of an experiment. If inaccurate or inconsistent observational techniques are used, a serious element of error is introduced. If interviewers are used to study behavioural changes in subjects, changes in their criteria of judgement over a period of time may provide unreliable and invalid information.

Regression — statistical regression is a phenomenon that sometimes functions in a pre-test, post-test design and makes the results difficult to interpret. Testees who score highest at the pre-test stage are likely to score relatively lower at the second test, whereas those who score lowest on the pre-test are likely to score higher at the post-test stage. In a pre-test, post-test design there is a normal regression toward the mean. The researcher should be able to recognise the effect of this regression in the interpretation of results.

Bias in the selection of subjects — the selection of subjects is the most important aspect in an experimental research. As pointed out earlier, some form of randomisation is essential in order to evaluate properly the influence of the treatment variable. Selection bias may be introduced in the experiment if, for example, intact classes are used as experimental or control groups. However, if randomisation is not possible, matching can be used to make the groups comparable.

Experimental mortality — mortality or loss of sample is another extraneous variable. Supposing that experimental and control groups were equal to begin with, but, if any subjects drop out of one group during the experimental period, the researcher may not be able to know what kinds of members dropped out, and this loss may affect the outcome of the study. That is, any differences between the experimental and control groups on the post-test may be attributed to the biased composition of the samples. In a long term research the loss of subjects is fairly common.

Contamination — this is a type of bias introduced when the experimenter has some previous knowledge about the individuals participating in the study. This knowledge of participant characteristics may affect the objectivity of the researcher's judgement. In educational research contamination can be minimised if outside observers are utilised to assess or rate the subjects without any knowledge of their traits or characteristics.

Types of experimental design

As we noted earlier, experimental research is concerned with studying relationships between independent and dependent variables. Selection of particular experimental design should be based on the purposes of the study, the type of variables to be manipulated, the way variables are to be manipulated, and the circumstances under which the experiment has to be conducted. The design should clearly state how subjects are to be chosen for the experimental and control groups, the way extraneous variables are to be controlled and the type of statistical analysis to be used for analysing the data.

There are many different types of experimental designs available which can be utilised by researchers. In this section we have outlined a few simple experimental designs that have proved useful for use in education.

1   The single-group design   In this design a reliable form of pre- and post-testing is necessary. Broadly, it consists of three stages. The first stage is the administration of a pre-test measuring the dependent variable. In the next stage the experimental treatment or the independent variable is applied. At the third and final stage a retest is administered measuring again the dependent variable. The amount of change from pre- to post-tests is obtained, and a statistical technique is applied to ascertain whether the change, if any, is significant. Thus, this design uses a single group which is tested twice. The following is a paradigm for this design:

Pre-test	Independent variable	Post-test
Test 1	X (treatment)	Test 2

This design has a number of weaknesses. The researcher, by examining the overall performance on the pre-test and the post-test, assumes that any gains between the two testing situations are attributable to the experimental treatment. As mentioned earlier, it is extremely difficult for the researcher to know whether the change or gain between the pre- and post-test is produced by the experimental treatment or by pre-testing, the instrument used, statistical regression, maturation, extraneous variables etc. Because of the lack of a control group it cannot be ascertained whether the above mentioned factors have influenced the outcome of the experiment. Thus, the design is lacking in internal validity.

Although the single-group design does not meet all the requirements for 'scientific' experimental methodology it is often used for preliminary research or when it is impossible to obtain a control group.

2   Two groups design (post-test only)   In this design, both control and experimental groups are used. These two groups are equated by randomisation. At the conclusion of the experiment the dependent variable is measured. In other words, no pre-test is given. The mean test scores of experimental and control groups are subjected to a 't' test. The assumption is that, since subjects are randomly assigned to the experimental and control groups, the two groups will differ only to the extent that random samples from the same population differ. The design is shown below:

Group	Pre-test	Treatment	Post-test
Experimental	–	X	Test
Control	–	–	Test

This design is widely used in the educational context because of its efficiency in terms of time and economy. Randomisation is one of the main strengths in the design which assures statistical equivalence of the groups prior to the experiment. The influence of extraneous variables should be balanced in the two groups. This design may be susceptible to low internal validity because of experimental mortality. A major limitation of this design is that it cannot assess change.

3   The classical design (pre-test post-test control group design)   In this design the experimental and control groups are often equated by randomisation and hence the problem of selection bias is minimised. If the researcher is in any doubt that the groups are not comparable, analysis of covariance can be used to adjust for any initial differences between the experimental and control groups. Pre-tests are administered prior to the application of the treatment. At the conclusion of the experiment the groups are retested. The difference between the pre-test and post-test is obtained for each group, and these diffcrence scores are compared by subjecting to a 't' test in order to ascertain whether the treatment produced a greater change than no treatment. Thus, this design allows the researcher to study change over a period of time. The design is as follows:

Group	Pre-test	Treatment	Post-test
Experimental	Test 1	X	Test 2
Control	Test 1	—	Test 2

Although this design has strong internal validity, making generalisations of the results introduces some problems. That is to say, the main concern is external validity. Since both the experimental and control groups are pre-tested, it is not known whether or not the same findings will be obtained for other individuals who are selected from the same population but who were not pre-tested. The problem therefore is not lack of control but of generalisation. There is always the possibility of an interaction occurring between the pre-test and the experimental treatment. For example, if a pre-test increases or decreases the subject's sensitivity to the treatment, then the findings may be unrepresentative of the impact of the experimental variable for the unpre-tested population from which the experimental sample was drawn. The problem becomes obvious in such studies as attitude change, values, etc. It should be mentioned that the pre-test effects are dependent to a large extent on the nature and dimension of the study. For instance, in a piece of research concerned with racial attitudes the effects of pre-testing may be more marked than in a study concerned with cognitive abilities.

Another shortcoming of this design is that control subjects are likely to be contaminated by experimental subjects. Although the control group is not exposed to the experimental treatment, they would have the opportunity of interacting with experimental subjects between pre- and post-tests. For example, in a school based research, experimental and control group pupils meet in many situations except when the experimental pupils receive specific treatment.

4   Two or more experimental groups design   In some studies the researcher is concerned with two or more experimental groups whose performance has to be compared with the control group. One of the most popular of such designs is the randomised groups design which involves the random assignment of individuals to each of the experimental groups as well as to the control group. A design for three experimental groups and one control group is shown below:

Group	Pre-test	Treatment	Post-test
Experimental 1	Test 1	X	Test 2
Experimental 2	Test 1	X	Test 2
Experimental 3	Test 1	X	Test 2
Control	Test 1	—	Test 2

Let us assume that the independent variable is a film aimed at improving race relations in society. The length of the film varies between the three experimental groups. An attitude test is administered to all the four groups before and after the experimental manipulation; the control group is not exposed to this. The test data can then be analysed by comparing the change (at the post-test stage) in the three experimental groups with that manifested in the control group. In this way the researcher can compare the effects of different degrees of exposure to the film. This design has similar weaknesses to that of the classical design.

5   *Two control group design*   Solomon (1949) has developed a design which is an extension of the classical design described earlier. In this design there are two control groups and one experimental group. Subjects are randomly assigned to groups. The advantage of this three group design becomes evident in situations where the pre-test is expected to interact with the experimental manipulation. The second control group is not pre-tested but is exposed to the experimental treatment. Their post-test scores are then used to determine the interaction effect. Thus, the Solomon design of a pre-post experiment with two control groups is aimed at providing both an estimate of the magnitude of any such interaction and an estimate of the effect of the experimental treatment alone. The design is as follows:

Group	Pre-test	Treatment	Post-test
Experimental	Test 1	X	Test 2
Control 1	Test 1	—	Test 2
Control 2	—	X	Test 2

6   *The Solomon four group design*   In this design, there are two control groups and two experimental groups. Individuals are randomly assigned to groups and treatments. The effects of pre-test are controlled because only one control and one experimental group are given pre-tests but all four groups are post-tested. Expressed in table form we have:

Group	Pre-test	Treatment	Post-test
Experimental 1	Test 1	X	Test 2
Control 1	Test 1	—	Test 2
Control 2	—	X	Test 2
Control 3	—	—	Test 2

It should be noted that although the third group is exposed to the experimental manipulation it functions as a control group. One of the strengths in the four group design is that it can make several comparisons to study the impact of the independent variable. Since only one-half of the groups are pre-tested the investigator can ascertain the impact of the pre-test; he can determine the effect of the treatment in both the pre-test and non pre-test situations; and he can assess the interaction effects of pre-test and experimental treatment.

The main limitation of this design is the problem encountered in implementing it in a practical situation. The researcher requires sufficient time and resources in order to conduct two experiments simultaneously (i.e. one with pre-tests and the other without pre-tests). There is also the problem of locating enough subjects needed for this kind of design. Because of the complexity of the design rigorous statistical analysis is applied to the data.

7   *Factorial design*   The experimental designs described thus far take into account only one variable at a time. In other words, the researcher systematically manipulates one independent variable in order to produce an effect on the dependent variable. However, very often in the educational field the researcher is interested in studying the effect of two or more variables simultaneously, and in such cases he employs a factorial design. This type of design contains two or more independent variables, and each is varied in two or more ways. Thus, in a factorial design the researcher manipulates two or more variables simultaneously in order to study the independent effect of each variable on the dependent variables as well as the effects due to the interaction among the several variables.

Factorial designs have been developed at varying levels of complexity. The simple one is the 2 x 2 design. The number of digits indicates the number of independent variables being studied. The numerical value of the digits shows the number of levels for each independent variable. Suppose that a researcher is interested in comparing the effectiveness of two types of teaching strategies (discussion and lecture method) on pupil learning in the humanities in secondary schools. His experience suggests that the effects of these methods may be different according to the length of time spent. The variations of school periods are, say, sixty minutes and thirty minutes per week. Thus, in this experimental design there are two experimental treatments (discussion and lecture methods), and two conditions of learning (one hour and half-an-hour); there are four combinations of variables. The researcher assigns the subjects randomly to one of the four experimental treatment groups. Group 1 is involved in sixty minutes discussion, group 2 in thirty minutes, group 3 is assigned to sixty minutes lecture and group 4 to thirty minutes. At the end of the school term pupil learning in the humanities (dependent variable) is assessed by means of a standardised test. In this design each of two independent variables has two values. The factorial design 2 x 2, for assessing the effects of two methods of teaching on pupil learning, is shown below. It should be remembered that a 2 x 2 design requires four groups of subjects.

Method of teaching		
Time spent every week	Discussion	Lecture
60 minutes	X	X
30 minutes	X	X

The four cells represent the scores of the four groups on the dependent variable, i.e. the humanities achievement test. Thus, by using this design, the researcher can first determine the main effects for the two independent variables (discussion and lecture methods) and then the main effects of time spent on achievement scores.

It should be mentioned that the factorial design can be extended to more complex experiments. For instance, an experiment using four teaching strategies, three ability levels (bright, average and dull) and five age groups (ages 12, 13, 14, 15, 16) would be represented as a 4 x 3 x 5 factorial design. As the number of experimental treatments is increased, the number of experimental groups increases since all kinds of one independent variable are considered in combination with all kinds of the other independent variables. However, such an experiment becomes complex because too many factors need to be manipulated or con-trolled simultaneously. It is true that the complex statistical analysis can now be handled by computers, still it is advisable that beginners in educational research should try and answer their questions with the simplest possible designs.

There are a number of advantages to the factorial designs. First, the researcher can treat as independent variables what otherwise would be regarded as extraneous variables. Secondly, many independent factors can be considered simultaneously in a single study which would provide savings in effort and work on the part of the researcher. Thirdly, the factorial design claims to have high internal validity. Fourthly, the interaction effects of many variables can be studied at the same time which is often essential in educational research.

The methods described above by no means exhaust the list of experi-mental research designs and procedures. There are *counter-balanced designs* in which all subjects are exposed to all treatments. One type of counter-balanced design is the Latin-square design. Because of the complexity of this design we shall not discuss this here. It is important to remember, however, that in the course of experimentation many plans and procedures may suggest themselves to the researcher. Such adaptations and developments in the design and procedure of research are often useful by-products of research, especially in the field of education.

Experimental research is the most difficult and complex task because of the multiplicity of problems inherent in the various kinds of research designs and because of the complex nature of human behaviour. However, well designed experiments manifest certain logical features that seem to eliminate certain forms of bias in the resulting data. Manipulation and control are some of the essential characteristics of well conceived and well conducted experimental studies. The findings of research should be such that they can be generalised to a larger population.

Before concluding this discussion it is necessary to mention that some kinds of research yield qualitative data, i.e. the data that are not easily converted into numerical values. For example, experiments carried out by Kohler on chimpanzees were of this nature. He studied how chimpanzees solved problems, and how the ways of problem solving determined the kinds of solutions that were produced. The data thus produced were descriptive, representing a starting point for many studies conducted since then. Another significant series of studies which have contributed to our understanding of human behaviour is that carried out by Piaget and his associates at Geneva. The Piagetian studies are focused on the conceptual development of children.

A concluding statement

In this chapter the nature and procedures of historical, descriptive and experimental studies have been discussed. A question can now be asked as to whether any relationship exists among these three methods of research. An important consideration is that any research should be based upon a systematic framework or rationale. No particular method of research is superior to another. There are certain problems and deficiencies in all the methods which have been described in this chapter. Although it is widely believed that experimentation is the best approach to the solution of educational problems, it should also be remembered that there are many educational questions that cannot be answered by employing experimentation. Other methods of research are also needed. A good piece of research is characterised by careful attention to the way in which the data is collected. The researcher must be certain that, regardless of the procedure used to collect the data, his method is reliable, valid and trustworthy.

5 Tools of research in education

At some stage in the design of a research programme consideration must be given to the collection of data. This stage is an important part of the research process and many data gathering tools or techniques have been developed to aid the researcher in this task. The tools of research vary in complexity with regard to their design, administration and interpretation. A research worker therefore needs to know about the techniques or tools available to him and something of their strengths and weaknesses. He may find that the existing instruments do not serve his purpose, and he may need to modify them or even to construct new ones.

Techniques or tools will be discussed in this chapter. Before proceeding however, we must first consider the reliability and validity of those techniques which are often utilised to evaluate behaviour, and which have been designed for use in a standardised way.

When we attempt to determine the success with which a certain measurement has been undertaken, we generally evaluate it by reference to the concepts of reliability and validity. We shall see about this in a moment. Other concepts equally important in the process of test construction are those of item analysis and sampling. In the context of educational and psychological measurement each of these concepts has a set of special meanings not common in everyday use.

1 Tools and techniques in collecting data

Reliability

Reliability in educational and psychological measurement refers to the degree of accuracy with which a given test or a set of tests scores measures whatever it is measuring. It can also indicate the trustworthiness or stability of the test itself. Since reliability of the test is estimated from test scores it is subject to their errors. Certain chance events occur during the process of assessment which lead an individual to obtain a slightly different score from one measurement occasion to another. These chance errors are referred to as variable errors. The extent to which variable errors are present in any measuring device is estimated by means of some index of reliability.

The most commonly used evidence of reliability is the coefficient of internal consistency of a given test, or internal consistency reliability. This is usually obtained by the 'split-half method' in which scores for the testees are obtained in each of two comparable halves of the test, such as odd and even numbered items. Agreement between the scores in the two halves is determined by calculating the correlation coefficient (r). Since this is based on score obtained on only half the test, a correction is needed to determine the reliability of the complete test (R) which is given by the Spearman-Brown formula: $R = 2r/(1 + r)$.

Another way of thinking about reliability is in terms of consistency over time. This is called test – re-test reliability or test stability. To obtain this measure the same group of individuals is re-tested after an interval of time, usually of a few weeks duration, and the correlation obtained between the two sets of scores. At first sight this may seem an easy solution to the problem of estimating test reliability, but there is a difficulty with this procedure. Many human characteristics are not static, but rather in a state of flux. This is more true of personality qualities which are generally found to be somewhat unstable or liable to fluctuation. If a considerable time lapses between the first and the second testing, there may be fluctuation in the score because of intervening experiences. For this reason re-testing usually takes place after a fairly short period of time despite the possibility that some individuals will remember their previous answers.

A third approach to estimating reliability involves construction of parallel forms of the test. This method attempts to eliminate the effects of changed situation and remembering responses from one occasion to another. To do this, two tests composed of different but similar items are designed to measure the same trait in the same way and both are administered to the same set of testees. An estimate of reliability is obtained by calculating the correlation between the two sets of scores. This is called the parallel-form reliability. It is difficult, however, to ensure that the two tests are equivalent with regard to content.

In evaluating a test with respect to reliability it is essential to know which procedure was used. It is also important to remember that test reliability is affected by one or more of the following factors: the test items, the test length, the characteristics of testees involved in determining the reliability coefficient and the testing conditions. In addition, when time has lapsed since a test was standardised, norms may become out of date and changes in performance may occur due to different experiences and to irrelevance of some test materials.

The important question as to how reliable an instrument or tool should be before it is trustworthy is an extremely difficult one to answer. A carefully constructed test of cognitive ability or achievement might be expected to have a reliability in excess of 0.90, but instruments with much lower reliabilities are accepted in the areas of personality and attitude.

Validity

The concept of validity is perhaps one of the most complex in test evaluation. It refers to the degree of success with which a technique or other instrument is measuring what it claims to measure. The two concepts, reliability and validity, are not identical. For example, we may be measuring a certain ability, attitude or trait, very accurately, but we may be measuring something quite different from what we think we are measuring. Thus, a technique may be reliable, but it may not be valid. The opposite is unlikely, for if a technique is unreliable it cannot be valid.

There is, of course, no such thing as an absolutely valid technique. It is essentially a matter of degree. It is always necessary, therefore, to gather some sort of evidence which provides confidence that a particular tool really measures what it is supposed to measure. It should also be stressed that the validity of any tool depends upon its reliability and the aims that formed the basis for its construction. Since the aim and the content of researches vary, the type of validity needed is determined accordingly. There are four major kinds of validity: content, predictive or empirical, concurrent and constinct. Each of these calls for several kinds of evidence.

Content validity is concerned with how well the sample of items that is used represents the total domain of possible items. This kind of validity is especially important in the case of achievement and proficiency measures. Unsophisticated test designers when preparing these tests may look only for 'face validity' i.e. they judge what a test measures by what it looks like. This is particularly dangerous in testing personality where, in the past, some tests of 'neurosis' were made up from items which were supposed to represent it without careful validation through comparisons of actual behaviours of neurotic and normal individuals. There is also a danger in using questionnaires that some people will admit to neurotic symptoms more readily than others so that the test may seem to be measuring neurosis whilst, in fact, measuring willingness to be frank about such tendencies. Nevertheless, a test needs to have face validity to the extent of seeming relevant or it is likely to be rejected by those who might use it, for example, employers and candidates for assessment prior to employment.

Another possible danger lies in the logical validation of content. It is argued that if a subject is carefully analysed into the information, abilities and skills it involves, then a test, based on these is necessarily valid. Yet as Vernon (1969) points out, different tests in the same school subject often correlate only to a moderate degree showing that their authors were not justified in inferring from the items they selected, to all round achievement in the subject. However, it is also possible that the content of school subjects is not usually analysed in sufficient detail to enable teachers to design fully representative tests of achievement.

Predictive validity has a different purpose. A test is said to have predictive validity if it enables its user to select individuals who will succeed in a course or occupation. Usually a battery of tests is used in careers guidance to indicate in which areas an individual is most likely to succeed.

Another form of external validation is provided by a measure of *concurrent validity*. A test is said to have concurrent validity if it correlates highly with a well known test and may therefore be used for the same purposes, for example a test which correlates highly with the Terman-Merrill revision of the Stanford-Binet tests measures whatever this test measures. Another, less dependable, way of obtaining an estimate of concurrent validity is to administer a test of say, attitudes to authority, to a group of pupils, and at the same time to obtain teachers' ratings of the pupils' attitudes. The correlation between test results and teachers' ratings is then computed as the evidence of test validity. Concurrent validity is thus concerned with the technique's ability to provide an estimate of present performance. If test scores are checked against criteria with a different sample, this is termed cross-validation.

The last kind of evidence required before one feels confident in interpreting results of any technique is that of *construct validity*. Construct validity is evaluated by analysing meanings or test scores in terms of psychological concepts. This involves a long continued interplay between observation, reasoning and imagination. For example, the researcher is interested in such constructs as anxiety or extroversion-introversion, which are not directly observable, and for which no satisfactory external criterion is available. He develops a test from his observation of the responses that testees make to a heterogeneous series of test situations. The question is whether the test constructor's perceptions and evaluations of such a set of responses have sufficient internal consistency to constitute a viable construct. The extent to which he succeeds is an indication of the construct validity of the test under consideration. Thus, the process of establishing the construct validity of a test is not a simple one. It involves such diverse evidence as group differences, change in performance as a result of experimental manipulation of certain variables, correlational analysis and internal consistency information.

A brief appraisal of different types of approaches in determining the test validity suggests that there is no simple answer to the issue of validity. This is particularly true in assessing the validity of attitude and personality questions. These are more sensitive than factual questions with regard to wording, context and emphasis. A further difficulty arises with the lack of criteria in these areas.

Item analysis

In the two preceding sections of this chapter, we have described the major criteria in the evaluation of an instrument as a whole. It is also necessary to examine the concept of item analysis which is an essential property in the test construction. This statistical analysis is required to consider, in a meaningful way, the acceptability of items and thereby the appropriateness of the test in question. To put it another way: an examination of each test item to discover its strengths and weaknesses is known as item analysis.

Once the test items have been written, the next step in the process of item analysis is to try the items out on a group of subjects who are representative of the population for which the particular test has been developed. Usually this trial testing is carried out on a small number of subjects, and this means that judgements about individual items are made on limited evidence. To achieve a satisfactory degree of stability in items, an analysis group of about 400 subjects is considered to be appropriate. It should be mentioned here that an effective measuring instrument is more than a collection of individually 'good' items based on their face validity. Other considerations such as the test length, pilot sample, item difficulty, and discriminating power of items must be taken into account.

A review of the literature indicates that there are various kinds of item analysis techniques, depending on the type of tests and the aims one wants to achieve with the test scores resulting from the items selected. However, one of the widely used techniques is in terms of 'facility' (F) and 'discrimination' (D). The facility index is required for identifying items which are either too easy or too difficult, and thus determining the distribution of item difficulties in a set of items. The feature of an item is called its level of difficulty. If the value of facility is high, the item is considered to be an easy one; if it is low the item is regarded as a difficult one. Again the calculation and interpretation of facility values are guided by the type of test and its scoring methods.

The aim of discrimination analysis (D) is to establish internal consistency of the test by correlating the individual items with the total test score. This process helps to find the most homogeneous items which maximise variance of the total score. It has other functions as well; when the researcher fails to evaluate the reliability of any instrument with the strategy of repeated measurements, he has to rely upon the interrelations among the items of a test to establish its reliability. The correlations themselves, also provide some evidence concerning its validity.

Another method of determining the discriminative power of test items is to divide the test papers into two equal groups — high and low scoring subjects. Their responses are then analysed to determine which items discriminate best between the high scoring and the low scoring subjects. This procedure of item analysis, more useful in attitudinal and personality questionnaires, increases the degree of homogeneity (internal consistency) in the set of items. But it does not provide any guarantee that a single property is being measured by the set of items. However, the method makes it possible to eliminate many of those test items which indicate measures of different properties. Thus, internal consistency methods of item analysis at least provide some safeguard against the inclusion of unrelated items in a scale.

The selection of a criterion to specify the characteristics of the high and low groups is a purely arbitrary definition of the limits separating the groups. The most common approach is to use the upper and lower thirds (middle third discarded) of the score distribution.

Standardised tests

A standardised test is commonly defined as one which is carefully designed and has met the following requirements: the content is selected and checked empirically, uniform methods of administration and scoring have been developed, and adequate technical information has been provided. In the field of measurement the term 'standard-isation' has close connections with the concept of 'objectivity', i.e. standardised tests are designed to give standard measurements where-ever they are used and whoever marks them. Thus, the objectivity of a test refers to the extent to which the instrument is free from personal error — the personal bias of the person who is doing the scoring.

Most standardised published tests are accompanied by manuals which provide information on such practical matters as publication date, cost, directions for administrations and scoring; and such technical matters as reliability, validity, norms, test difficulty, techniques of interpreting test scores and reports of the research in which the test was utilised.

When using these tests with individuals, or reporting opinions and attitudes, results inevitably depend on the sample of individuals on whom the test was standardised or who were consulted as to their views. A test standardised in the USA is not applicable in England until it has been standardised, whilst an opinion poll taken in the North of England may have little bearing on the opinions of people in the South. For these reasons it is important to know which samples were used in either kind of situation when interpreting results. Several methods of sampling are therefore considered before discussing testing techniques.

Sampling

Under normal conditions it is neither possible nor desirable to study entire populations, whether these are populations of people or of resources; sufficient data can be obtained through study of a proportion of the population. Techniques have been devised to obtain a small scale representation or miniature model, of the population from which the sample is taken. A simple technique, but one which may lead to bias in small samples, is that of simple random sampling; individuals are selected by chance alone as in a lottery. Alternatively, members of the sample may be selected from correspondence with a table of random numbers such as those of Fisher and Yates (1963), but this is laborious even if a computer is employed and is little used.

Whatever the size of the sample, some sampling error is inevitable.

In a small sample extreme cases may be over represented by chance, or an excess of 'good' or 'poor' instances may be drawn. The more variable the population the more likely it is that a sample chosen in this way may be unrepresentative.

For this reason other types of sampling may be preferred. *Systematic sampling* is a method of choosing individuals at regular intervals from a list, perhaps in alphabetical order, or, say, in order of their incomes. If 250 individuals are to be studied from a list of 5000, since this is one in twenty every twentieth member will be selected, the first being taken at random from among the first twenty on the list, perhaps the 11th, and thereafter the 31st, 51st, 71st and so on. This is a method which works well if the individuals on the list are in random order with respect to the characteristic to be studied, or if the order is systematic and the system is known; for instance, if husbands and wives are listed, always with the husband first, the sample could consist predominantly, or entirely, of one sex unless the system is taken into account. If there is no existing list, e.g. an electoral roll or school rolls, simply listing individuals in this way before a sample can be taken is likely to be time consuming.

A more reliable way of selecting a representative sample is by *proportionate stratification*. In this technique the correct proportion is taken from each stratum which may have more relevance for the enquiry or experiment. A research worker might plan to take equal proportions of the sexes, and samples of one in twenty of representatives of each of the social classes 1–5, or, if the study was in schools, the sample might consist of equal numbers of the sexes, and perhaps, one in ten of children in nursery schools (2–4 years) and primary schools (5–11 years).

If sub-categories are to be considered in a sample of this kind, e.g. children from different ethnic groups, those who are handicapped in some way, or those 'in care', it may prove that the sub-group is too small to supply meaningful data. For that reason, disproportionate stratification may be used in which larger proportions are taken from small groups. For instance, all handicapped children may be included, if there are not very many of them.

Often a more practical way to select samples, especially in schools or industrial firms where testing and interviewing a few individuals can interfere with their work, is to select individuals from representative schools or firms, where entire classes or groups may be studied. This is a *clustering technique*. It is also a method of limiting travelling expenses for research workers if the schools or firms are located in representative areas. Cluster designs are examples of *multi-stage sampling* since areas must first be selected, then schools or firms and finally classes or individuals within them.

If areas or institutions differ substantially in size as do counties, or comprehensive schools as compared with village schools, sampling with *probability proportionate to size* may be employed. Taking schools as an illustration, a school having 2000 pupils will have a ten times greater chance of being chosen than a school with only 200 pupils. However, within the schools, if classes are 25 in number, a class will have a chance of 1 in 40 of being chosen in the large school, but 1 in 4 in the small school. Thus overall every class has an equal chance of being chosen.

Some useful references including further information about sampling include Butcher (1965) and Hedges (1978). More recently an attempt was made to illustrate some problems of sampling by describing its application to a practical situation — the evaluation of a complex and open ended curriculum programme (Verma and Humble, 1979).

2   Psychological tests

Since the beginning of the century when Binet first devised a test of 'intelligence' to enable him to identify children in need of special schooling, many tests have been prepared and for a diversity of purposes. These may be conveniently classified as tests of cognitive ability, educational tests (achievement, aptitude and proficiency), tests of personality, social adjustment and attitudes, and tests of motor or perceptual skills.

So long as children in Britain are selected for Grammar or Public Schools, tests of intelligence and achievement will be needed as a means of predicting which candidates are likely to prove most successful in the long run. And even where this kind of selection has ceased, tests still have a use in helping to determine whether children's achievements are commensurate with their abilities or whether they need either remedial help or more stimulating and demanding work to stretch them to their full capacities. Tests are also used in schools and careers guidance centres to assist pupils in choosing specialist subjects or in selecting jobs most suited to their abilities and personalities.

Diagnostic tests have been devised to assist in determining what underlies slow progress or other educational problems of some children. A battery of tests, including individual tests which allow observations of behaviours, may indicate whether this is due to brain damage, poor command of language, confusion as to left or right handedness, laziness, discouragement, or boredom with what school offers. Once a diagnosis is made it is usually possible to decide on suitable treatments.

A programme of testing for all kindergartners which has been initiated in California (Meyers, Ball and Critchfield, 1973) seems a desirable development since the training activities which are also part of the programme can be immediately introduced before serious problems develop from neglect. This testing sequence investigates hand preference, visual-motor perception, auditory association, ability to draw a person, bead stringing, body perception, and gross motor skills whilst the tester notes behaviours such as hyperactivity, distractibility or impulsiveness whilst she administers the tests.

Tests are also used, and new ones are sometimes developed in the course of enquiries and investigations by research workers.

A brief discussion of the main types of research will serve to show the diversity of their uses and to indicate some of their limitations.

Tests of cognitive ability

Perhaps the best known tests of cognitive ability are the 'intelligence' tests. Psychologists differ in their interpretation of 'intelligence', some seeing it as a unitary trait 'general intelligence', whilst others believe that it consists of a number of primary abilities such as verbal and abstract reasoning, spatial imagination, numerical ability. In either case there are many more specialised abilities such as clerical speed and accuracy which operate only in a few tests. Most British psychologists hold the first view, whereas American psychologists are more divided in their views.

The author of the well known Wechsler Intelligence Scale for Children (WISC) inclines to the first view. In the American preface to the 1974 revision of the test, he says:

> The author believes that general intelligence exists; that it is possible to measure it objectively; and that, by so doing, one can obtain a meaningful and useful index of a subject's mental capacity. He also believes that the much challenged and berated IQ, in spite of its liability to misinterpretation and misuse, is a scientifically sound and useful measure, and for this reason he has retained the IQ as an essential aspect of the revised Scale.

When first introduced the IQ was obtained by comparing a child's mental age with his chronological age. If, for instance a child of ten years performed as well as average children of twelve years in a large representative sample, he was said to have a mental age of twelve. His IQ was the ratio: mental age $\div$ chronological age x 100; in this instance, 120.

Use of mental age is growing less common, however, whereas the concept of IQ is still commonly used. The manual which accompanies a test gives tables of norms showing IQs corresponding with given scores and chronological ages, of the sample of children with whom the test was standardised.

Whereas those who are advanced for their years have IQs appreciably higher, and those who are retarded have IQs appreciably lower than 100.

Development of intelligence tests provides a good example of construct validation. When Binet devised a test of intelligence in the early years of the century he put together a diversity of tests representing all kinds of abilities on the assumption that general intelligence would operate in them all. Since then the statistical method known as factor analysis has been used to select items which test similar abilities and, in particular, to find items which are the best tests of 'g' or general intelligence. In modern tests both verbal and non-verbal tests are usually included. For example in Heim's AH4 test for use as a paper and pencil test with secondary school children, content is outlined in the test manual:

> Part I consists of 65 questions which have a verbal or numerical bias. Six types of principle are included: directions (some of which are primarily verbal, some primarily numerical), verbal opposites, numerical series, verbal analogies, simple arithmetical computations and synonyms . . . Part II consists of 65 questions which have a diagrammatic basis and which exemplify five types of principle: analogies, sames, subtractions, series and super impositions.

The WISC test which is administered individually, as the Binet test was, also contains verbal and non-verbal items, but the latter take the form of performance tests using apparatus. Whereas the verbal tests include information, similarities, arithmetic, vocabulary, comprehension and memory for digits, the non-verbal tests consist of picture completion, picture arrangement, block design, object assembly and coding and mazes. Marked differences between verbal and non-verbal performance, or failure in some particular aspect of performance is likely to lead to further investigation. Graded items of each variety make it possible to test children between the ages of 6½ and 16½ years.

Group tests tend to be more limited in content than individual ones; some even contain items of a single type whilst others consist of sections each limited to one type of item. It seems probable, however, that uniformity holds attention less well than a variety of item types presented at random or in cyclic order.

Familiarity with the method of testing also affects performance and therefore the IQ which a child obtains. Children who have had little schooling may do poorly in both verbal and non-verbal tests, whilst those whose language is limited for any reason, such as deafness, poor use of language in a child's home, or having to learn a new language following immigration may perform far better in non-verbal than in verbal tests. The Goodenough Draw-a-Man Test and Raven's Matrices are useful with such children. In this test a design must be chosen from a number illustrated to fill the bottom right hand corner after studying a series of increasingly complex designs in the horizontal and vertical directions.

Although these are easier than verbal tests for many children and adults, experience of using them in a College of Education with small groups of students over several years showed that the mathematics graduates could always gain at least 60 of a possible score of 65, whereas arts graduates rarely gained so high a score as 60 and in a few instances obtained astonishingly poor results. This suggests that it may be important to use a variety of tests and observations when assessing general ability. It demonstrates also what is now recognised: that these tests are not able to directly measure genetically inherited intelligence but can only estimate certain manifestations of it.

The new British Ability Scales, published in 1978, (Elliott et al, 1978), differ from earlier tests since all but three are not norm referenced; within a defined population, these tests are both sample free and norm free. There are twenty-four scales and a number of standardised conservation items. Since any scale (or any sub-scale within some scales) may be administered either on its own or in consideration with other scales, there is considerable flexibility. The scales are designed to assess: speed (speed of information processing); reasoning (formal operation thinking, matrices, similarities, social reasoning); spatial imagery (block design level, block design power, rotation of letter like forms, verbal-tactile matching); short term memory (immediate and delayed visual recall, recall of designs, recall of digits, visual recognition); retrieval and application of knowledge (basic arithmetic, early number skills, naming vocabulary, verbal comprehension, verbal fluency, word definitions, word reading). At least four of these scales must be administered to obtain an estimate of IQ. The Rasch Model which was used in designing the scales is explained in chapter 6. Although the British Ability Scales have been developed after many years of research it has failed to tackle some of the crucial issues concerning the nature of intelligence and its measurement (see Verma and Mallick, 1980).

Educational tests of achievement, aptitude and proficiency

As a rule, tests of achievement prepared by teachers in schools do not depend on detailed analysis of the skills and abilities which children learn. Indeed, seen from a psychologists standpoint, many tests and examinations in schools and colleges sample children's or students' achievements in a rather haphazard way.

In order to make comparisons between children from different schools and different areas of the country, psychologists need standardised tests. Tests of achievement are used to assess a child's performance in relation to that of his peers, or may be used to assess his performance in school subjects such as arithmetic and reading in relation to his abilities as estimated by an intelligence test or standardised test of ability in those school subjects. If a child is referred to a psychologist or trained remedial teacher because of educational retardation, a battery of tests may be used to diagnose his difficulties, including specially prepared diagnostic tests which identify his weaknesses in, say, reading skills, reading comprehension, and vocabulary. Batteries of tests may also be used to assist school children in their choice of specialist subjects or in careers guidance centres to help them to select suitable careers. In the United States standardised batteries of tests such as the Differential Aptitude Test or the General Aptitude Test may be used to help students in these ways. The former includes tests of verbal reasoning, numerical ability, abstract reasoning, space relations, mechanical reasoning, clerical speed and accuracy and language usage. Students' results are often presented in 'profiles' which show how far his scores deviate above or below the median score. In this way strengths and weaknesses can be seen at a glance.

Criterion referenced tests have been developed mainly since their introduction in the mid-1950s in connection with programmed texts and PSI (personalised, systematic instruction). The purpose of this kind of test is to determine how far the testee has mastered a skill or ability; thus it is a test of proficiency. To devise the learning programme and post-test requires careful analysis of the performance required into 'objectives' or successive stages of achievement.

Test items may be prepared and used with a sample of pupils or students similar to those for whom the test is intended, to ensure that they are clear and of a suitable level of difficulty. A satisfactory standard of achievement is decided beforehand and may be as high as 90 per cent.

Norm referenced achievement tests are standardised in the same way as are 'intelligence' tests. The Edinburgh Reading Tests, for example, are standardised for children aged 7–12 and adolescents of 12 upwards. For the younger groups three kinds of item are included. The first kind requires children to read a short passage and then to ring 'true', 'false' or 'doesn't say' after a number of statements relating to the passage. Or a statement is read and the children must make sure that they remember its content before answering multiple choice items on it. In the second type, the children read statements and put them in the order of their occurrence. The third kind of item, the views of several groups of persons are described and the children decide which of these groups is responsible for a number of statements which follow. Thus, in each case reading comprehension is required as are memory and reasoning, to a greater or lesser degree depending on the item.

The Manual provides conversion tables giving 'reading quotients' from age in years and completed months and test score. For instance, a child of 11.7 who scores 130 has a reading quotient of 117. Reading ages have been calculated by finding for each age group the mid-score that divides their results 50 : 50; any child whatever his actual age, who obtains a certain mid-score is said to have a reading age equal to the chronological age of the group which has that mid-score. Reading ages corresponding with scores are given separately for Scotland and England/Wales. A score of 79, for example, corresponds with a reading age of 10.9 in Scotland, and of 10.11 in England and Wales.

Analysis of reading difficulties is made by use of diagnostic tests. The Neale Analysis of Reading Ability requires checks on a child's hearing, eyesight, interests, pertinent emotional difficulties and attitude to reading before the test begins. During the test the psychologist, (or a teacher trained to use tests), notes whether the child needs encouragement to begin reading, refuses to try unknown words, habitually repeats words or phrases and whether he reads quietly or loudly, mumbles or is hurried. A score sheet lists other specific observations which should be made while the child reads passages of increasing difficulty. As a result, the tester obtains a record of mispronunciations, substitutions, refusals, additions, omissions and reversals. Questions on the passages lead to an estimate of reading comprehension. Reading ages corresponding with scores are supplied as for the Edinburgh scales.

Like most carefully standardised tests of achievement, this test claims to have high validity and reliability. Using a parallel form of test with ten boys and ten girls from each year group from 7 to 11 years of age a reliability was obtained of about 0.98. The validity coefficient determined by a measure of agreement between this test and factors common to other well standardised tests (i.e. a kind of concurrent validity), is 0.95.

Well validated tests exist, similarly, for achievement in mathematics and for diagnosing difficulties in arithmetic (Schonnell, 1942). A large number of such tests are outlined in Vernon's *Intelligence and Attainment Tests* (1961) and in Cronbach's *Essentials of Psychological Testing* (1961).

98

A wide variety of techniques has been devised in an attempt to measure personality traits. These include psychometric techniques, inventories, projective techniques, observational techniques, the sociometric method, nomination techniques including the Guess Who game, peer ratings and self reports. All of these techniques are designed to help psychologists in identifying typical responses of individuals in the absence of opportunity to continuously observe their behaviours.

Before discussing some of the techniques in common use and their different purposes, it may be helpful to consider difficulties which arise in attempting to assess personality by questionnaires or interviews and by observation. Firstly, if individuals are asked to say what are their own ways of behaving e.g. whether they are sociable, co-operative or honest, they are apt to report their behaviour as more socially desirable than it really is. This can occur for various reasons: they may genuinely believe what they say, or they may consider it inexpedient to tell the whole truth or advantageous to represent themselves as better than they are, or they may respond in this way because they have been trained to give acceptable answers. In addition, when answering questions, a 'tendency to agree' has been observed. Bligh (1974) found that 'Yes' was underlined far more frequently than 'No' although consistency would have led to their being underlined with equal frequency. Moreover, if an item enquires how a person feels, e.g. Do you often feel tired?, the answer is apt to reflect recent experience since memory is fickle. Thus, even over a short period of time, some of these techniques have rather low test-retest reliabilities: and where reliability is high it may indicate that people are consistent in the kind of misleading answers which they give; it need not indicate that a test is a reliable measure of a given trait. These points should be borne in mind when considering the various techniques now to be outlined.

The British scale most commonly used to assess personality traits is the Eysenck Personality Questionnaire (the EPQ). In addition, the American 16PF developed by Cattell, Eber and Tatsuoka is frequently used in clinical psychology, careers guidance and research.

The Eysenck Scale (1975) tests three main variables: emotionality (neuroticism) versus stability (N), extroversion versus introversion (E), and tough mindedness (Psychoticism) (P). In addition a lie-scale (L) is included as a measure of dissimulation. Eysenck claims that these variables account for much of the difference between normal personalities. A scale of criminality has been developed from items in which individuals known to have a criminal tendency score high; many of these items come from the P-scale. In the questionnaire items measuring the three main variables are mixed, so reducing the possibility that the testee will realise what is being measured. Nevertheless, the tendency to give socially desirable answers is likely to operate in the adult scale when answering items such as:

11 : Would it upset you a lot to see a child or an
    animal suffer?   YES   NO

15 : Are you an irritable person?   YES   NO

70 : Can you get a party going?   YES   NO

89 : Are you always ready to admit it when you
    have made a mistake?   YES   NO

So that the scale becomes less valid, even if it is relatively easy to be objective in answering:

1 : Do you have many different hobbies?   YES   NO

5 : Are you a talkative person?   YES   NO

52 : Do you like mixing with people?   YES   NO

74 : When you catch a train do you often arrive
    at the last minute?   YES   NO

The test manual provides information about each scale including their test-retest reliabilities, internal consistency, reliabilities and age norms for adults. Mean and standard deviations are given for more than a hundred occupations and for some abnormal groups. Similar statistics are given for the Junior EPQ. Test re-test reliabilities lies between 0.78 (P) and 0.89 (E) which is comparable with those for other published tests of personality traits. Internal consistency reliabilities range from 0.74 (P) to 0.85 (E) for males and from 0.68 (P) and 0.85 (N) for females. If the latter reliabilities were very high this might indicate a rather too narrowly restricted range of items to cover the area adequately.

The 16PF Scale is designed to test sixteen personality traits but as each measure is estimated from fewer items than in the Eysenck Scale, the estimates obtained are less reliable. The authors claim that since the 16PF is designed to measure the total personality, its predictions have the widest possible applicability in any field where personality is important, e.g. in business and industry to select personnel, in education as a predictive measure, an aid to planning programmes or a means to assess characteristics leading to behaviour difficulties such as delinquency or anxiety. It is also recommended for use in vocational guidance and clinical diagnosis.

Numerous tests have been devised to measure specific personality traits. The Rokeach test of dogmatism has been used extensively in research in studying prejudice and in relating dogmatism versus open mindedness with other traits and attitudes (Rokeach, 1960). Rokeach claims that dogmatism characterises the whole structure of a person's attitudes and expectations, and is thus more general than fascism, or other political, ethnic or religious prejudices. It is associated with intolerance in a variety of beliefs and behaviours.

Another personality characteristic is identified by the Mehrabian Need for Achievement Scale which has been validated in Britain for use with college of education students (Cohen, Reid and Boothroyd 1973). Students high in n Ach tend to engage in energetic, innovative activities but work hard only when there is some challenge in a situation. They constantly seek novelty or new solutions to old problems; thus they seek success but determine their own goals and may reject those offered in schools or colleges.

Many other tests are mentioned and areas of disagreement between research workers are discussed by Vernon (1964).

Inventories

Although inventories, like personality questionnaires, depend on self report, they do so in situations in which there is no intention of hiding their purposes from individuals who answer them.

An early example, the Woodworth Psychoneurotic Inventory consists of one hundred and sixteen questions based on psychiatrists descriptions of psychoneurotic behaviours, e.g:

58 : Are you ever bothered by the feeling that people are reading your thoughts?

79 : Do you feel like jumping off when you are in high places?

Such an inventory is most likely to be used with individuals who have asked for help and so are quite willing to check items corresponding with their particular problems. Its chief use is to assist in diagnosis and to act as a talking point between psychiatrist and patient.

Inventories most commonly used with normal individuals are those designed to match vocational choices with the interests of young adults wishing to enter skilled occupations and professions. Since the analysis of results is complex and requires electronic scoring, these inventories are used mainly in Vocational Guidance Centres. Cronbach (1961) discusses three such inventories which have been developed in quite different ways. The best known, Strong's Vocational Interest Blank, is based on studies of the interests of successful men in a variety of careers. Lee and Thorpe (1956) developed an inventory following a study of the duties undertaken in a range of occupations. Kuder (1956) began instead from a set of personality traits identifying clusters which distinguished between individuals and only later matched them with vocational choices based on a logical analysis of occupations.

Five areas of interest are enquired into in the Strong Interest Blank: occupations, amusements, subjects of study, miscellaneous activities and types of people. Each interest has to be rated L, I or D, indicating like, indifference or dislike, respectively. Scores corresponding with each rating differ with occupation. Thus, for engineers ratings based on interests of many successful men for liking to be the author of a technical book results in scores 3 for L, -1 for I, and -2 for D, but for liking to be the author of a novel, the scores for engineers are -1 for L, 1 for I and 0 for D.

When all 400 items have been answered and scored for a range of occupations, the patterns of interests displayed by an individual can be used in advising him as to which variety of careers he might enter, assuming that he has the necessary ability and qualifications. Patterns of interest have proved fairly stable in adults. Correlations for Stanford University students over a period of eighteen years were 0.76 for physician, 0.54 for personnel manager, 0.68 for sales manager and 0.73 for lawyer, (Strong 1959, Darley and Hagarah 1955), but profiles of the interests of a few individuals showed marked changes even to the extent of reversing likes and dislikes.

The Kuder blank is more suitable for use with older adolescents in schools. Pupils can take the test, score it and plot their own profiles showing their strengths and weaknesses in different kinds of interests or patterns of activity. However, a teacher skilled in careers guidance is needed to interpret results in terms of interest categories such as technical, social service, etc. Of these two inventories the Strong and Kuder are reported to be about equally reliable.

A variety of other vocational interest tests have been developed for use in America but, since careers guidance in Britain is not usually conducted so systematically, the use of tests is relatively uncommon.

Projective techniques

Projective techniques probably began with the use by Freud and Jung of word associations. They are still mainly of use in obtaining insight into the problems of maladjusted individuals. In using these techniques, it is assumed that anything the patient or testee contributes will reflect his own preoccupations, anxieties and beliefs. Thus, unless he refuses to respond or does so in a stereotyped way, his contributions will necessarily cast light on his personality characteristics and his problems.

A number of techniques have been devised. Paper and pencil tests such as sentence completion and cross out tests are suitable for use with groups. In the former the first few words of sentences are presented with space for the testee to add the conclusions, e.g:

I regret . . . . .

My mother . . . . .

My three worst habits are . . . . .

Initial phrases are chosen to elicit such responses as guilt, fear, anxiety, hostility, suspiciousness, disgust and so on.

The Pressey cross out $(X - 0)$ test includes four activities. In the first the testee is invited to cross out words he finds unpleasant, e.g. white, drunk, choke, flirt, unfair. The second provides a list of stimulus words each followed by five other words; the testee is required to cross out the words associated with each stimulus word. A third section asks him to cross out anything wrong, e.g. extravagance, sportiness, boasting, deformity, taking back. In the last he is asked to cross out words which cause him worry or anxiety, e.g. injustice, noise, self-consciousness, discouragement, germs. Thus this test is a controlled form of word association.

A test which allows patients to display ideas, motives and feelings about interpersonal relationships is the Thematic Apperception Test (TAT). In this test the patient is invited to make up a story about each of a series of pictures showing, for instance, a grey haired man looking at a younger man who is sullenly staring into space or the silhouette of a man or woman against a bright window, the rest of the picture being totally black. Stories are interpreted on the assumption that each person mentioned represents some aspect of the testee's personality, aspects most acceptable to him being represented by someone of the same age and sex as himself. The TAT has also been used in educational settings (Verma 1973; 1980).

A very well known test which allows considerable freedom of interpretation is the Rorschach Test in which a number of symmetrical ink blots are presented for the testee to say what he sees in them. A fairly substantial book has been written on scoring responses; this instructs the scorer to take note of various aspects of location (the portion of the blot selected), content (whether human, animal or specific disturbing topics), determinants (whether there is good or poor form and how far this is congruent with the blot), movement (human, animal or natural forces), colour (used alone, as a symbol or to add to perception of form), shading (whether to represent three dimensions or a specific texture). Originality is also noted and the number of responses to each blot. It is claimed that scores can give a measure of intellectual ability in addition to emotionality, and pointing to specific preoccupations. However, despite the continued use of the task and its popularity with some psychiatrists and psychologists, interpretations tend to differ as they may, and often do, for responses to any projective test.

Observational techniques

It is well known that if a number of teachers are asked to rate children for such qualities as independence or confidence, they tend to differ; what one teacher sees as commendable in dependence another may consider is excessive self-sufficiency. The 'halo-effect' operates too. If a teacher has a generally high opinion of a child he is likely to rate her high in everything. Indeed as a good relationship develops between a teacher and his class he may be apt to rate them all unduly high, with the possible exception of a few 'black sheep'. In addition, everyone tends to observe selectively, looking for qualities which seem important to them. For these reasons a number of methods have been developed to assist in the making of objective observations. These include schedules in which specific behaviours have to be checked, perhaps noting their frequency, and time sampling in which specified behaviours of an individual or group are recorded at, and for, stated intervals.

Schedules

Two useful schedules for assessing social adjustment and social development respectively are the Bristol Social Adjustment Guide (Stott, 1963) and Doll's Vineland Social Maturity Scale (Doll, 1947). The Adjustment Guide is designed for assessment of behaviour in school; the teacher matches a child's behaviour with one of a number of brief descriptions under a series of headings: greeting, school work, games and play, attitudes to other children, personal ways, physique (including speech), and makes a rating of school achievement in English and maths. Behaviours under the first of these headings are described as follows: waits to be noticed/hails teacher loudly/greets normally/can be surly: never thinks of greeting/is too unaware of people to greet/nn (nothing noticeable).

The Vineland Maturity Scale fulfils a different purpose in assessing a child's social development in relation to that of other children. Since this requires no more than factual observation it can be checked by someone in the child's home and by teachers too, if behaviours may differ in the home and school environments. Kellner Pringle

(1966) has improved the normative data of this scale with British children. The original scale of one hundred and seventeen items was based on children's behaviours in daily living, such as capacity to feed and dress herself, to dry her own hands (2¼ years), to go out alone, to be trusted with money (5½ years), to occupy herself at a level suitable for her age, ability to communicate, control of movement and socialisation. It is possible to obtain a 'social age' and 'social quotient' for comparison with other measures such as IQ. Interestingly the correlation between mental age and social age is not very high. An over protected but intelligent child may be unable to dress himself even at six years, but may obtain a high IQ, whereas a child of lower intelligence from a poor home may be socially very competent. A main use of the Vineland Scale is in helping to assess a child's need for special education.

Few scales are produced commercially since it is customary to develop a scale to fit the purposes of a particular study, but established scales may be useful initially as models. Cronbach (1961) mentions a parent behaviour rating scale, for instance. He suggests that raters using a scale should be asked to state the kinds of situations in which observations were made and whether they had sufficient opportunity to observe any trait, instead of making an estimate from insufficient information.

Time sampling

A method of observation which has become familiar to school teachers owing to trial uses of the Flanders technique by students from Colleges of Education is observation of specified teaching behaviours at, say, three second intervals throughout a lesson. From a record of this kind it has been shown that many teachers talk for about 75 per cent of the time during lessons and that, in some classrooms, there is little scope for pupils' questions or comments about the subject of the lesson.

Observations of particular pupils at intervals over a period of time can give a fair picture of typical behaviours. A recording of the whole of the behaviour of young children, in terms of movement, activities and conversation say for periods of ten minutes throughout a day can supply an anecdotal record which is likely to be more representative than observation for a few longer periods. Time observation of this kind can be a prelude to the introduction of behaviour modification techniques in the case of young children having difficulties in school or who cause disruption by excessive activity or annoying other children, or they may be used to supplement case studies of children sent to psychological centres owing to more severe problems.

Sociometric techniques

Sociometric techniques were developed by Moreno (1953) to study group interactions. If school children are asked to say who they would like to sit next to, to work with, or to go out with, they may choose different individuals for each activity, but their choices overall serve to show who is popular and who is rarely chosen. From information of this kind a teacher may rearrange groups in order to bring together children who will work together effectively and she may incidentally introduce an 'isolate', or a pupil who is positively rejected, into the group containing individuals which he or she has chosen. In this way hostilities may be reduced, or avoided and children formerly ignored or rejected may gradually come to be accepted.

It may also get over the difficulty of choosing teams in school games where, commonly, the good players are chosen quickly whilst those who have little talent are left conspicuously last. Prior choice of teams on the basis of friendships can result in more amicable relationships between players and involvement of most or all team members in the game.

How reliable such data is may be difficult to assess, but it has been suggested that sociometric status among elementary school pupils in the USA is at least as stable over a one-year interval as intelligence or attainment quotients (Gronlund 1959).

Guess who techniques

To avoid problems which arise in asking individuals to rate their peers for various traits, such as the 'halo-effect' in which individuals seen as likeable tend to be rated high for every characteristic, a nomination technique has been developed. Typical descriptions of individuals are provided and members of the group or class respond by suggesting names to match each description, e.g. this one is good at everything, this one is the class athlete, this one is always annoying other people, etc. In this way a description of each child can be built up from the number of times he or she is identified with particular descriptions. When testing young children, Hartshorne and May (1929) used this technique in the form of a guessing game.

Motor and perceptual tests

The chief uses of motor and perceptual tests are in diagnosing abnormalities in young children which may cause, or has already caused, slow development of physical skills or educational abilities and, among adolescents or adults, in identifying abilities required in a variety of occupations.

Some of the abnormalities which can be identified by tests are colour blindness, inability to distinguish similar words or sounds, poor motor co-ordination leading to clumsiness, poor hand-eye co-ordination shown in difficulty when drawing and writing or in throwing and catching, and failure to establish dominance of either the right or left hand which tends to cause difficulties in learning to read and write. More serious problems in visual-motor co-ordination may be indicated by difficulties in distinguishing figures from the ground, in locating objects in space, in the discrimination of detail, or a memory for the sequencing of events. In exploring serious problems it is, of course, necessary to make a thorough case study including measures of intelligence, and use of a variety of perceptual and motor tests together with enquiry into his emotional/social adjustment and conditions in his home.

Performance tests of intelligence suffice to indicate some perceptual deficiencies. For example, in the case of an eleven year old boy referred to the psychologist for difficulty in reading, writing and arithmethic and a growing tendency to bully other children, he seemed socially poised and proved normally intelligent in an orally conducted intelligence test; but when given the simple performance task of re-assembling a manikin from a separate head, arms, body and legs, he seemed perplexed; after much anxious thought he placed the head at the top, arms and legs in the middle and the body below. His performance therefore suggested a serious perceptual handicap possibly arising from brain damage. This might be explored by use of the Koppitz modification of the Bader Gestalt test, designed for use with five to ten year olds, which consists of eight designs that are to be copied under standard conditions.

Douglas-Savage (1968) recommends use of the Lincoln Oretsky Motor Development Scale (Sloan 1955) which is a standardised motor proficiency scale for clinical use. It consists of thirty-six items arranged in order of difficulty, so allowing comparison of a child's motor development with that of his peers and of older and younger children. Percentages are given of children at each age level passing each item, together with estimates of validity, reliability and tentative percentile norms for the sexes. A wide range of performance can be expected at any age in normal children owing to differing rates of maturation, boys on average being somewhat slower in development than girls.

Other tests, including peg-boards, form-boards, picture completion and activities using blocks, can assist in diagnosing poor ability to recognise shapes or in manual dexterity. A rail walking test devised and standardised by Heath (1942) tests ability to balance, but failure seems indicative also of neuroticism.

Relationships between performance in perceptual tests and personality characteristics have been found with a number of tests. The most notable and thoroughly researched are those of Witkin (1954). People taking these tests are required to identify the vertical in abnormal conditions. In one experiment the subject is strapped into a tilting chair in a dark room and is asked to judge when an adjustable luminous rod, shown against a luminous square frame several feet away from him, is in the upright position. Since we normally judge 'upright' from a combination of visual and kinaesthetic cues, this is mainly a test of kinaesthetic skill. Since the subject is apt to think that a side of the square is vertical he tends to be influenced into giving a compromise solution between what he feels and what he sees. In a second test the entire room in which the chair is mounted can be tilted also, and the subjects' task may be to straighten the chair or the room. The third test introduces additional complexity since the room is also rotated. The orientation score on each of the three tests is the angle between the subjects' setting and the true vertical.

Subjects differed widely in performance, men on average being more successful than women. The tendency to be influenced by visual cues was named 'field dependence' by Witkin and his colleagues; continued experimentation throughout a period of ten years showed that this perceptual trait was fairly stable. In relating 'field dependence' with personality traits, it proved that individuals high in 'field dependence' tended to be low in confidence, but this data could have been contaminated by prior knowledge of scores in the Witkin tests.

Paper and pencil embedded figures tests in which subjects are asked to identify simple figures within increasingly complex ones, seem also to be measuring field dependence although in a very different context. These tests, based on the Gottschaldt tests (1926), correlate significantly with Witkin's tests of orientation.

A factor similar to Witkin's field dependence was identified by Thurstone as one of two 'closure' factors. The second factor involved the ability to recognise incomplete figures, letters or pictures. Pemberton (1952) who studied the relationship between the closure factors and personality factors found that subjects who excelled in speed of closure tended to rate themselves as sociable, quick in reactions, artistic, self-confident, systematic, neat and precise and dislking logical and theoretical problems. In contrast those who scored high in flexibility of closure, required in the embedded figures test, rated themselves as socially retiring, independent of the good opinions of others, analytical, interested in theoretical and scientific problems, and disliking rigid systematisation and routine.

The other main use of performance tests is in careers guidance and personnel selection. The DAT battery as we have seen, includes tests of mechanical ability and of clerical speed and accuracy. Tests of mechanical ability may consist of gadgets to take apart or reassemble, or of paper and pencil tests designed to assess more generalised skills, e.g. co-ordination of eye and hand in speed and accuracy in placing a dot in each of a sequence of circles, or in copying figures, spatial imagination in working out from a diagram of a block construction how many blocks touch each marked with an X, or visual accuracy in following intersecting curving lines to determine their ends. The former depend too much, perhaps, on past experience, whilst the latter may be too general to indicate ability for a particular job.

Tests by the US Air Force (Fleishmann 1954) showed that paper and pencil tests had little in common with more complex co-ordination such as following an irregular course or a moving target as in gunner, radar operation and high speed manoeuvring, but it could estimate wrist-finger speed for aiming and steadiness.

In the United States where testing is commonly used in careers guidance in schools the General Aptitude Test Battery (GATB) produced by the United States Employment Services (USES) includes six motor or perceptual tests: spatial aptitude (3-dimensional), form perception (tool matching, form matching), clerical perception (comparing tested names), motor co-ordination (mark making), finger dexterity (assemble-disassemble), manual dexterity (place, turn). Thus, these are tests which assist in selection for many different courses or occupations. Tests specific to occupations of course, can be used with applicants but are too numerous to be used more generally.

Until the 1950s no basic list of psychomotor abilities had been established, but between 1954—56, Fleishmann (1956) with associates, identified eleven major factors: reaction time, arm-hand steadiness, rate of arm movement, finger dexterity, manual dexterity, postural discrimination, fine psychomotor co-ordination, multiple limb co-ordination, rate control (e.g. continuous adjustments in tracking a target), response orientation (signals call for different responses); response integration (two-hand co-ordination or other co-ordinated activities resulting in a simple integrated motor response). Since some of these factors seem quite independent, the idea of a general factor of psychomotor ability is ruled out.

Since, normally, none of these factors is highly predictive for any specific job, where training is expensive development of highly predictive batteries of tests is important. The Air Force has a complex co-ordination task, simulating the action of a pilot in using a stick and rudder bar which he has to move in response to signals similarly to the way a trained pilot does. This test has a validity of about 0.40 for predicting pilot success and therefore has an important place in the battery of tests for pilot selection.

Attitude scales

Attitudes, like personality traits, may be difficult to assess from observation of behaviours and are at least as difficult to assess by questionnaire or interviews. Questionnaires cannot directly assess 'enacted attitudes', i.e. attitudes which are displayed in action but are limited to assessing 'avowed attitudes', i.e. the attitudes people say they have. As we have already seen in discussing personality tests, many people tend to give socially desirable responses to questionnaires, especially if these may influence their future in any way. An applicant for a managerial post, for instance, may represent himself as more tolerant than he really is if he believes this to be advantageous. To assess people's 'enacted attitudes' involves putting them in situations in which attitudes affect decisions and this is not easy to do.

Garfinkel, an ethnomethodologist whose name is now used to identify the technique he invented, recommends following avowal of attitudes by some apparently unrelated request for action by the testee; thus someone who agrees that hereditary wealth is undesirable might be approached by a friend (an ethnologist worker for the investigator) offering assistance in tax evasion with a view to accumulating wealth for his children or grandchildren, or some other appropriate 'garfinkel'.

Notable contributors to the development of paper and pencil tests to elicit avowed attitudes are Thurstone (1929), Likert (1932) and Guttman (1950).

Thurstone prepared a large number of statements, for instance about the Church, expressing a diversity of attitudes, and presented these to three hundred judges, put into eleven piles representing a range of attitudes from extremely unfavourable to very favourable. Items in which judges disagreed were discarded, but where agreement was quite close, scale values were obtained by determining the median of the judges ratings (i.e. the point above which half the judges' ratings fell). Thus items rated 8.6, 5.4 and 1.2, for example, would indicate very unfavourable, neutral and very favourable attitudes. After checking the scale with a further group who were invited to identify items with which they strongly agreed, 45 statements representing the entire range of attitudes were selected to form the final scale. The attitude of a testee responding to these items is measured by the summation of the scale values of items with which he agrees.

That avowed attitudes are apt to change rather rapidly is shown by studies of student teachers. Their attitude after three years in college has been found to correspond with the pupil centred views of their tutors; after only a year teaching in schools their attitudes reverted to what they were initially, i.e. to those commonly expressed by school teachers. Yet there may have been little change in enacted attitudes, for these were not tested. A reasonable explanation is that students tend to agree either with tutors in college or senior teachers in schools since their good opinions are advantageous to them; that is to say, they change their idea of what is socially acceptable depending on the environment in which they find themselves.

Likert's method requires fewer items than Thurstone's. Instead of selecting a range of items he chose items about which people felt differently, most having a neutral attitude, and only a few holding either extreme attitude. If each item is scaled 1−5, then the ratings assigned to it should fall approximately in a normal distribution: in a sample of one hundred, about forty should rate it at 3, about twenty-four each at 2 and 4, and only about six each at 1 or 5. In this way some twelve to fifteen items suffice to provide an estimate of quite a wide range of avowed attitudes.

Guttman (1950) differs from Thurstone in interpreting the term 'scale' more narrowly. He aims to select items which obtain ratings from respondents in the order of their total scores. Although, like Likert, he might start with five categories per item, he would analyse results on the item for the entire sample and would expect respondents having a high total score to rank the item at 5, those achieving fairly high totals to rank the item at 4, and so on, until those with very low total scores should rank the item at 1. Taking only twenty respondents in illustration and numbering them 1, 2, . . . 20 in order of their total scores, he might find;

Rating	5	4	3	2	1
Subjects	1 2 5	3 4 6 8	7 9 12	10 11 13 14	15 16 17 18 19 20

The item seems to fit Guttman's requirements only moderately well. His 'coefficient of reproducibility' should be calculated and if it fails to equal or exceed 90 per cent, the categories must be altered. Here, for instance, it might be better to group 5 and 4 together and 3 and 2 together. This leaves three categories which discriminate almost perfectly in the way Guttman requires:

Rating	5 or 4	3 or 2	1
Subjects	1 2 3 4 5 6 8	7 9 10 11 12 13 14	15 16 17 18 19 20

Guttman's method is useful not only in scaling attitudes but in scaling, for example, levels of children's thinking when their answers to questions are matched with Piaget's stages of development.

Since tests of attitudes are not very difficult to devise this has been a popular exercise for post-graduate students of education.

Social distance scale

A method of determining attitudes from ways in which people say they would behave to other groups, or how they wish them to be treated is that of the social distance described by Bogardus (1970).

The method has been used recently by Lovegrove and Poole (1975) in a study of attitudes to immigrants in Australia. This using only part of a table, shows differing attitudes for different groups.

	Italians	Mainland Chinese	Other Chinese	English
Keep them out	11	41	19	3
Let only a few in	39	32	32	17
Allow them to come	44	21	29	60
Try to get them to come	4	2	3	19
Not stated	1	3	2	1

The semantic differential

This method, developed by Osgood et al. (1957), Osgood (1957) measures directly the connotations of words or objects. The stimulus is rated on a seven-point scale, for example.

It is again suitable for identifying attitudes to different racial groups, e.g.

English	kind	.	.	.	cruel
German	soft	.	.	.	hard
French	volatile	.	.	.	phlegmatic, etc.

but equally mat be applied to persons and characteristics, e.g.

my mother	kind	.	.	.	cruel
love	weak	.	.	.	strong
control	good	.	.	.	bad, etc.

In this way clusters of attitudes may be determined by a group of people towards other groups, or by an individual towards groups or towards other persons or towards inter-personal relationships in his family circle. The method has been found particularly revealing in the case of a woman having three disassociated personalities (Thigpen and Cleckley, 1953).

Questionnaires

It is a fairly common experience when asked to complete a question-naire for the recipient to find that she neither agrees nor disagrees with a statement but is expected to decide one way or the other. If this happens in several successive items she may decide that the questionnaire is a poor one and so refuse to either complete or return it.

A good questionnaire should not only represent the aims of the research workers who send it out, but should also allow for the full variety of possible answers. This will almost certainly necessitate a pilot study to determine how people are likely to answer, which questions will retain their interest, and how to present them in a way which, so far as possible, elicits the truth.

Concern to obtain maximum information must be balanced against the reluctance of recipients to complete long questionnaires or, indeed, any that are time consuming, whatever the reason. The questionnaire should therefore be brief, and should be persuasively introduced in a covering letter by some authoritative figure or in a personal approach by an interviewer. Each item should include all common responses and a space to add comments or unexpected alternatives.

The form of question should avoid any suggestion that one kind of answer is preferable to another and must not assume facts not in evidence; e.g. to ask which of the following reasons would you give for thinking that teaching in small groups is preferable to lecturing? . . . assumes that the recipient believes that small group teaching *is* preferable, although he may think the reverse.

Finally, the suitability of items and the validity of the questionnaire should be assessed by trying it out in the field before a revised questionnaire is prepared and circulated.

More detailed information on questionnaire construction can be obtained from Courtenay (1978).

Interviews

Since interviewing individuals may involve talking for an hour or so and perhaps travelling to and from the interviewee's home or workplace this is an expensive method of gathering information, which is used only when other methods seem inadequate.

There are, of course, obvious advantages in interviewing since it is then possible for a trained interviewer to put the interviewee at ease and so to obtain his full co-operation. It is also possible to gain additional information about the person interviewed such as his intelligence, the way he organises his answers, and his attitudes to other people. On the other hand the person interviewed may assess the interviewer and decide to give answers he thinks she will like.

There are two main approaches to interviewing. One is to use a structured questionnaire, allowing a little comment and a few additions from those interviewed. This is suitable for collecting factual information, for instance, the way in which a school organises its careers guidance. In such a case it is important that the questions should be as brief as possible, that all likely alternatives are included so that the correct one can be indicated by a tick, and the administrator must, of course, keep strictly to an agreed procedure except for initial courtesies and a few words here or there to keep the interviewee at ease or to define a term.

If, however, more personal information is required, such as the way in which a parent brings up her child, it may be more satisfactory to memorise the specific questions to be answered and to include these in an unstructured interview conducted through conversation which can be continuous and informal. An interviewer having a very good memory might risk recalling answers, but it is more common to record interviews provided that the interviewee is satisfied that the tape is only an 'aide memoire' for the interviewer. It seems likely, however, that tape would not be acceptable if the interviewee was asked to divulge very personal information, as in interviewing prior to the Kinsey Report; in such a case brief notes or memory alone might have to suffice. In this kind of interview much depends on the rapport the interviewer is able to establish, her sensitivity to the interviewee's feelings and ability to avoid remarks likely to arouse anxiety or to embarass the interviewee. Indeed, if a question does cause anxiety, annoyance or embarassment it may be important to leave it, returning to it later, if possible.

A great deal more about interviewing has been written in books about research techniques e.g. in Wood (1978).

6 Some key statistical concepts in educational research

A girl says that she tossed six coins together three times and each time six tails turned up. Could it happen? Is it likely that there was something unusual about the coins or that she cheated? A nine year old boy, given a vocabulary test at school, scores 144. The average score at his age is 100. Is he very exceptional? In a test of spatial imagination given to the third year of a middle school the average score for boys was 67 and that for girls was 59. Is such a difference likely to occur by chance, or does it indicate a real difference in their achievement? Two teachers in a school say that they compared an individual method of teaching with class teaching; when tested at the end of term their pupils did better in the topics they learned by individual methods. Can this result be trusted to the extent of re-commending the new method to their colleagues or is further investigation needed? These are just a few of the questions that a statistician or research psychologist might be asked. In order to answer them he must be familiar with theoretical distributions which enable him to say what is the probability of each result.

A very simple theoretical distribution which most secondary school pupils can understand is that which arises when pennies are tossed. Unless a penny is biassed there is an even chance that heads or tails will turn up. If two pennies are tossed together, there are four possibilities: both turn up heads, the first turns up heads and the second tails, the first turns up tails and the second heads, or both turn up tails. Using H for head and T for tail, the four possibilities are HH once, HT twice and TT once. Similarly, when three coins are tossed together there are eight possibilities, i.e. HHH; HHT, HTH, THH, HTT, THT, TTH, TTT. The frequencies of these possibilities may be written as in Table 6.1.

Table 6.1.

Possibility	all H	2H 1T	1H 2T	3T	Total
Frequency	1	3	3	1	8

A pattern of possibilities is beginning to appear which can be extended by simply adding adjacent pairs of numbers in the line above, keeping 'all heads' to the left and 'all tails' to the right, it is shown in Figure 6.1 and so on, indefinitely.

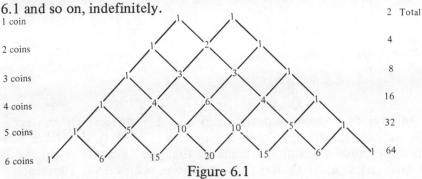

Figure 6.1

(Readers who have learned algebra may recognise these lines of numbers as the coefficients in the binomial expansions $a+b$, $(a+b)^2$, $(a+b)^3$, $(a+b)^4$ etc; those who took A-levels in mathematics will know how to calculate $6C_o$, $6C_1$, $6C_2$, etc. to obtain the last line in the triangle). The last line in the triangle gives the theoretical distribution or *'expected frequencies'* when six coins are tossed together. If the six coins are tossed together 64 times, we expect on average that 6 heads will appear together once, 5 heads and 1 tail six times, 4 heads and 2 tails fifteen times, 3 heads and 3 tails twenty times, 2 heads and 4 tails fifteen times, 1 head and 5 tails six times and 6 tails once. This looks neater in a table: see Table 6.2.

Table 6.2

Possibility	6H	5H1T	4H2T	3H3T	2H4T	1H5T	6T	Total
Frequency	1	6	15	20	15	6	1	64
Probability	1/64	6/64	15/64	20/64	15/64	6/64	1/64	1

116

The probability of each event is calculated by dividing each frequency by the total. Thus the total of the *probabilities* of all these events is 1.

Already we can answer the question at the beginning of the chapter. The probability that the girl would toss six tails together once was 1/64. The probability that she would do so three times in succession was $(1/64)^3$, i.e. $\frac{1}{262,144}$, which is less than one in a quarter of a million tosses. In other words, the probability that this event would occur by chance is less than one in a quarter of a million; it is very unlikely indeed. When some twelve year old girls who claimed this result saw the probability worked on the board and were asked whether they had perhaps influenced the result in some way, they laughed heartily!

The triangle of expected frequencies which can be extended indefinitely is known as Pascal's triangle. The mathematician Blaise Pascal (1623–62) discovered it at the age of sixteen following a question put to him by the Chevalier de Mere who, like most aristocrats of the time, enjoyed gambling.

Normal distributions and the normal curve

From this discovery has developed the use of *parametric statistics* based on the study of *binomial distributions* and the *normal curve.*

As we take frequencies further down the table of possibilities to Pascal's triangle, so the distribution of frequencies looks more like a curve: e.g. for 10 coins see Table 6.3.

Table 6.3

Distribution	10H	9H1T	8H2T	7H3T	6H4T	5H5T	4H6T	3H7T	2H8T	1H9T	10T	Total
Frequency	1	10	45	120	210	252	210	120	45	10	1	1024
Probability	$\frac{1}{1024}$	$\frac{10}{1024}$	$\frac{45}{1024}$	$\frac{120}{1024}$	$\frac{210}{1024}$	$\frac{252}{1024}$	$\frac{210}{1024}$	$\frac{120}{1024}$	$\frac{45}{1024}$	$\frac{10}{1024}$	$\frac{1}{1024}$	1
To 3 dec. places	0.001	0.010	0.044	0.117	0.205	0.246	0.205	0.117	0.044	0.010	0.001	1.010

The distribution can be represented as a column graph: see Figure 6.2. Since the columns are of unit width, and represent successive probabilities, their total area is 1. We can read from the table the probability of tossing, say, eight or more heads:

it is $\dfrac{45+10+1}{1024}$ = $\dfrac{56}{1024}$ = $\dfrac{7}{128}$

or $0.044+0.010+0.001$ = 0.055

i.e. it may be expected to happen a little more often than one in twenty times.

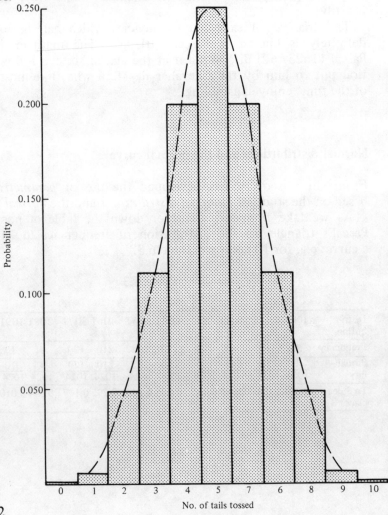

Figure 6.2

It can be seen that the tops of the columns lie approximately on a curve and that the area under the curve is equivalent to that of the columns. However, to obtain the probability of 8 or more heads by using the curve we need to obtain the area under the tail of the curve from 7.5 to 10.5. Since tables of areas under the normal curve are obtainable in books they are often used to obtain probabilities in large distributions. Although laborious, it would be possible to work out the probabilities if a hundred coins were tossed together. If the results were represented in a column graph, the tops of the columns would form an almost perfect curve. The *normal curve* is the limit of the binomial distributions.

Many distributions of measurements of human beings such as heights, weights, sizes of shoes, gloves or hats, distances individuals of the same age and sex can throw a ball etc. fit very well to the normal curve. So do many test scores, although in the case of standardised tests this may be partly because psychologists designed them to do so.

Before we can make use of the normal curve in order to say how exceptional a pupil's score is as compared with other children of his age, we need to turn his score in a test into a *standard score*. To do this we must first obtain the *mean* and *standard deviation* for the distribution of scores.

Taking a simplified example initially:

In six tests a boy obtains marks of 36, 49, 52, 60, 65, 74

The mean score is defined as the total score divided by the number of scores, i.e. the boy's mean score is $\frac{336}{6} = 56$.

(In symbols, if m is the mean, x is a score, N is the number of scores, and Σ (the Greek capital letter sigma) means 'sum' or 'add up' then $m = \frac{\Sigma x}{N}$)

Deviations of the scores above and below the mean are as follows:

Score	52	49	65	36	60	74	
Deviation from 56	-4	-7	9	-20	4	18	
Squared deviation	16	49	81	400	16	324	Total: 886

∴ mean squared deviation from the mean (*the variance*) =

$$\frac{886}{6} = 147.67$$

standard deviation = $\sqrt{\text{variance}}$ = $\sqrt{147.61}$ - 12.1 approx.

[The formula for standard deviation is $s = \sqrt{\Sigma \dfrac{(x-m)^2}{N}}$]

The standard score (z) can now be obtained in each subject, using the formula

$$z = \frac{x - m}{s}$$

When the scores in different normal distributions are treated in this way it has the effect of reducing them all to similar normal distributions having mean zero and unit standard deviation. This facilitates comparisons between, say, distributions of examination scores originally having different means and different spreads.

Some examples will serve to show uses of the normal curve and of standard scores.

Example 1

For the normal curve, and therefore approximately for all normal distributions

about $^2/3$ of the scores (68.26%) lie in the range $m\overset{+}{-}s$
about 19/20 of the scores (95.44%) lie in the range $m\overset{+}{-}2s$
about 998 in 1000 (99.74%) lie in the range $m\overset{+}{-}3s$

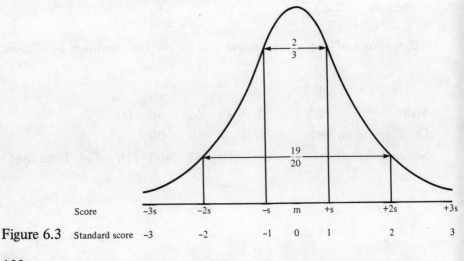

Figure 6.3

Score	-3s	-2s	-s	m	+s	+2s	+3s
Standard score	-3	-2	-1	0	1	2	3

This is shown in Figure 6.3. If information concerning, say, a standard-ised test of arithmetic achievements gives the mean score for eight year olds as 60 and the standard deviation as 12, then for the entire population, or a large representative sample, about two-thirds can be expected to gain scores in the range 48–72, about nineteen-twentieths in the range 36–84, and almost all in the range 24–96.

Example 2

Since many achievements in, for instance, reasoning, reading vocab-ulary, arithmetic, etc. seem to be distributed normally, this has an interesting bearing on the range which can be expected in 'mixed ability' classes.

As an example, scoring of individual tests in the Terence Merrill tests of intelligence (largely reasoning), the scores obtained are said to correspond with mental ages. A six year old who passes all the six tests for six year olds, four of the tests for seven year olds and three tests for eight year olds has a mental age of 7 years 2 months, (using each test as two months after the bare year). A child whose *mental age* is the same as his chronological age is said to have an *Intelligence Quotient* of 100. The standard deviation in terms of quotient points is given as 16. For this, therefore, nearly all IQs will lie between $100 \pm 3(16)$ i.e. 100 ± 48 or 52–148. What does this imply in terms of 'mental age'? Since 16 is about a sixth of 100, at six years, the standard deviation is about one year (a sixth of 6 years) and almost all 'mental ages' will, therefore, lie in the range 3–9, i.e. a range of six years. Similarly at twelve years, the standard deviation will be about 2 years and consequently almost all 'mental ages' will then lie in the range 6–18 years, a range of 12 years. Table 6.4 shows results in more detail.

Table 6.4

IQ			52	68	84	100	116	132	148
Approx. MA)		6 yrs	3	4	5	6	7	8	9
in years and)	at	8 yrs	4	5.4	6.8	8	9.4	10.8	12
months)		10 yrs	5	6.8	8.4	10	11.8	13.4	15
)		12 yrs	6	8	10	12	14	16	18

Since reading and other achievement ages follow a similar pattern, it is not so surprising, perhaps, that some children on entry to middle schools at nine years are found to have reading ages not much higher than six years.

Whilst such ranges undoubtedly raise problems for teachers of mixed ability classes, usually the lowest group (more than two standard deviations below average) are in special schools or remedial classes, and the school catchment area tends to limit the range of achievements amongst the children each school receives. We do not see this wide range as an argument for giving up mixed ability teaching. Where it is used well it has been found not to handicap able children whilst having good effects on the motivation and skills of the less able; in effect, the achievement range is reduced by a movement upwards at the lower end. There is some evidence too that delinquency is less prevalent in schools where all streams are equal, perhaps because there are no bottom streams to feel rejected. Alternatively, or in addition, teachers attitudes may influence the performance of the less able children differently in different schools.

Example 3

In a mathematics test having mean score 50, and standard deviation 16, a boy scored 74. In an English test, with mean score 48 and standard deviation 10, he scored 65. In which subject did he do better?

$$\text{Standard score (maths)} = \frac{74-50}{16} = \frac{24}{16} = 1.5$$

$$\text{Standard score (English)} = \frac{65-48}{10} = \frac{17}{10} = 1.7$$

Although his raw score was lower in English than in maths, when the distributions are equated it is evident that he did rather better in English than in maths.

Example 4

To answer the second question at the beginning of the chapter, we need to know the standard deviation of the scores for nine year olds. If it is 17, then the boy's standard score is $\frac{144-100}{17}$.

To obtain the probability of obtaining such a high score we use tables of areas under the normal curve. This requires a correction: if we had a probability distribution we could add the probabilities represented by successive blocks. In using the curve, however, the end points of the blocks are 143.5, 144.5 and so on, (see Figure 6.4).

Table 6.5

Standard score														
0	25	50	75	1.00	1.25	1.50	1.75	2.00	2.25	2.50	2.75	3.00	4.00	5.00
Probability area under the normal curve														
.500	0.401	0.309	0.227	0.159	0.106	0.067	0.040	0.023	0.016	0.006	0.003	0.001	0.0000317	0.000000287

To calculate the probability of a score of 144 or more, we obtain the normal curve 'standard score'

$$\frac{143.5 - 100}{17} = 2.56 \text{ (nearly)}$$

If, however, we require the probability of scoring *more* than 144, we calculate the normal curve 'standard score'

$$\frac{144.5 - 100}{11}$$

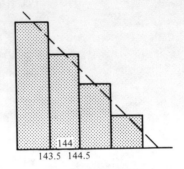

Figure 6.4

Using a simplified table of areas under the normal curve, see Table 6.5, the probability of a score so high as 2.56 is about 0.006; i.e. only 6 in 1000 nine year olds would be expected to do so well.

Testing populations and large samples

The discussion of normal distributions so far applies to large populations, where the population is the group of people under consideration, e.g. all nine year old school children, all five year olds in their first term at school, all entrants to universities in 1979, and so on. Often these populations are too large to be studied *in toto*; it would be too time consuming and expensive. However, entire populations are sometimes studied if an enquiry is considered sufficiently important — such as the ten-yearly census of the population — and is generously staffed and funded. Bodies such as the Scottish Research Council, the National Foundation of Educational Research and the Department of Education and Science have sometimes obtained funds for studies on a very large scale. Currently the DES is funding a series of substantial enquiries into standards of basic skills of children throughout the country. A large sample is being used which enables the research workers to compare performance in different parts of the country and between the sexes, but it is chosen in such a way that the performance in individual schools will not be identifiable.

Concern that children should achieve a high standard in basic skills has also led a number of local authorities to test substantial samples of children, or all children, in their areas. It is, of course, very important that these tests should be well chosen. Most, if not all, are likely to be norm referenced and so need to have been standardised fairly recently on a similar sample of children. Since educational methods are changing children can be expected to show rather different strengths and weaknesses from those of their predecessors. If tests are selected which are unsuitable they can give very misleading results. Their administration, too, is important, for if they are administered incorrectly results are no longer comparable with those of the standard population. Whilst if an administrator, teacher or councillor misunderstands what the test measures he may reach unsound conclusions when interpreting results.

As we have seen in chapter 5 a standardised test is one in which the procedures, apparatus and scoring have been predetermined. Usually there is a standard way of putting questions, detailed directions to administrators which must be clearly followed, instructions as to time to be allowed for each page, when to turn over or to wait, the method of indicating answers and so on. Indeed, every condition which affects performance must be specified if the test is to be regarded as standardised.

In addition, norms may be given which show means and standard deviations for different age groups, for boys and girls separately and, sometimes, for children attending different types of school. This enables psychologists and teachers to compare a child's performance with that of others. In criterion referenced tests this is not possible, but children's performances can sometimes be assessed by comparing their performance in terms of different difficulty.

Even when using standardised tests, the results of any one child can be expected to vary on different occasions. Interestingly, the sex or race of the tester may influence results; children usually perform rather better with a tester of their own sex and race. In addition, of course, children cannot be expected to perform at their best when they are tired, hungry or emotionally distrubed. The environment, too, may affect results if ventilation or light is poor, or if extraneous noise or the size of a hall makes listening to instructions difficult. For these reasons more faith can be put in high marks than in low ones.

Familiarity with test conditions, or with the kind of test items, may also considerably affect a child's score. For instance, in testing seven year olds with a group 'intelligence' test, their headteacher found IQs for Max and Barbara of 95 and 98 respectively. Earlier conversations with them suggested that these scores did not do them justice. When tested individually by a research worker using an interesting variety of test items and in a situation where instructions could be clarified, Max obtained an IQ of 137 and Barbara an IQ of 128. This makes the difference between seeming about average and demonstrating exceptional ability. A teacher who accepted the group test IQ would have been seriously misled.

Younger children and those retarded for any reason are more likely to display their full abilities when with one sympathetic adult. But a highly intelligent girl of twelve, unpracticed in group test technique, spent so long trying to solve a few difficult items that she failed to complete the test and so gained an IQ of 105. Retested with an individual test, her IQ was 165, and in a different group test, after she had been instructed to omit difficult items until the end, her IQ was 160. These quotients are quite unusually high; the test in which she was not adequately briefed was wholly misleading and denied her a place at Grammar School.

Varieties of tests available have already been outlined in chapter 4. A few additional concepts will be introduced here. When preparing norm-referenced tests of achievement the research team not only excludes confusing or ambiguous items but also calculates measures of *item difficulty* and *item discrimination*. The difficulty index of an item is the correlation between item score and test score for the sample members. If subjects who do well in the test overall do well in an item, whilst subjects who do poorly overall do poorly in the item, its discrimination index is high. Knowledge of difficult and discrimination indices enable the research team to put items of the test in order of difficulty, having selected first those with high or fairly high discrimination.

It is from results in group tests standardised on a carefully selected sample, and having items that were subjected to item analysis, that tables of norms are prepared showing how different scores compare with ages. In this way it is possible to say that a child aged 9 years 6 months performs like an average child aged 8 years 6 months in reading, but achieves the score of average children of 10 years 3 months in mathematics. Reading and mathematics quotients can be calculated if this is desired.

A different way of devising tests which does not depend on comparisons between children, and therefore does not need a large sample of children to standardise it (i.e. it is not norm referenced) has been proposed by Rasch (1966). Requirements of items and tests to fit the Rasch model are that they must present a reasonable chance of success to the subject taking the test, the test must be of a unitary trait (if different abilities are to be tested, there must be a test of each), items must have equal discrimination indices and there should be minimal guessing and carelessness. In this model, success in an item depends only on the ability of the testee and the difficulty of the item.

The estimate of a testee's ability, obtained from the test, is:

1 independent of any reference group,
2 independent of the particular items employed in the test (the abilities of two children can be estimated from different ranges of items),
3 a single scale can cover the full range of ability and development on which all individuals can be measured, (for instance in vocabulary, reading comprehension or mathematical skills),
4 scores and differences between scores (inter and intra-individual) can be interpreted as falling on a ratio or interval scale. This means that difficulty levels of items can be compared.

Elliott (1976) showed that in tests devised in this way, items proved to be in the same order of difficulty for either high or low scoring subjects. Also sub-tests, e.g. odd versus even items, give the same ability estimates for the children. A single scale covering the full range of ability prepared from a chain of shorter tests with linking items covering abilities from low to high. In addition, when preparing the tests some subjects can take two successive tests in order to compare difficulties of their items. Once the degree of difficulty of all tests in a chain has been determined, the ability of a pupil can be estimated from any test or set of tests which is suitable for him.

Sampling from a population

In order to answer the third question at the beginning of the chapter, and similar questions, we need to consider what are the effects of sampling from a population. Let us consider first how the means, m, of random samples of size, N, may vary from the population mean, μ, (μ is the Greek letter m, pronounced mew) using a simple example in illustration.

Suppose a population of 4,000 children take a test for which each individual is given a mark in the range 0–10. If there is reason to think that the distribution in the population is normal, then the theoretical or 'expected' distribution of marks will be approximately as shown in Table 6.6. A set of cards can be made to represent the population, i.e. four marked 0, forty marked 1, one hundred and eighty marked 2, and so on, and samples can then be drawn. Suppose 50 random samples of 36 individuals are drawn, each thirty-six cards being returned to the population and well mixed before the next sample is taken. On calculating the mean and standard deviation of each sample it will be found that both vary. The population mean is 5.

Table 6.6

Score	0	1	2	3	4	5	6	7	8	9	10
Frequency	4	40	180	480	840	1008	840	480	180	40	4

Mean 5, s.d.

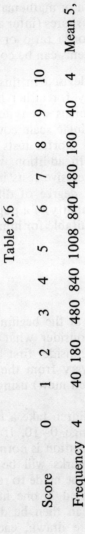

The sample means will be found to spread around this roughly in a normal distribution, two-thirds of them approximately lying in the range 4.73–5.27 and about ninety-five per cent of them in the range 4.48–5.52. It can be shown mathematically that the theoretical mean of the sample means is the population mean, μ, and that their standard deviation is $\dfrac{\sigma}{\sqrt{N}}$ where σ is the population standard deviation (here 1–6), and N is the size of the sample.

$$\frac{\sigma}{\sqrt{N}} \text{ is called } \textit{the standard error of the mean}$$

Since the samples are small compared with the population, their standard deviations will be smaller than that of the population.

In most statistical work the mean and standard deviation of the population are not known and must be inferred from a single sample. Since it is uncertain where m, the sample mean lies in the range about the population mean, it is safe only to say that there is approximately a 95 per cent probability that the true mean lies in the range $m \pm 2 \dfrac{\sigma}{\sqrt{N}}$.

. The *best estimate of the population standard deviation* can be shown to be,

$$\sigma = \sqrt{\frac{\Sigma\,(x - m)^2}{N - 1}}$$

Where
$$s = \sqrt{\frac{\Sigma\,(x - m)^2}{N}}$$

is the sample standard deviation, dividing by N–1 instead of N, gives a larger value, nearer to the population standard deviation than that of the relatively small sample.

Since the standard error (se) of the mean, when calculated from the sample is $\dfrac{s}{\sqrt{N}}$ it follows that as sample size increases, the se of the mean decreases, but inversely to the square root of the size of the sample. To halve the standard error, therefore, it is necessary to quadruple the size of the sample.

The 't' test   Although it might be expected that the distribution of sample means would be normal if the population from which the samples is drawn is normal, this is only the case for large samples. For small samples the distribution is taller and thinner than the normal distribution and is known as a 't' distribution. A simple example using the t-distribution, introduces two other concepts.

Example 5

Two teachers assessed the same ten essays and assigned the marks shown in Table 6.6. Determine whether their assessments differed significantly.

Table 6.6

Essay	A	B	C	D	E	F	G	H	I	J
Mark (Teacher 1)	2	3	4	5	5	5	6	6	7	9
Mark (Teacher 2)	0	1	3	6	4	5	7	3	8	9

Table 6.7

Calculation

											Total
d = difference (+N−)	2	2	1	1	1	0	1	3	1	0	12
d^2	4	4	1	1	1	0	1	9	1	0	22

$$\text{Mean difference} = \frac{12}{10} = 1.2$$

$$\text{Estimate of } \sigma = \sqrt{\frac{1}{9} \ \Sigma \ (d-m)^2}$$

$$= \sqrt{\frac{7.6}{9}}$$

$$= \sqrt{0.84}$$

$$\frac{\sigma}{\sqrt{N}} = \frac{\sqrt{0.84}}{\sqrt{10}} = \sqrt{0.084} = 0.29 \text{ approx.}$$

useful equivalents:
$$\Sigma \ (d-m)^2 = \Sigma \ d^2 - Nm^2 = \Sigma d^2 - \frac{T^2}{N}$$

$$\Sigma \ (d-m)^2 = 22 - \frac{144}{10} = 22 - 14.4 = 7.6$$

The test starts from an hypothesis concerning the expected or true state of affairs: *the null hypothesis*. In this instance, since the teachers would be expected to agree, the null hypothesis is that the mean difference between the teachers' marks is zero. Using the formula for t:

$$t = \frac{m-\Sigma}{\sigma/\sqrt{N}}$$

where Σ is the expected mean difference, ie zero, and
$\sigma/\sqrt{N}$ is the standard of the mean

$$t = \frac{1.2}{0.29} = 4.1 \text{ approx.}$$

Probability tables of t show that this is very high, see Table 6.8.

Table 6.8

Degrees of freedom	t				
	0.10	0.05	0.02	0.01	0.001
1	–	–	–	–	–
5	–	–	–	–	–
6	1.94	2.45	3.14	3.71	5.96
9	1.83	2.26	2.82	3.25	4.78
10	1.81	2.23	2.76	3.17	4.59

For ten pairs of marks (9 degrees of freedom)

The probability that $t = 3.25$ or higher is 0.01, i.e. one in a hundred
The probability that $t = 4.78$ or higher is 0.001, i.e. one in a thousand
Since 4.1 lies between 3.25 and 4.78, we conclude that so great a difference between the teachers marks is improbable unless they genuinely differ in standards or opinions. The difference is said to be significant.

The concept of *degress of freedom* is closely related to the number of observations, in general the number of observations minus the number of constraints put on the system. This will be recognised from

131

experience of examples. If two distinct samples are to be compared, e.g. girls' and boys' marks in a mathematics test, a different formula for 't' is available. Degrees of freedom in the comparison are given by (number of girls + number of boys − 2).

To anyone lacking experience in statistics, it is tempting to think that a difference in mean score between two samples is necessarily meaningful. But if samples are small the difference between them needs to be quite large to be significant when tested by the 't' test.

Use of the test enables us to say whether the difference obtained is quite likely to occur by chance or whether it is significant, i.e it is improbable. In the latter case the difference may be due to some underlying cause which deserves further investigation.

If populations differ, comparisons should be made with caution. In a letter to *The Times* in 1978, a comparison was made between the performance of comprehensive schools, grammar schools and independent and direct grant schools as to the success of their pupils in obtaining two A-levels. The figures given were 6 per cent, 30 per cent and 35 per cent respectively. I do not remember where the writer claimed to have obtained the figures, but he certainly concluded that the latter schools were better. It must be remembered, however, that comprehensive schools take almost 100 per cent of the population (with the exception of very backward and, usually, of very able children). Grammar schools take on average the top 20 per cent, and the last group, which is more mixed, takes pupils on the whole from the top 10–15 per cent of the population. Since 30 per cent of 20 per cent *is* 6 per cent, the grammar schools were doing no better than the comprehensive schools even if the latter took the full range of able pupils. Since they do not, the comprehensives were doing better; some of their rather less able pupils were evidently successful in obtaining two A-levels. The case of the last group is more remarkable: 35 per cent of 10 per cent is only 3.5 per cent, whilst 35 per cent of 15 per cent is 5.25 per cent. Thus these schools on average obtained at most 5.25 per cent successes and so did less well than the grammar schools.

In this example we do not need 't' tests if we are comparing entire populations. If, however, the figures arose from samples, the differences should be tested for significance. Assuming that the letter writer's figures were correct and applied to whole populations or to large samples, we may speculate on the cause of these differences. Is there a tendency perhaps, where entry to schools and universities is competitive, to encourage the brightest at the expense of the relatively less able? In grammar schools, independent schools and direct grant schools, the less able are in fact well above average for the whole population, but they may be referred to and treated as stupid and so become discouraged. Alternatively, or in addition, teachers may tend to teach classes at an average pace, so that those below average (a very high average) fall behind and so do not obtain the successes which their abilities merit. Thus, if the figures are correct it might be worthwhile to make further enquiries to see whether some schools avoid this unfortunate effect.

Some other theoretical distributions

So far we have discussed the normal distribution and have seen how to use areas under the normal curve in studying populations or large samples. The 't' distribution has been discussed and the 't' distribution used in comparing the mean of a small sample with an expected value. Sometimes, in addition, variances of samples have to be compared. To test whether one sample is more variable than another, i.e. whether the variances in the two samples differ significantly, the *F-test* is employed.

The theoretical distribution, known as the *F-distribution*, is not even nearly normal for small samples and differs in shape depending on the relative sizes of the samples being compared. Three tables are commonly available showing the probability of obtaining different values of F for samples of different sizes; the three tables correspond with probability levels 0.05, 0.01 and 0.001.

Example 6

Scores for 25 pupils taking a history test have standard deviation 11, scores for 19 of these pupils who took a maths test had standard deviation 16. Do the variances differ significantly?

The variances are 11^2 and 16^2 respectively, i.e. 121 and 256.

$$F = \frac{\text{larger variance}}{\text{smaller variance}} = \frac{256}{121} = 2.4 \text{ approx.}$$

Table 6.9 gives degrees of freedom (df), i.e. ones less than sample size in each case, here 18 and 24. Upper numbers of the pairs in the table are 5 per cent points, lower or bold face numbers are 1 per cent points.

The value F = 2.4 lies between the 5 per cent and 1 per cent for 24 and 18 df values; so the null hypothesis that the variances do not differ is rejected. Their difference is significant; it is a difference which would occur by chance less frequently than 5 in a hundred times.

Table 6.9

Degrees of freedom for smaller variances	Degrees of freedom for larger variance							
	1	2	...	16	20	24	30	40
1								
2								
.								
.								
17				2.29 / 3.27	2.23 / 3.16	2.19 / 3.08	2.15 / 3.00	2.11 / 2.92
18				2.25 / 3.19	2.19 / 3.07	2.15 / 3.00	2.11 / 2.91	2.09 / 2.83
19				2.21 / 3.12	2.15 / 3.00	2.11 / 2.92	2.07 / 2.84	2.02 / 2.76
.								
24	3.40 / 5.61							

Table 6.10

									Total	Sum of Squares
10 year old :	7	9	10	11	11	13	16	18	19	125	1703
12 year old :	10	11	12	13	14	15	17	19	20	145	2401
14 year old :	5	6	7	9	10	12	15	16	18	107	1311
										$T=377$	$S=5415$

The F-test is analysis of variances. Frequently a research worker will deal with more than two samples and so will wish to compare their means simultaneously. To take a simple example a psychologist might be interested in comparing attitudes of three different age groups of children towards learning science at school. A more complex comparison would be required if the purpose was to compare the performance of boys and girls aged 12, 14 and 16 years in problems at two different levels of abstraction. In a still more complex experiment the purpose might be to compare performance of five year olds or four different kinds of tests, using four different kinds of items. Numerous designs are possible, depending on the number of variables, to be integrated whether or not the experimenter is interested in all their interactions and, of course, the availability of subjects.

The first of these comparisons is quite easy to handle, but as additional complexities are introduced, it is advisable to look up possible designs of experiments in such well known texts as *Experimental Design* by Cochrane and Cox or in rather less mathematical texts such as *Design and Analysis of Experiments in Psychology and Education* by Lindquist. These enable a research worker to find the most economical design in order to study the effects of different variables and their interactions. A simple one-way analysis and a few illustrative designs will suffice here.

Example 7

The scores of random samples of 10, 12 and 14 year olds in an attitude scale towards learning science in school were as shown in Table 6.10 (high scores indicate more favourable attitudes). The purpose here is to see how far the means of the three samples differ from the mean of the whole set of observations i.e. $\frac{T}{30}$. We therefore calculate the variance of the sample means about this mean and the variance of all observations about the overall mean. Their difference is the variance of scores in samples about sample means. This is called the residual variance.

Overall sum of squares about the overall mean = $S - \frac{T^2}{N}$ (using the alternative formula in example 5)

$$= 5415 - \frac{377^2}{30} = 5415 - 4734.3 = 680.7$$

Sum of squares of sample means about overall mean

$$= \frac{125^2 + 145^2 + 107^2}{10} - 4734.3 = 4809.9 - 4734.3 = 75.6$$

136

Table 6.11

	SS	df	variance	
Ages	75.6	2	37.8	$F=\dfrac{37.8}{24.2} = 1.56$ for 2 and 25 df
Residual	605.1	25	24.2	
	680.7	27		

An analysis of variance is shown in Table 6.11. Looking up this value of F in the table under 2df, 24 df is the nearest obtainable to 25, we see that 1.56 is less than 3.40 so the difference is not significant. Thus, the null hypothesis that the means do not differ can be accepted. However, the samples are small. Similar differences in larger samples might prove significant. The following examples give designs of experiments which enable the research worker to make the desired comparisons in the other experiments.

Example 8

Insertion of a few illustrative scores serves to show how totals and hence means can be obtained for each group. An interesting possibility suggested by Table 6.12 is that there is an interaction effect with age, boys doing more poorly than girls at 12 years but better than girls at 16. It would require a fairly large sample to verify this. Age and abstractness of test seem likely to prove significant.

Table 6.12

	Age 12		Age 14		Age 16		Total	
	B	G	B	G	B	G		
	1	3	3	4	5	5	21)	This is a
Concrete	3	4	5	5	7	6	30) 86	three-way
	4	4	6	5	9	7	35)	analysis of
								variance with
	B	G	B	G	B	G		main effects
	0	1	2	2	4	3	12)	due to age,
Abstract	2	1	4	3	6	5	21) 61	type of test
	2	2	6	5	8	5	28)	and sex.
Total	12	15	26	24	39	31	Total (B) 77	
		27		50		70	Total (G) 70	

Example 9

The third problem can be handled most economically by using a *Latin square* design, see Table 6.13. In this design groups of subjects are used in such a way that all groups are represented in each row and column: pupils are assigned to the groups at random. The design enables the research worker to compare main effects due to items, tests or groups and any interactions between test type and item type.

Table 6.13

		Item type			
		A	B	C	D
	1	G_1	G_2	G_3	G_4
Test	2	G_4	G_1	G_2	G_3
type	3	G_3	G_4	G_1	G_2
	4	G_4	G_1	G_2	G_3

If the order of the methods used is likely to influence the results, a different Latin Square should be used, e.g. G1 G2 G3 G4
G2 G1 G4 G3
G3 G4 G1 G2
G4 G3 G2 G1

An assumption in using the F-test is that individuals tested are drawn at random from normal populations. However, an experiment by Norton, reported in chapter 2 of Lindquist's book (mentioned previously) shows that populations need not be normal. If they are not it is advisable not to reject the null hypothesis unless the probability of so large a value of F is 0.01 or less.

To compare observed frequencies of events with expected frequencies, another theoretical distribution is required. This is the X^2 *distribution*, (pronounced Chi Square) $X^2 = \Sigma \frac{(O-E)^2}{E}$, where O is the observed frequency and E is the expected frequency.

Example 10

A simple example is obtained from an experiment in tossing 6 coins. The null hypothesis is that there is no difference between the distributions of observed and expected frequencies. For four degrees of freedom, the probability shown in Table 6.14 that X^2 will exceed 11.67 is 0.02, therefore so great a value at 12.3 would occur by chance in less than one in fifty experiments. This value is therefore significant. The null hypothesis is rejected. We might repeat the experiment to

138

see if a similar bias occurred again, see Table 6.15. The X^2-test is frequently applied in the case of the two-by-two table.

Table 6.14

	Observed frequencies			Expected frequ.s	O	E
6H 0T	1111	4	1		13	7
5H 1T	1111 1111	9	6			
4H 2T	1111 1111 1111 1111 1	21	15		21	15
3H 3T	1111 1111 1111 111	18	20		18	20
2H 4T	1111 111	8	15		8	15
1H 5T	11	2	6		4	7
0H 6T	11	2	1			

To avoid expected frequencies less than 5, the first and last two categories, are grouped leaving five categories, with four degrees of freedom

$$X^2 = \frac{-(O-E)^2}{-E} = \frac{6^2}{7} + \frac{6^2}{15} + \frac{2^2}{20} + \frac{7^2}{15} + \frac{3^2}{7}$$

$$= 5.14 + 2.4 + 0.2 + 3.27 + 1.29 = 12.30$$

Table 6.15

Table of Chi Square

df P	0.99	0.98	0.95		0.10	0.05	0.02	0.01	0.001
1					2.71	3.84	5.41	6.64	10.83
2									
3	0.115	0.185	0.352	– – –	6.25	7.82	9.84	11.34	16.27
4	0.297	0.429	0.711	– – –	7.78	9.49	11.67	13.28	18.47
5	– – –	– – –	– – –	– – –	–	–	–	–	–

Example 11

Comparing choice of career (professional/non-professional) with children's social class (1, 3/3, 4, 5) gave the results shown in Table 6.16.

Table 6.16

Career choice

	Professional	non-professional	Total			
1, 2	55	20	75	a	b	a+b
Class				c	d	c+d
3, 4, 5	27	68	95	a+c	b+d	N
	82	88	170			

For this square, an equivalent form of the X^2 formula is

$$X^2 = \frac{(ad - bc)^2 \times N}{(a+b)(b+d)(c+d)(a+c)}$$

Thus $X^2 = \frac{(55 \times 68 - 20 \times 27)^2 \, 170}{75 \times 88 \times 95 \times 82} = 23.5$ approx.

For 1 degree of freedom, (1 each way, and 1 x 1 = 1) the probability of a value exceeding 10.83 is 0.001. Since 23.5 is much greater, its probability is small. The null hypothesis, that there is no difference in career choices between the classes is therefore rejected; the difference between the groups is highly significant.

The X^2 distribution can be used with non-normal distributions and even with discrete variables. Thus it is a useful and powerful test. Statistics relating to non-normal distribution is known as *nonparametric statistics*.

Non-parametric distributions and tests

So far we have considered distributions which are distributed normally or samples drawn from normal distributions. In some studies skew, bi-modal, U-shaped or T-shaped distributions may be found and for this we may need different tests. For instance, in sociometric studies in which children say who they would like to sit next to, to work with or to play with, one or two children may prove popular. These are the 'stars'. The majority receive far fewer choices or even none at all. If we plot the distribution of frequencies against number of choices the distribution is *positively skewed*, i.e. the tail is towards the positive end, see Table 6.17 and Figure 6.5. In an easy class test in which nearly all children do well, the distribution is *negatively skewed*; the tail of the curve will then be to the negative end.

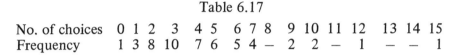

Table 6.17

No. of choices	0	1	2	3	4	5	6	7	8	9	10	11	12	13	14	15
Frequency	1	3	8	10	7	6	5	4	–	2	2	–	1	–	–	1

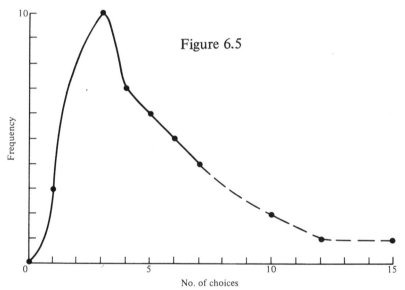

Figure 6.5

To compare scores in distributions of these kinds it is more meaningful to obtain median scores than means and to obtain deciles or percentiles to compare performance than to obtain standard scores. The median score is defined as the point on the scale of measurement above which are exactly half the measures and below which are the other half. It is defined as a point and not as a score or any particular measurement. It may be obtained accurately from a graph or by making a calculation. Similarly the upper quartile (or 75th percentile) is the point above which are exactly a quarter of the measures, and the lower quartile is the point below which are exactly a quarter of the measures. These measures are suitable for use in comparing large samples of O- and A-level marks which often are, but need not be, normally distributed.

Table 6.18

Mark	Frequency (Pure maths)	Cumulative frequency	%	%	Cumulative frequency	Frequency (Physical)
89.5 – 100.5	20	5100	100	100	1700	0
79.5 – 89.5	120	5080	99.5	100	1700	16
69.5 – 79.5	390	4960	97.6	99.0	1684	60
59.5 – 69.5	950	4570	89.9	95.5	1624	231
49.5 – 59.5	1239	3620	71.1	82.0	1393	337
39.5 – 49.5	1221	2391	46.6	62.1	1056	461
29.5 – 39.5	810	1170	23.0	35.0	595	392
19.5 – 29.5	289	360	7.1	13.3	203	159
9.5 – 19.5	64	71	1.4	2.5	44	38
0 – 9.5	7	7	0.1	0.3	6	6
Total	5100					1700

Example 12

Table 6.18 shows distributions of marks in pure mathematics and physics papers taken by some sixth form pupils. End points of intervals have been corrected so that the scale of marks becomes continuous. It is evident that marks in physics are poorer than those in pure mathematics. This suggests that either the physics paper was harder or that the candidates who took physics were less able than those who took pure mathematics. This is easy for an examiner to investigate as many candidates take both subjects. Here the candidates are about equal in calibre so the physics paper was evidently more difficult. Drawing cumulative frequency graphs for both samples by plotting cumulative percentages against the mark at the upper end of an interval gives the results shown in Table 6.18.

It is now possible to compare marks so that equal standards are required for pass mark and successive grades in the two subjects. If it is agreed to fail one third of candidates, the pass mark in pure mathematics is 45 and in physics is 38. If only the top 7 per cent are to receive A grades the corresponding marks are 73 in pure mathematics and 67 in physics.

The median and upper quantile (75th percentile) are also marked on the graphs; the method is applicable if the distributions of marks deviate substantially from normal.

Non-parametric tests   have been devised to provide tests of significance for distributions which are not normal. It may not be possible to specify the functional form of the population distributions but only that the accumulated distribution function is continuous. An alternative term for the tests is *distribution free*. The best known non-parametric test is the X^2-test, but many other tests have developed. Some of the more important ones are clearly explained in *Non-parametric Statistics for Behavioural Sciences* by S. Siegel.

In practice such tests have the advantages of simplicity and wide application, but they have certain disadvantages as compared with parametric tests. The conclusions drawn are weaker and the use of parametric tests as approximations may give more information than the use of a suitable non-parametric test.

Here only two fairly common tests are mentioned: these are the Signs Test and the Median Test. The *Signs Test* can be used for pairs of observations, for instance, for measures for the same sample on two occasions, when it is suspected that the population is changing.

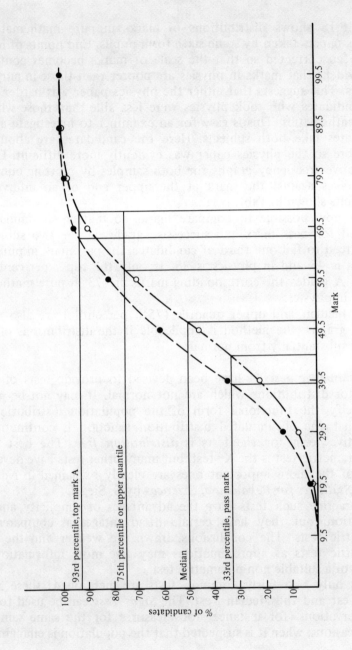

Figure 6.6   Comparison of marks in pure mathematics and physics

Example 13   Use of the signs test

If the differences were due solely to chance we should expect that about half the differences were positive and half negative. This is like tossing pennies again. We want to know the probability of 4 negative differences (tails) among fifteen trials (tosses). We need the probability that this number is less than 4, i.e. the first three probabilities from the fifteenth line of Pascal's triangle:

$$\frac{1}{2}15 \ (1 + 15 + 105 + 455 + 1365) = 0.0592$$

Since the probability of four negative differences is greater than 5 per cent the two sets of observations do not differ significantly at this level, i.e. we accept the null hypothesis that the sets of observations do not differ.

Table 6.19

Pair No.	1	2	3	4	5	6	7	8	9	10	11	12	13	14	15
y	34	28	29	45	26	27	24	15	15	27	23	31	20	35	20
x	33	36	50	41	37	41	39	21	20	37	21	18	29	38	27
$d = y - x$	-1	8	21	-4	11	14	15	6	5	10	-2	-13	9	3	7

Example 14   Use of the median test

The IQs of two remedial classes are as shown in Table 6.20. Do they differ significantly?

Table 6.20

IQ

Class A	Class B
98	96
139	89
93	117
120	100
103	110
106	98
115	105
108	92
107	86
121	128
91	
118	
135	
123	
105	

145

When the IQs are put in order it is possible to find the overall median of the 25 scores, i.e. the 13th score. The first 13 are: 139, 135, 128, 123, 121, 120, 118, 117, 115, 110, 108, 107, 106. Thus the median is 106, see Table 6.21. The null hypothesis that IQs of the two classes do not differ is therefore accepted.

Table 6.21

	Class		
	A	B	
Above 106	9	3	12
106 or below	6	7	13
	15	10	25

$$X^2 = \frac{(63 - 18)^2 \times 25}{(12)\,(13)\,(15)\,(10)} = \frac{225}{104} = 2.17$$

for one degree of freedom X^2 must be 3.84 or more to be significant at the 0.05 level

Correlation regression

So far in this chapter we have looked at differences between scores, means or variances but in some investigations social scientists are more interested in how far variables agree with each other. If so, they are likely to prepare contingency tables or to calculate a correlation coefficient between each pair of measures.

Table 6.22 for instance, is a *contingency table* showing the relationship between scores obtained in students' three best A-levels (A=5, B=4, . . . E=1) with class of degree in physics, obtained three or four years later, from first class (I), upper second (II_1) . . . to pass (P) or fail (F) (King 1973). It is obvious that, although there is a tendency for those who were well qualified initially to obtain better class degress, there are quite numerous exceptions.

If however, all those obtaining over 11 for A-levels had obtained first class degrees, those obtaining 11 had obtained upper seconds, and so on, whilst those scoring less than 9 initially had all obtained pass degrees or had failed or withdrawn, the table would have looked

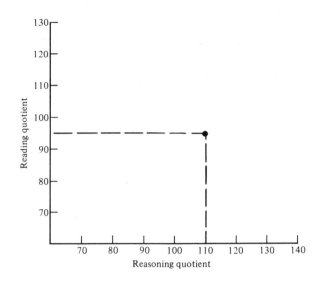

Figure 6.7   Score for child A,B

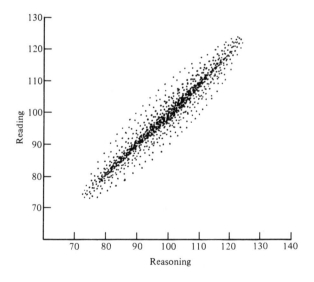

Figure 6.8

very different. On combining the P and F columns, 100 per cent would have appeared in each main diagonal space and all other entries would have been zero. the *correlation* would then have been perfect and would have been 1. Whilst in the extremely improbable event that those who began with the highest scores ended with the lowest and so on in reverse, the correlation would be perfect and negative and would then be −1.

Table 6.22

Degree Class A-level points	I & II$_1$	II$_2$	III	P	F	Total %
over 11	40	30	20	10	0	100
11	20	30	25	18	7	100
10 or 9	6	25	33	24	12	100
less than 9	9	7	35	22	17	90

For Table 6.22, the correlation is 0.39 (it is calculated from frequencies, not from percentages); and this is exceptionally high as, on average, A-level results correlate about 0.2 with degree results.

Low correlations can occur simply because the range of abilities of the tested sample of students is very narrow. This is evident from consideration of a *scatter diagram*, see Figure 6.7. If Tests of verbal reasoning and of reading quotients of a single child (A,B) say 110 and 95, can be shown by a point in a scatter diagram.

When all the children's scores are represented in this way the result is a roughly elliptical scatter of points with a concentration along the main axis, see Figure 6.8. The narrower the ellipse, the higher the correlation. Here it is about 0.7. For *parallel forms* of the same test of reasoning, or of an achievement test, the correlation should be at least 0.8 and may be as high as 0.9 or 0.95 (for tests of personality or attitude correlations of parallel tests or the same test on two occasions may be much lower than this). However, if only the average children are selected for consideration, say those who gained between 85 and 115 (see the points inside the square) the points are relatively more scattered, so the correlation for them is considerably lower, probably about 0.4 in this instance.

Since A-level candidates are already highly selected because they have all passed O-levels and have been chosen for the academic sixth form, they represent a fairly narrow range of ability; whilst those who take degrees are probably of a still narrower ability range. This is one reason why correlations obtained between A-level and degree results are low. Other reasons may be that pupils who were coached at school do less well in university where they must think for themselves, distractions occur due to changing interests as the students mature, they may be bored with a course or far more interested in university studies than those at school, or they may take a new subject entirely which was not available for study at A-level so making their results difficult to predict.

Care is needed in interpreting correlation. A correlation of 0.9 between two variables does not necessarily imply a causal relationship between them. For example, the production of pop records in the UK over the past twenty years probably correlates quite highly with the incidence of violent crime, since both have increased fairly steadily, but this does not imply that one has directly influenced the other! There may be another variable, or more probably a complex of variables which accounts for both. People wishing to prove a case will often cite high correlations as 'evidence', but causes must be sought elsewhere.

When incidence of lung cancer was first shown to correlate quite highly with numbers of cigarettes smoked regularly over a period of time, the distinguished statistician Fisher (1959) pointed out that this did not show that cigarette smoking was necessarily a cause; since smoking is a voluntary activity, people who smoke may differ in some way, such as genetic constitution, from those who do not. Subsequent experimentation with animals has established that cigarettes do contain a carcinogen, but genetic constitution may still determine which smokers, or animals exposed to smoke, succumb to it and which do not. Thus, further investigation is needed to fully establish causes. Comparison of smokers and non-smokers certainly shows that more of the smokers will develop cancer and still more will develop bronchial or cardiac symptoms.

A number of different correlation coefficients are needed depending on the kinds of scores or measures and their distributions. If two sets of normally distributed scores have been obtained for the same sample, the *product moment correlation (r)* is calculated. When candidates are marked in order on two occasions or by two different judges, the *rank order correlation coefficient (p)* should be used. Where there is a range of normally distributed scores for one variable and only a dichotomy, e.g. pass-fail, for another variable (which is also normally distributed) the *tetrachoric correlation coefficient* is obtained. If both sets of scores for the sample are registered as pass-fail, although both variables are normally distributed, the *bi-serial correlation coefficient* should be calculated.

A clear account of these coefficients with illustrative examples can be obtained in Guilford's book (1956) chapter 13.

Another important concept in studying relationships between variables is that of *regression*. If we take the average score, y, in an arithmetic test for all 7 year olds, all 8 year olds and so on to 14 years, and plot these scores against average age (x) we may obtain points which are roughly on a straight line, see Figure 6.9.

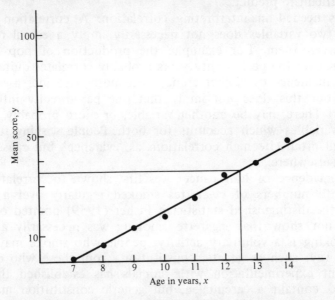

Figure 6.9

If so, it is possible to calculate the equation of the line which fits best, and this is called the regression line of y (mean score) on x (age). Given a child's age, e.g. 12½, the 'best estimate' of his score in the arithmetic test can be obtained from the regression line and is about 33. If all the separate points of the scatter diagram are entered, showing each child's score, the regression line is still the same, but the possibility of a substantial error in the estimate made from only one other measure is then more obvious.

Sometimes the regression line is curved. This happens when testing students under pressure, if they differ appreciably in level of anxiety. Those who are not anxious at all (often the extroverts) and those who are paralysed with anxiety (more likely the introverts) tend to do poorly, whereas students who experience just sufficient anxiety to be aroused to maximum effort, do best, see Figure 6.10.

150

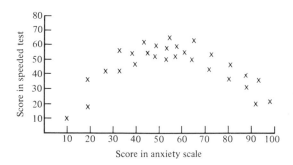

Figure 6.10

Since the test scores are clearly not normally distributed the product moment correlation coefficient should not be calculated. Instead a coefficient M (eta) can be calculated to measure the degree of relationship (e.g. see Downie and Heath 1974, p.110).

When correlations have been obtained between a number of approximately normally distributed variables it is possible to detect relationships between them by *factor analysis* or to estimate scores in one variable from a *multiple regression equation* containing several other variables. If a table or matrix of correlations is obtained between, say, twenty variables of achievement in school, it may be possible to identify four or five factors which account for much of the difference between pupils, e.g. verbal and non-verbal reasoning abilities, verbal fluency, spatial imagination, numerical speed and accuracy. Attempts to predict success in various specialised studies might be made by using multiple regression equations based on a battery of tests to assess these factors and relevant personality factors. Factor analysis is explained by Child (1970). Multiple regression is often used in research and is discussed in Guilford (1956) chapter 16.

7 Educational research and the teacher

As mentioned in earlier chapters a number of significant advances have been made in the field of educational research during the last two decades. There has not only been an increase in the quantity of educational research but some improvement in the quality has also taken place (see Ward, Hall and Schramm, 1975). In fact, our knowledge and understanding in many areas of the learning-teaching situation has been improved through research. The nature and functions of such areas as learning, motivation, group dynamics and teacher effectiveness are better understood today than, say, a few decades ago.

Indirect contributions to methodological and operational strategies of educational research have also been made in the last twenty years. For example, since the launching of Sputnik in 1957 a great amount of time, effort and money have been expended on curriculum development programmes in science and in other topics in America and on this side of the Atlantic. Most of the work has gone into designing a new set of teaching materials and preparing classroom teachers to use them. The new course materials were intended both to replace existing materials in conventional school subjects (e.g. mathematics) and to add new areas of study (e.g. humanities, social studies) to the school curriculum.

The work of the psychologists, namely, Tyler, Skinner, Bruner and Piaget has also contributed to a body of organised knowledge concerning education and this has had a significant impact on the design of educational materials. It should be mentioned, however, that their work was undertaken primarily as 'scientific' enterprises and with no immediate practical purpose in mind. There is no doubt that such research has influenced educators and researchers to some extent, but it is difficult to determine how far. It can be said, however, that this curriculum reform movement (between 1960 and 1975) has contributed significantly to the advancement of educational theory, research, evaluation and practices.

Educational research ultimately focuses on problems related to learning and social, emotional and personal development in the classroom. Some (but by no means all) outstanding social scientists still prefer to work within the ivory towers of academic institutions rather than in practical problem-oriented establishments (e.g. schools). There are other scholars who, from these watch towers, can survey accurately movements and trends which the practitioner often cannot see because he or she is too close to the situation. However, the gap between educational research and practice has remained a yawning chasm. Such a gap has to be narrowed by changes not only in research strategy but by changes in teacher education as well. Attempts to narrow that gap, therefore, present a stimulating challenge to both researchers and practitioners as we will see in a moment.

The expansion of educational research has also come about, partly because of the increased confidence society seems to have placed upon the educational enterprise. Bloom (1966) pointed out for example that, 'Education is looked to for solutions to problems of poverty, racial discord, crime and delinquency, urban living, peace, and even for problems arising from affluence'.

In spite of the financial nourishment and methodological advancement research related to education has had the least direct impact when undertaken for the purpose of solving practical educational problems. It has failed to give educators answers they seek concerning many of the classroom problems. Some teachers and administrators believe that educational problems can be solved by a direct research attack. Let us consider an example: the problem of discovering the best method of teaching, say, social studies has been investigated by a number of researchers. Yet, no-one seems to know the precise answer as to the best method of teaching this subject because a method which is effective with one group of students may be ineffective with another group. There are factors such as the previous experience of students, their motivation and ability, the ethos of the school, the personality of the teacher and many others which might contribute to the effectiveness of a particular teaching method. In other words, teaching effectiveness depends upon the situation in which it occurs and the learners to whom it is directed as well as the technical skills and the personality of the teacher. Nevertheless, the emphasis of much educational research in recent years has been on the solution of educational problems by tackling them through research techniques (Travers, 1978). Many studies have been undertaken, but their influence on classroom practices has remained relatively small. In spite of some advancement there is still much ignorance about classroom dynamics, and the amount of verified knowledge is still limited.

There seems to be no quick way of solving educational problems through educational research, given the gulf between the findings of educational research and the classroom pay-off. Yates (1971) states that:

> In the natural sciences widely generalised and applicable findings may reasonably be expected from fundamental research. In the social sciences, and in educational research particularly, such expectations are likely to be frustrated because of the extent and significance of the differences among the institutions and situations involved. The 'local' variables are so potent that they call for special attention from the researcher . . . in the educational field. Much firmer distinctions are, of course, forced upon us. Among schools of the same 'type', for example, the range of variation is so great that it is most unlikely that a prescribed method of teaching will yield the same results in each.

Let us examine some of the other reasons why educational research has been a painfully slow process in producing educational change. In other words, why educational research has failed to provide teachers, administrators and all those concerned in the field with effective means of solving educational problems and why teachers have not been able to utilise existing research, and ultimately improve the quality of life.

Generally speaking, obtaining knowledge through research is a demanding task. Education processes are often more complex to research than the biological or the physical world. The educational researcher has to deal with so many variables simultaneously, most of them cannot be controlled or experimentally manipulated.

As a discipline educational research has no clear cut boundaries at either the conceptual or the practical levels (as pointed out in earlier chapters). It borrows and applies methods and techniques or tools from other fields such as psychology, sociology, history, anthropology and many others. What in effect this means is that disciplines other than educational research are always the centre of discussion concerning the methodology of education. Traxler (1954) argues that the overlapping of educational research with research in the other social sciences is inevitable because of the nature of the educational process itself. According to him education means providing conditions

154

and using techniques to foster the maximum development (intellectual, physical, social and emotional) of an individual in relation to his or her capacity, and any discipline that is concerned with the growth and development of an individual can be used by education. Furthermore, techniques and procedures of educational research are primarily the methods of the behavioural and social sciences. For example, studies of growth and development in children utilise the procedures and tools originally developed in psychology while longitudinal studies of individuals make use of the case study methods which have their origins in social and clinical work.

Although there are certain positive aspects in Traxler's remarks, it can also be said that the progress of educational research has suffered from subordination to differing modes of approach and methods derived from fields other than education. Once the alien techniques have been adopted in the educational sphere, they have tended to maintain their distinctive languages and strategies. Simon (1978), therefore, emphasising the need for educationally oriented research states that:

> . . . the focus of educational research must be education, and that its overall function is to assist teachers, administrators, indeed all concerned in the field, to improve the quality of the educational process . . .

There have been efforts by some educationalists to define educational phenomenon more specifically with a view to establishing its identity and pursuing its goals. Simon (1978) quotes an American philosopher who attempted to define educational phenomenon as:

> What occurs in the classroom, in the process of teaching, is neither a chance happening, nor determined by anything comparable to a law of nature. Here is a planned, deliberate, explicit intervention designed to promote learning which may differ from place to place and from time to time, but which is observable and subject to analysis.

Simon suggests that the educational researcher should deal with methodological issues in the light of some such definition of educational phenomena. This view suggests that the researcher should try to minimise the influence of his previous discipline!

Another problem associated with educational research has been the recent emphasis on the development of an educational technology which represents an extension of the Thorndike model. Attempts to introduce the computer assisted learning (CAL) have also been made which falls into this model. Much of the so-called modern educational technology tries to bring an engineering model of production to the classroom situation (e.g. Bloom's taxonomy, and Tyler's objectives model in education). In reality, classrooms are not manufacturing enterprises and they present very special problems in the development of a technology. The teacher has to deal with many variables; rigid control of these variables is extremely difficult to achieve.

There are also ethical issues which need to be considered by the researcher. Unlike the biological sciences, subjects in the social sciences (including education) can refuse to take part in the experiment. They have the right to ask the researcher to guarantee the confidentiality of research data, and to remain anonymous. It is also quite legitimate on the part of subjects to seek assurance that their participation in research will not affect them in any way, i.e. educationally, socially and professionally. Thus, the researcher's relationships with human subjects are based on personal trust. He must respect them at all times. The ethical considerations must be adhered to by researchers, though this does make educational research more difficult.

Research and the teacher

The teacher's conceptions, expectations and perceptions of educational research is quite different from that of the researcher. Most teachers would like to know simple and immediate solutions to their specific classroom problems. For example, how to deal with a disturbed child? How to motivate children in the class so that they can concentrate on their work? What is the most effective method of teaching a school subject? How to minimise disruptive behaviour in the school? Teachers expect that the researcher should provide meaningful and reliable information on these specific issues that may be encountered in their everyday activities. Thus, they typically want practical advice for handling particular problems. Obviously these are relevant questions for teachers. But educational research can never provide a prescription for the teacher or educational planner; it can provide some general guidelines, though these guidelines may not be very specific like, say, physics. However, when answers to such questions as mentioned above are not forthcoming they sometimes become sceptical of educational research enterprises.

Our own experience of working with school based research over a number of years has shown that there are many prevalent misconceptions amongst teachers about the nature and function of educational research. At one extreme are those who have complete faith in educational research technology, ignoring the methodological limitations and failing to differentiate between good and poor research design. They simply lack knowledge of discrimination between faulty, trivial investigations and sound studies. Whether or not they have an intelligent appreciation of research, they seem to accept research findings uncritically. Such teachers believe that research can provide reliable and meaningful solutions to many of their classroom problems. At the other extreme are the teachers who have a fearful distrust of research or new ideas, completely ignoring the evidence that in many situations a well designed research can provide them with some useful information on which to base a decision. Also, at this extreme are those who view change or innovation as unnecessary. They often reject research findings which present ideas that depart too far from prevailing beliefs or practices. They are unwilling to apply the outcome of relevant research in the schools.

One of the grounds for distrust of researchers by some teachers seems to be the suspicion that the researcher is trying to dictate to the teacher what he should do. Traditionally, teachers consider themselves autonomous. The training of teachers seems to have failed to convince them that there are valid generalisations which apply to teaching. This is obviously a misunderstanding of the role of research in the total educative process (Thouless, 1966). Interestingly, many of the recent innovations have their origin in the initiatives taken by the schools, and such initiatives can often be termed as a form of research. For example, in 1967 the DES (Department of Education and Science) mounted a large scale study of comprehensive education, because certain LEAs (Local Education Authorities) and groups of teachers had independently pioneered ways of breaking away from the 11+ selection procedures. However, it would seem reasonable to say that the majority of teachers are often cautious and conservative in their classroom practice.

Teachers dislike theory. This may be due to the fact that they have been offered conflicting theories in the past. Indeed, a number of research studies currently carried out in education are not based on any theoretical position. It is also fair to say that many teachers operate under implicit theories which, they feel, are threatened by explicit, reasoned and well confirmed theories. Theory increases our understanding of the world which can help us to decide how to act as researchers.

The estrangement between theory, research and teachers can also be explained in terms of the part played by the producer of research. It is often said that many research workers are not sufficiently aware of the practical classroom problems, and that their hypotheses are based on wild speculation. Criticisms of such nature are not wholly unjustified. The reports of much research are often technical which make them difficult for teachers to interpret and apply in their own situation. Thus, the formidable terminology and tactics of some research alienate many teachers from reading findings or reports. Researchers have also a responsibility to adapt their findings to the language of practitioners.

Another reason why educational practice has advanced less than other areas of professional activities is that most research reports are published in academic or technical journals which are not easily available to teachers. This situation suggests that teachers are unaware of many educational studies conducted by competent scholars. Researchers ought to remember that professional educators at all levels are consumers of research who must have an access to the findings if they are to be of use in school. In recent years some publications in Britain (e.g. British Journal of Teacher Education, British Educational Research Journal, New Society, New Community) have aimed at the creation of the means of increased communication of research findings to teachers.

The above factors, among others, seem to have contributed to the slow progress of educational research, and consequently the practice of education to the degree necessary in a research oriented world. It is apparent that some of the reasons are inherent in research itself (i.e. education being a very complex field to research), some resulting from the attitude of teachers and educational decision makers and some connected with the defects of communication between researchers and teachers. Increased research mindedness among teachers and classroom mindedness amongst researchers will depend on effective communciation between the two parties.

Tyler (1978) points out that, 'Persons in research and development who want their work to be employed immediately by the practitioner can be helped greatly by working with practitioners to understand their problems and perceive the context through their eyes'. Writing about the presentation and dissemination of research findings Wrigley (1976) suggests that the difference in attitude between the educational researchers and their audience is one of the main problems in promoting research. He lists five possible audiences: 1) other researchers in the field; 2) teachers in the classroom; 3) policy makers at local and national levels; 4) the general public interested in educational matters; 5) the press.

Our experience has also shown that a large proportion of the teaching force neither plan nor conduct research in their classrooms. Lack of 'know how' in planning research seems to be one of the possible explanations for such an attitude. This can be related to the paucity of training in research techniques in teacher training programmes throughout the world. Such programmes have actually been designed

158

to put practitioners into the school equipped to teach specific subjects and carry on routine work within the school system. The power structure within the school system is also not geared toward the use of research. Rarely do specific aspects in the teacher training curriculum focus on research methodology, even though those who train teachers have a key role in enabling teachers to translate educational research findings into practice when they enter their profession. This might be one of the reasons as to why researchers and teachers do not seem to appreciate each other's concerns and difficulties. It seems necessary that preparation as a teacher should not only involve acquiring knowledge of subject matter but the ability to operate educationally at different levels: as a class teacher, as consumer of research conducted outside the school and as producer of research. All teachers should have a grasp of what research is so that they are able to translate the findings into practice. This should enable them to question some of the traditional practices and ideas about the learning-teaching situation. By redesigning the curriculum in teacher training colleges and institutes of higher education and by giving particular attention to the research process, teachers can become both consumers and producers of research. There is a growing movement, linked with curriculum innovation and its evaluation, to induct teachers into classroom research. It is difficult to ascertain the degree of success of this movement.

The role of the educator/researcher

Given the gap which exists between research findings and practical application in education, the question is often raised whether teachers should participate in research activity, and if they do, what should be the nature and degree of his or her involvement. Opinions differ with regard to this question.

There are some who say that teachers have no right to research into their teaching, because it is unethical and unprofessional to use children like guinea pigs. Lieberman (1956) asserts that the teacher's job is to apply the educational findings while it is the responsibility of social scientists to generate these findings. Justifying this proposition he points out that the average classroom teacher is always under pressure of work, and is not acquainted with the principles and techniques of research. Lieberman further adds that, 'Developing, testing and confirming knowledge is not something the practitioner can do as a hobby or in his spare moments at work. The discovery of new knowledge is a full time job'. On the other hand, Lieberman suggests that teachers may conduct research in their classroom and obtain information regarding interpersonal attitudes of pupils, but such exercise is not carried out to add to the existing knowledge in the field.

There are many social scientists who would support the view of Lieberman that the function of the teacher is to conduct research only in his own classroom in order to acquire certain information, skills and attitudes, and which will encourage him to become creative rather than merely a reproductive individual. A number of early curriculum development projects had viewed the teacher as a kind of technician who had learnt certain techniques for transmitting knowledge, skills or habits but who in the main is simply for putting into practice ideas that have been developed elsewhere.

Other writers (Gage, 1963; Van Dalen, 1966) do not support the proposition that all educational research should be designed to add to 'scientific' knowledge. Van Dalen (1966) points out that although the problem and rationale of research may be different in 'pure' research and 'applied' research, techniques may be very similar. Corey (1953) arguing for teacher participation in research stated that keeping educational research within the domain of a professional researcher is to take too limited a view of the educator's role. He added that teachers can make better decisions and can become more effective practitioners if they conduct 'action' research. Action research, according to Corey (the originator of the term), is done by practitioners so that they may improve their classroom practices. It is a type of applied research which is conducted to find solutions to immediate problems in the schools.

Some people are of the opinion that action research conducted by teachers is lacking in sound methodology whereas basic research is generally of a superior quality. In fact, whatever may be the argument regarding the relative importance of basic and applied types of research, both will continue to be done, because there seems to be no rational grounds for conflict between them. Basic research is designed to discover principles whereas action research is conducted to find out the best way of applying those principles in practical situations. The role of teacher as consumer of research is extremely important for both types of research. Action research is obviously of value to the teacher as the consumer, and the practical values to be obtained from basic research must be acquired by the consumers.

In spite of the points both in favour and against action research, more and more educational researchers seem to think that a study in action research is valuable in the sense that its methodologies and findings contribute to improvements in educational practices. Getzel (1978), in a thorough and well documented account of educational research, gives the following opinion which argues that theoretical research has little effect on school practice:

> The fact is basic research produces only tiny 'bits' of knowledge
> about an infinitely complex world. Given time, such incremental
> gains in knowledge may have some effect on practical situations,
> but schoolmen have long been aware that research findings usually
> have little practical bearing on the actual operation of schools.

Turning to the teacher's role as researcher there seems to be little
doubt expressed in the literature that teachers are the main consumers
of the findings of educational research. We believe, however, that
if teachers are to understand the implications of research data and
critically to examine practice in the light of these implications, then
they must be involved at some level in the research process. We hope,
therefore, that more and more teachers are inducted into the research
role from both practical and theoretical positions. Research in education can neither be efficient nor effective in its objectives without
the full co-operation of teachers.

Tyler (1978) states that, 'If educational research is to have any
real impact on schools, then it is imperative that teachers be involved
in research processes and that the existing barriers between the so-
called 'doers' and 'thinkers' be thus broken down'.

A teacher may undertake various forms of research. For example,
he/she may like to explore a particular aspect of any academic discipline connected with his/her own subject specialism or with the
theory of education. On the other hand the teacher may decide to
conduct applied research into an aspect of the school for which he/she
is not directly responsible. The term 'educator/researcher' used for
this section of the chapter refers only to the teacher who is also a
participant within the situation he/she is researching. Thus, the edu-
cator/researcher is not only a teacher doing research, but a teacher
doing research into his/her own classroom.

Admittedly, the role of educator/researcher is a complex one.
There might be a role conflict! For example, as researcher the teacher
would like to develop his/her own understanding of the classroom,
but as teacher he/she is responsible for developing the understanding
of his/her pupils. Herein lies the problem. Obviously it is essential
that the role conflict between the teacher as educator and the teacher
as researcher should be avoided by setting out clear guidelines. That
is to say, participation in research should not be undertaken at the
expense of the pupils' learning. The risk of inhibiting pupils' learning
may be reduced if the teacher/researcher focuses upon empirically
observed problems in the classroom rather than imported problems.
At the initial stages the teacher ought to be concerned with diagnostic
rather than prescriptive judgements. Having gained such an insight

he/she should move beyond the boundary of diagnosis towards the prescription of remedies. It is in this respect that the educator/researcher differs from professional researchers. The teacher must be in a position to convince his or her colleagues that the findings obtained are meaningful and trustworthy (reliable and valid in psychometric terms). Furthermore, he or she needs to implement the findings in order to judge their usefulness. However, the teacher who succeeds in combining teaching and research is likely to gain a greater awareness of classroom dynamics. Eggleston (1979), concluding an article titled 'The characteristics of educational research: mapping the domain' writes:

> Constantly teachers are regarded . . . as the objects of communication and consumers of research findings. While I would agree that it is our responsibility to write accounts of our researches and their implications in comprehensive prose which give teachers access to our minds, and share the hope that our work does yield usable findings, I am even more concerned that we think of teachers as professionals with whom rather than on whom we do research. Effective teaching is more likely to be achieved when the teacher himself/herself is operating in reflective and empirical modes. Teachers operating in this way cease to be tiresome intervening variables and become self-conscious instruments of educational processes.

Research activity is one of the most effective ways for a teacher to do better what he/she is expected to do, i.e. teach. Research is likely to sensitise the teacher to the whole educational process in a way that should promote his/her effective use of personal resources, in order to help pupils learn. By engaging in research, sources for facts can be tapped and a certain structure in the perception of classroom problems can be achieved through research on educational problems. The teacher needs to demonstrate that he/she is more than a high level technician.

As mentioned earlier the teacher who is planning to conduct research in his or her own classroom should set out clear guidelines for the dual role of educator/researcher. The teacher is expected to create an environment which is conducive to learning; as a researcher he/she must be concerned with the diagnosis of problems, and ultimately moving beyond the diagnosis of problems towards the prescription of remedies. It is in this respect that the teacher/researcher differs perhaps from other research workers. Although most classroom teachers are appliers rather than producers of research, the teacher has an important role to play in certain kinds of research. In the future, more and more teachers must be called upon to play the dual role of educator/researcher, and only then can they become proficient consumers and producers.

8 Examples of some educational research

As indicated in chapter 7 some significant studies relating to education have been carried out in recent years. It is difficult, however, to select optimally designed studies to illustrate the ways in which research procedures have been employed, partly because of the controversial nature of some of the studies and partly because of the complexity of the educative process itself. Most of the investigators have recognised the limitations of their research with regard to structure and/or operationalisation.

However, in this chapter examples have been drawn from recent studies conducted in Britain which are fairly well known amongst educators and researchers. These studies have received considerable publicity in the mass media, and were aimed at a fairly wide audience.

It should be mentioned at the outset that only brief descriptions of these studies are given in the following pages, and readers should study the original references for fuller information. Each study attempted to identify certain characteristics of individuals and their behaviour. We have taken the liberty of summarising the research reports, hoping that the summaries are valid. At the end of each summary, we have presented some comments and questions. These are intended to help readers focus on specific characteristics of the study, and to supplement the questions they would like to ask after reading the original reports.

Each of the studies had focussed upon a specific educational problem, claimed to have followed a carefully designed plan, collected and interpreted data, and has been published in book form.

1 Streaming in the Primary School
by Joan C. Barker Lunn (1970)
England, Slough:
National Foundation for Educational Research

This study was initiated in 1963 by the NFER in response to a request from the Ministry of Education (now Department of Education and Science). It set out to investigate the effects of streaming and non-streaming on the personality, social and intellectual development of junior school pupils over their junior school career. It was hoped that the findings would provide some evidence for the Plowden Committee which was being set up to report on the primary school.[1]

The broad aim of this large-scale study was broken down into a series of questions (e.g. Are there any personality, attitude or interest differences in children of the same ability level in the two types of school?). The enquiry consisted of three parts, but the materials contained in this report were concerned with the results of the second and third phases. The second phase was a comparative study which adopted both a cross-sectional and a longitudinal design. The third stage was an intensive study involving nine schools.

The main part of the research was concerned with the follow-up study of 5,500 pupils in 72 junior schools in England and Wales. Of these schools 36 were non-streamed and 36 streamed. A streamed school was defined as 'one in which the allocation of each yearly intake to classes is on the basis of ability or attainment, so that the most able are assigned to the top or A-streams, the less able to other streams' (Barker Lunn, 1970, pp.11–12). A non-streamed school was conceived as the 'one in which pupils within each year group are assigned to classes made up of children from all ability levels' (p.12). This is done either by assessing pupils on a standardised test; or by allocating pupils to classes randomly, perhaps based on alphabetical order of the children's surnames; or by allocating them on the basis of age.

In order to obtain comparable samples of streamed and non-streamed schools matching procedures were adopted, utilising a number of criteria such as type of school, number of classes in the school, average number of pupils in each class, etc.

The pupils were assessed in terms of their performance and attitudes in nine different areas:

1   Attainment in reading, English, number concept, problem and mechanical arithmetic;
2   Verbal and non-verbal reasoning;
3   'Creativity' or 'divergent' thinking;
4   Interests;

5 School-related attitudes;
6 Personality characteristics;
7 Sociometric status;
8 Participation in school activities;
9 Occupational aspirations.

The instruments to measure intellectual development (reading, English, mechanical arithmetic and problem arithmetic) were specifically designed to be suitable for all ages, from seven to ten plus. It was hoped that measures of gain in achievement could be made during the longitudinal study. There were two parallel versions of each test, and Sample A (half the matched pairs of schools) took the A version, and Sample B took the B version of the tests. These tests were administered at the end of each school year in the Junior School. Furthermore, a Free Writing assessment, in the form of two tests – one of which entailed writing essays and the other testing creative thinking – was made at the end of the 3rd and 4th year respectively.

One of the aims of the research was to examine achievement; another was to find out the effects of streaming and non-streaming on children's personality, attitudes and social adjustment (the affective domain). In order to assess meaningfully social, attitudinal and personality development a series of measures were used. A number of attitude scales were devised which attempted to measure attitude to school, interest in school work, relationship with the teacher and the importance of doing well at school. Furthermore, two other tests were used to assess attitude to class and 'other' images of class – these were included to tap possible levels of dissatisfaction of lower streams of children with their classroom situation. Other measures included in the battery were sociometric techniques and a self-report social adjustment scale, and these were designed to assess the pupil's ability to get on with his classmates. The pupil's self-concept in terms of school work was also assessed and the effects of the school as an organisation noted. The level of anxiety was also explored which can have a damaging effect on the pupil's achievement.

Various personality variables were studied in relation to maladjustment. Such instances of the relationships assessed by teachers' ratings were bullying, social withdrawal, disobedience etc. General information on the child's background, and behaviour in school was also obtained from the school.

In assessing the children's attitudes, personality and behaviour, a note was also made of the teachers' attitudes to streaming and other educational topics and this proved to be significant. Two main teacher types were found: Type 1 and Type 2 i.e. non-streamers and streamers. Type 1 teachers who believed in non-streaming showed favourable attitudes to slow children, were tolerant of noise in the classroom, were generally permissive in terms of less discipline, favoured group activities rather than traditional lesson formats, and were against the use of corporal punishment. Their approach was essentially 'child-centred' (Barker Lunn). On the other hand Type 2 teachers advocated streaming, and good academic attainment. They adopted traditional lesson formats and patterns of seating; were not permissive and less tolerant to noise and talking in the class. Furthermore, they advocated corporal punishment.

In addition, a limited study was conducted of parents' attitudes. Two other studies made were: an intensive study of six schools and problems and methods of organisational change.

One of the interesting findings concerned the role of the teacher. This was quite revealing when considered in relation to the two teacher types, and two types of school organisation (non-streamed and streamed). Teachers in streamed schools seemed more united in both their views on educational matters and teaching methods as compared to non-streamed schools where there was a wide divergence of opinion. Another interesting pattern which emerged was that about half the staff in non-streamed schools held attitudes more typical of teachers in streamed schools. In other words, they had created 'streamed atmosphere' within the non-streamed classes.

Children with above average ability were found to have no difference in academic self-image between the streamed and non-streamed school, and teacher type 1 and type 2. However, in the case of average ability children, those taught by non-streamers, type 1 in non-streamed schools had a more positive self-concept and academic image than children taught by streams, type 2 in streamed schools. It is also worth noting that poorest attitudes identified were held by pupils taught by typical streamers, type 2 teachers in non-streamed schools.

It is interesting to note that streaming seemed to have beneficial effects in the sense of a good academic self-image for pupils of below average ability in streamed schools.

With regard to academic performance there was no difference in the average academic achievement of boys and girls of comparable ability and social class. Teacher type seemed to bear little relationship to academic progress. However, the researcher suggested that any effect might have been blurred by children changing from one teacher type to another in consecutive years (Barker Lunn, chapter 5).

The results on 'divergent thinking' tests showed that a higher level of this type of thinking was associated with non-streamed schools when children were taught by typical non-streamer teachers. Perhaps the higher scores were due to the teaching techniques, and 'permissive' atmosphere created by these teachers (Barker Lunn, chapter 6).

It was not found in the study that on the whole social class played an important part in academic performance of children in either type of organisation. But there was some evidence that pupils coming from the lower social class background 'deteriorated' in reading attainment over the junior school course in relation to children of higher social class. As one would expect there was a tendency for teachers to over-estimate the ability of higher social class children and under-estimate the ability of pupils coming from lower working-class. Teachers' low estimations about the abilities of lower working-class pupils may be accounted for the children's decline in performance (Barker Lunn, chapters 5 and 7).

This study clearly shows that the wider range of attainment of English children is to a large extent due to the operation of the self-fulfilling prophecy based on teacher expectations. This implies that such underlying attitude plays an important part in the educational achievements of pupils.

An attempt to assess the extent to which children can be accurately allocated to school classes on the basis of attainment shows that approximately 15 per cent of pupils were wrongly placed in a stream at the end of the school year. The criterion of allocating them in different ability groups was their performance in arithmetic or English. Children who were allocated to high streams showed academic improvement whereas those who remained in too low a stream deteriorated. However, this was not a common pattern in this research (Barker Lunn, chapter 7). It is important to point out that upward mobility between streams was rather low.

There is evidence from many different sources of the need to reflect upon the methods which are used to assess the abilities of children, particularly those of ethnic minority groups and indeed of any other disadvantaged children. Because of the inherent problems in conventional methods of assessment one cannot help wondering if some of the children are really in the right ability streams. If they are wrongly placed this could have a crucial bearing on their achievements throughout life.

Generally speaking, the findings of Barker Lunn's research showed that neither school organisation nor teacher type had much impact on the social, emotional or attitudinal development of pupils of above average ability, but the effect was noticeable in case of average and below average ability children.

The school's streaming or non-streaming seemed to have influenced the development of school related attitudes (e.g. attitudes to class, and motivation to do well in school) in pupils of average and below average ability. In these areas, pupils in non-streamed schools showed more favourable attitudes than pupils in streamed schools (Barker Lunn, chapter 9). An aspect of the study was concerned with friendship patterns which indicated that pupils in both streamed and non-streamed schools taught by either teacher type tended to choose their friends who were of similar ability and social class. However, a number of mixed ability friendship patterns emerged in non-streamed schools. With regard to the social popularity of children of different ability levels no difference was observed between those in streamed schools and those taught by typical non-streamers in non-streamed schools.

Overall, Barker Lunn's work points to the differing effects of streaming and non-streaming on average and below average ability children; little difference was found between children of above average ability. The findings also showed that streaming for the average ability child can endanger self-soncept; such a child in the streaming system would tend to have lower self-concept. The whole of the research indicated a closer unity in the objectives and teaching strategies of teachers in streamed schools, while there was a tendency on the part of many non-streamed school teachers to hold attitudes or implement educational policies at variance with the declared policy of their school (Barker Lunn, p.276). According to the obtained results the children's academic attainment, on the whole, was not affected by their school's organisational policy or their teachers' attitude to streaming. However, the academic achievements of pupils seemed affected as a result of upward or downward mobility. The most interesting finding was that the emotional and social development of average and below-average ability pupils was significantly affected by streaming/non-streaming dimension and also by teachers' attitudes.

This research has also shown that progressive methods of teaching do not necessarily lead to lower attainment in the basic skills as suggested by many critics of progressive education. It has also demonstrated that there are significant factors other than streaming in the primary school which can account for children's attainments.

However, no clear-cut conclusions can be drawn from this research. Given enthusiastic and skilful teachers, non-streaming had obvious advantages, particularly for the motivation of pupils. But even in unstreamed schools, about half the teachers supported streaming explicitly. The researcher has failed to recognise that social scientists have not yet reached a complete understanding of the environment, or factors which would enable them to produce optimum conditions for the encouragement of creative children or self-initiated learning. Furthermore, Barker Lunn seems to have ignored the limitations of the techniques and methods used for the assessment of cognitive and non-cognitive variables.

2 Teaching Styles and Pupil Progress
by Neville Bennett et al. (1976)
London
Open Books

Since the publication of the Plowden Report[1] and Black Papers[2] the need arose for some research evidence to inform educators and researchers on particular aspects of the 'traditional' versus 'progressive' debate. Very little research on teaching styles was available.

A study was designed by Neville Bennett and his co-workers to determine the effect on pupils' cognitive achievement of formal, informal and mixed teaching styles. The nature of enquiry was a controversial one.

The research team set out to answer two broad questions: a) Do differences in teaching styles differentially affect the cognitive and emotional development of pupils? b) Do certain types of pupil perform better under certain types of teaching styles? In creating the research design, the investigators kept a number of points in mind:

1 Teaching styles should be broken down into their constituent behaviours with a view to achieving a clearer definition;
2 The range of teaching behaviours contained within a style should be widened to increase the validity of the description;
3 A multi-dimensional approach to teaching style ought to be adopted;
4 Efforts should be made to validate the description;
5 A large and representative sample of teachers should be involved in the study;
6 The time between the two testing situations should be long enough to enable the pupils to become familiar with the teaching style;
7 The study should be based on relevant and viable theory.

Teachers in Lancashire and Cumbria from some 871 schools responded to a 28-item questionnaire which covered six broad areas: classroom management and organisation, teacher controls and sanctions, curriculum content and planning, instructional strategies, motivational strategies and assessment procedures (see chapter 3 of Bennett's book for a detailed discussion).

On the basis of responses, twelve groups of teachers were formed for research purposes. The groups ranged from Type 1 (the most informal) to Type 12 (the most formal) (see pp.45—7). The teaching styles were categorised and validated by the research team and LEA advisers who visited and observed classrooms, and also by content analysis of pupils' essays.

Responses to questions on aims and opinions, educational issues and teaching methods were related to teaching styles. In the analysis seven styles were used.

Responses to the questionnaire and analyses indicated that informal teachers were of the opinion that formal methods are relevant in terms of teaching basic skills and providing children with structure, and such methods do not make heavy demands on teachers. These teachers disagreed over discipline problems. Informal teachers also thought that informal methods could create discipline problems.

Formal teachers, on the other hand, thought that formal methods of teaching encouraged responsibility and self-discipline, create balance between teachers and their work, develop pupils' full potential, and are better for bright pupils. Formal teachers also felt that informal methods encourage responsibility amongst pupils, help pupils to think for themselves, make heavy demands on the teacher, can teach basic subjects less effectively and can create discipline problems.

Pupils taught by 37 teachers (a sub-sample selected), who were regarded as typical of their style, were tested (400 pupils per style). Twelve of the 37 teachers chosen were at the formal extreme of the continuum, 13 were at the informal extreme and the remaining 12 represented intermediate or 'mixed' teaching styles. These three groups of teachers representing formal, informal and mixed teaching styles constituted the levels of treatment in a quasi-experimental analysis of pupil performance in reading, English and mathematics.

In June 1973 objective tests of reading, mathematics and English were administered by classroom teachers to pupils at the end of their third year in junior school. In September 1973 personality tests were given to the same children by the research team. In November/December 1973 pupils wrote imaginative and descriptive stories. In 1974, cognitive tests were re-administered and pupils' behaviours were also observed.

Analyses of data showed that with regard to the performance in reading, mixed-style teaching had the greatest gain. The differences between formal and informal styles of teaching were highly significant (approximately 3–5 months reading age). This pattern was consistent across sex and ability groups.

The formal styles of teaching showed the greatest gain on the test of mathematics; and the sex differences were slight. The low-ability boys did less well in formal classrooms on this dimension.

In English the formal style of teaching proved superior except for boys in the lowest achievement group, and for girls of English Quotient below 100.

By observing pupils' behaviour in the classroom the researchers had hoped to find an answer to the question of *why* formal teaching styles attained greater progress. A Pupil Behaviour Inventory was utilised to observe 101 pupils — 53 informal and 48 formal. They were grouped into high, medium and low achievers. Behaviour items were sorted into four categories — work activity, interaction, watching and movement. Analyses of data showed that formal pupils were engaged in more work activity. Informal pupils co-operated and talked more about work, and social interaction was higher too. Teacher interaction was highest in formal classrooms for all abilities.

Formal pupils watched their teacher more, irrespective of achievement level. The behavioural aspect of movement increased with informal classrooms and lower ability.

An analysis of samples of imaginative and descriptive writing indicated that pupils in formal and mixed-style groups were better at punctuation than pupils in informal groups (but not significantly inferior in creative and imaginative writing). On both the aspects girls were better than boys, and scores across teaching styles were very similar.

The personality inventory was meant to measure extroversion, neuroticism, conscientiousness, self-evaluation, anxiety, motivation, associability and conformity. The self concept was assessed by a semantic differential. There was little change between the two testing situations; teaching styles had little effect on changes, except for anxiety and motivation. There was no evidence of differential change in self concept across teaching styles.

Some differential gain was attributable to personality type. For reading higher gain was related to stable extroversion. Overall differences in mathematics were slight, but neurotic introverts gained least. The results in English showed few differences of type.

The 101 pupils whose classroom behaviour was observed and analysed by personality type. Pupils seemed to behave differently under different teaching styles; for example, all personality types did more actual work in formal classrooms and social interaction was more frequent in informal classrooms. The researchers concluded that teaching style had a more powerful effect on pupil progress than had pupil personality.

The link between work activity and performance suggests that, 'it is important how pupils spend their time and on what, and what content and learning experiences the teacher provides' (Bennett, 1976, p.160). The researchers, as a result of this investigation, concluded that:

> formal teaching fulfils its aims in the academic area without detriment to the social and emotional development of pupils, whereas informal teaching only partially fulfils its aims in the latter area as well as engendering comparatively poorer outcomes

in academic development.
(p.162)

This is an example of a piece of research which received considerable publicity when the findings were made available. However, the main report is an intelligible account, obviously aimed at a large audience.

There are a number of points which readers may wish to raise with regard to this study:

1 Teachers were classified by teaching styles on the basis of what they said they practiced in the classroom, rather than how they actually operated in the learning-teaching situation. Therefore, one of the criticisms directed at Bennett's study was its failure to sample teaching through systematic observation and case study of classroom practice.

2 No attempts were made by the investigators to ensure that teachers who participated in the study agreed on the precise nature and function of formal/informal teaching styles. They were simply asked whether they preferred formal or informal teaching methods.

3 Bennett's analysis of teaching assumed that a teacher characteristic such as formal-informal, direct-indirect, is a fixed attribute. It may be argued that one study could classify the same teacher as 'formal' while another classifies him/her as 'informal', depending upon the situational factor.

4 The researchers used a one-year time span to ascertain the impact of teaching styles. It would seem to be too long a gap; other variables (e.g. school organisation, parental influence) might have contributed to the significant differences in the pupils' cognitive domain.

5 The researchers took no account of cultural and religious factors in their analysis. For example, some religious cultures are academically oriented, and hence the teaching style could in some ways be irrelevant.

6 Teachers were classified on the basis of their responses to a questionnaire. Since confidentiality was not regarded as an important factor, it was difficult to ascertain whether teachers discussed the questionnaire amongst themselves and with the head.

7 The researchers had no control over assigning children or classrooms to experimental treatment. The study also failed to differentiate type of pupils. The weaknesses in the sampling procedure have been recognised by the investigators.

In view of the various limitations of the study, readers should take a careful and balanced view of its design and analyses. Furthermore, it can be argued that teaching need not be either traditional nor progressive; there is much of value to be derived from both styles in practice. There is no strong evidence to suggest that the two should not be combined in the classroom, giving a concern both for the personality of the pupil and for the stringency demanded by the need to master knowledge and skills.

3 Fifteen Thousand Hours: Secondary schools and their effects on children
by M. Rutter et al. (1979)
London
Open Books

Educational researchers, in their study of factors affecting pupil performance and behaviour at school, have for far too long concentrated on variables which are extrinsic to the school. The reasons offered for poor academic performance, for example, would be attributed to numerous factors such as poor home background, low socio-economic status, social deprivation, innate ability and so on. But what about the effect of the school itself on the pupil? For a long time it has been suggested that its effect is limited since factors such as home and social backgrounds are much more crucial i.e. if a school happens to have poor results and behaviour problems it is really due to a poor intake of pupils who have various types of social and psychological problems. However, a major study has recently appeared which considers that the role and effect of the school on the pupil is much more dynamic than was hitherto realised. Do a child's experiences at school have any effect on his future development; does the type of school make a difference; which particular characteristics of school matter most? These ideas gave rise to the study summarised in this section.

Rutter and his co-researchers (1979) in a study entitled 'Fifteen Thousand Hours' found that differences between schools in terms of academic performance, levels of attendance and behaviour could not merely be attributed to the type of pupil intake alone. Other factors were at work which were intrinsic to the school itself. The study is called 'Fifteen Thousand Hours' after the number of hours a child spends at school from the age of five to school-leaving age.

The researchers investigated a sample of twelve comprehensive schools in the inner London area — with a view to finding out why there are differences between schools in terms of various measures of their pupil's behaviour and attainments; and to discovering how schools influence children's progress. The study was evolved on the basis of earlier work carried out on ten year old children within the inner London area (Rutter et al. 1974, 1975) and on the Isle of Wight in 1970. This work revealed the possibility that schools seem to affect considerably the way children functioned. Hence the need for the present study which started in 1971. 1,487 from the original 1970 London survey were included in the total sample of 3,485 children taken from the twelve schools. This meant that fairly detailed primary school records were available for a sizeable portion of the sample — and provided an extra insight as to their progress through secondary school. How for instance, did academic attainments compare between pupils of initially similar ability who attended different secondary schools? How indeed did this apply to the total sample — and how was attendance, pupil behaviour, examination success and delinquency affected? The research team examined aspects of the school organisation, (e.g. size and resources) and other external factors and internal school practice.

Three main measures of the pupils' backgrounds were used, and the data were obtained from Inner London Education Authority records. The measures were: the pupils' scores at the age of ten in a 'verbal reasoning test', parental occupation and the pupils' scores on a behavioural questionnaire completed by their primary school teachers.

The findings were quite revealing. The schools' rates of success were considerably different on all the measures. Even when factors such as pupil ability at entry, social and home background were taken into account — there was evidence to show that the individual school could dramatically affect their pupils' achievement, attendance and behaviour. The process seems to be a causal one, e.g. what the pupil achieves or does not achieve hinges very much on the set up in a particular school. Thus pupils were found to make better progress academically, and were better behaved generally in schools which stressed academic matters. For instance, indications of this would be where the curriculum is well-planned; where teacher expectations are high and homework is set; where co-ordination is good between teachers, and a lot of preparation is put into the planning of lessions; where a sizeable proportion of teaching time is spent on the subject. Where academic matters were not stressed, and pastoral care stressed to the detriment of everything else — then pupil behaviour was observed to be worse. Marked variation between schools was noted on all the variables investigated. The effect of the school is consequently seen to be a rather pervasive one.

Rutter and his co-workers also measured day-to-day behaviour of the pupils in school and combined this data with their observations of the pupils in class. In addition, a confidential questionnaire was completed by the pupils, and this was aimed at gaining information on unobserved behaviour. The researchers concluded that schools do make a difference — and a large one. The differences between the schools were so great that the average exam score for the least able children in the most successful school was as good as that for the most able children in the least successful school.

However, these findings must be viewed within certain limitations. There are several aspects of the study which require careful interpretation: sampling, the measured differences in intake, and the observational techniques adopted. The nature of the data collected was rather limited, e.g. the data on children at the intake stage. The data on 1,487 'cohort' children (i.e. 1970 London survey pupils) involved an assessment of pupil behaviour by teachers of these pupils when they were 10. The questionnaire used was designed to detect children with possible behavioural problems in the primary school. Such a questionnaire was very much context limited and aimed to make an assessment at the age of 10. Obviously a child's behaviour is subject to change — and may influence the nature of the assessment considerably. Further assessments ought to have been made — and furthermore some indication given as to the validity of the questionnaire — for instance, the nature of its reliability coefficient. Incidentally, this teacher questionnaire on pupil behaviour was also used to assess behaviour in the secondary school — it was claimed to be equally valid but figures were not given. Assessing the behaviour of a fourteen year old pupil as opposed to a ten year old pupil may require evaluation of different features of behaviour, and what is more, teachers in the secondary school situation may assess problem behaviour by different criteria. What is considered troublesome in the secondary school situation, may not be considered as such in the primary school; furthermore, what is considered troublesome in one secondary school, i.e. a low level of tolerance of disruptive behaviour — may be accepted as the norm in another, where semi-delinquent behaviour may be quite common. As Rutter and his co-researchers mention — one teacher's action may be construed quite differently in different schools, or the same must be true for pupils action in different schools and even in different classes. So a much tighter control in the assessment of pupil behaviour is needed.

With regard to the assessment of the pupil's performance and attainment in school, in relation to the school processes, e.g. the social organisation of the school, the methods of teaching used — the data obtained is limited by the constraints of one week's observation of an average ability pupil in the third year — certain classes were followed for a week. The data obtained, although useful, should have been checked at a later stage, since this is a longitudinal study. What is also apparent is that in the researcher's observation of pupils and classes only average ability pupils were observed — which implies that not all the cohort children's classes were observed. All the schools were situated within the same city and the same authority. A cautious interpretation concerning generalisation of the sample seems necessary. However, most educational research studies are conducted within the constraints of time and resources.

Despite the various limitations of the data this study is an important contribution to the emerging body of research on schooling and teaching. It has pointed to the rather dynamic part which the school and teachers play in shaping pupils' behaviour and affecting achievement. The school can no longer be seen merely as a passive agent to outside influences — it is rather very active, creating its own sphere of influence. It raises the basic question, are schools really what they are because of the intake, or do children behave as a consequence of school influence? It is probably a mixture of both — but it is evident that schools do have a considerable degree of say in how they are organised — and teachers equally have a similar choice in their decisions on how to respond to the children they teach.

Notes

1 Department of Education and Science: Central Advisory Council for Education (1967). *Children and their Primary Schools* (Plowden Committee Primary School Report), London: HMSO.

1 as above

2 Cox, C.B. and Dyson, R.E. (Eds), Black Paper I - Fight for Education (1969); Black Paper II — The Crisis in Education (1969); Black Paper III — Goodbye Mr. Short (1970). London: The Critical Quarterly Society.

Glossary of educational research terms

The terms included in this glossary are those often encountered in educational research reports and in the literature. This glossary is intended primarily for readers with limited knowledge of conducting research in education.

Acculturation　　　The term implies a particular kind of cultural transmission; two culturally distinct groups come together in time and place.

Achievement test　　An instrument designed to measure the extent to which a student has attained certain concepts or skills in a given content area (e.g. reading or arithmetic), usually as a result of specific teaching.

Action research　　A type of research which is normally undertaken by practitioners, i.e. it calls for the researcher's involvement in the action process. For example, if the classroom teacher is involved in research activity it is probably in the area of action or decision oriented research. Thus, action research is concerned with the immediate application of the results in a specific situation.

Analysis of variance　　A statistical technique which takes the total variance of a series of tests or variables into account and analyses the aggregated variance along certain lines. This technique is useful in educational research, especially for comparing groups and at the same time allowing for the varying effect of different methods of teaching or treatments. Basically, this technique is a series of methods which allow the researcher to measure differences between scores or sets of scores.

Applied research   This type of research is often designed to solve an immediate practical educational problem. Much of the modern research on psychological issues and in education has as its objective the immediate application of its findings.

Attitude test   A test designed to assess an individual's feelings and tendencies toward action with respect to social objects, situation or people – for example, attitude toward ethnic minority groups. Attitude tests are relatively crude measuring instruments.

Audiences   An individual (e.g. teacher) or group (e.g. local education authority) that might use the research information produced by the investigator. For example, a classroom teacher might be interested in finding a more effective way of teaching his subjects, and hence he is the audience addressed by research through its findings.

Basic research   A type of research which is normally designed to extend the boundaries of existing knowledge in a particular discipline and the results may not necessarily be of immediate practical use. The findings of basic research are expected to add to our store of information.

Battery of tests   A group of tests or sub-tests arranged to be administered together that measure different aspects of the same characteristic (e.g. questionnaire and projective type personality tests). Sometimes the term is loosely used for any group of tests administered together to the same sample.

Behavioural objectives   In most educational programmes goals are stated in a way that specify what the learner will be able to do after specific instruction, i.e. the learner's changed behaviour.

Behavioural validity   A method of assessing the quality of a psychological test by direct observation of actions associated with the measurable variable. For example, in order to ascertain the validity of an attitude scale, the attitude as denoted by the test score is compared with observable behaviour in a corresponding situation.

Behaviouristic model   That conceptualisation which considers all behaviour as conforming to the principles of conditioning and learning (e.g. Skinner and Tyler).

Bias   The researcher's conscious or subconscious influence in the process of data collection, analysis and interpretation of results can distort the conclusion of an investigation. Furthermore, his biases also operate in the selection of problems for research.

Biased sample   The outcome of a sampling procedure that systematically excludes certain kinds of subjects or systematically under-represents certain kinds of subjects that should have been included in the study (c.f. random sample).

Case study   A research technique which emphasises observation, interview, description and anlaysis of a single individual or situation (e.g. a single child, group, school or research project). The case study is essentially research in depth rather than breadth.

Checklists   Tools which are used for the collection of data about events, materials or people; certain characteristics are judged to be simply present or absent rather than rated along a continuum. For example, research articles can be evaluated by using a checklist which may contain questions such as, 'Is the problem clearly stated?'

Chi-squared statistic   A statistical technique appropriate for frequency based data is called the chi-square test. The analysis determines the probability that the frequencies observed in the study differ from some theoretical hypothesised frequencies.

Class interval   The range of scores treated within one group is called 'class interval'. For example, if the researcher had to treat all scores/ values from 10 to 20 as one group, and from 21 to 30 as another group, these ranges would be called 'class intervals'.

Coefficient of correlation   A statistical measure of the degree of relationship between two sets of scores or measures for the same group of individuals. The correlation coefficient most frequently used in educational research is known as the Pearson 'r' or as the product-moment correlation. Coefficients of correlation can have values ranging from −1, (indicating inverse relationship) through 0 (showing no relationship) to +1 (positive relationship). As a general rule, the rank-order correlation coefficient is preferred when the number of cases is small, (say 15 to 20) and when there are few ties in ranks.

Comparative studies　　　　A type of research in which attempts are made to ascertain common factors or relationships among phenomena. Although studies of this type often employ statistical correlation to determine relationship, correlation is one of the ways of making comparisons.

Consumers of research　　　　Those individuals or agencies that are interested in research findings. For example, a classroom teacher may be interested in finding a more effective way of teaching, parents may like to understand their children better and a local education authority may wish to know the impact of mother-tongue teaching on pupil learning for the purposes of educational planning.

Construct validity　　　　It addresses itself to the problem of determining to what extent a test or tool measures a particular, theoretically defined aspect of the variable being considered.

Control group　　　　A group of subjects that is comparable (not necessarily identical) to the experimental group, but is not exposed to the treatment. The function of the control group is to indicate what would have happened to the experimental group if it had not been exposed to the experimental treatment.

Criteria　　　　Standards or dimensions on which a research programme, outcome or process is to be judged or evaluated.

Criterion-referenced test　　　　A type of test that attempts to assess performance in tasks on given criteria. The essential feature of criterion-referenced test is that it intends to show specifically what the person can do rather than comparing one person with others. It contrasts with a norm-referenced test.

Cross-sectional studies　　　　A method of research in which developmental trends are based upon comparisons of groups who differ in age at a given time.

'Culture-fair' tests　　　　Tests that attempt to show that the test items or questions are equally difficult or easy for all groups, regardless of race, nationality, social class or cultural background.

Deductive method of reasoning　　　　The method involves a thinking process in which one begins with the recognition of a universal law or principle and applies it to the interpretation of particular phenomena.

Degree of freedom   This refers to the number of observations or scores minus the number of parameters that are being estimated. For example, in using N sample observations to estimate the mean of the population the degrees of freedom will be N−1.

Dependent variable   The variable that is affected or influenced by the experimental treatment is called the dependent variable, that is, the outcome of the experiment. There may be more than one dependent variable in an experimental design.

Descriptive research   The type of research which is primarily concerned with the nature and degree of existing situations or conditions. Descriptive research obtains information based on empirical observation or research whose purpose is to describe rather than to judge or to interpret.

Diagnostic test   A psychological test which is used to locate specific areas of weakness and to ascertain the nature of weaknesses rather than to assess the level of attainment.

Empirical research   This type of research is based on observation, case-study, experience of factual information rather than on reason, logic or theory alone.

Empirical validity   This kind of validity provides the evidence that a test score can be interpreted in a particular way because of the relationship between the test performance and behaviour in some other activity. In other words, empirical validity is based on the correlation of the test with a suitable criterion.

Evaluative research   This term is often used in curriculum development to refer to the procedures adopted to collect and analyse data concerning the effectiveness of a particular programme. However, this type of research can range from simple appraisal of particular aspects of social practice to complex educational investigations taking several years.

Evidence   The term is often used in research to refer to findings or results which may contribute to the consideration of a particular issue.

Experimental group   The group that is exposed to a particular treatment which is being studied.

Experimental research   In this type of research the investigator seeks to determine what can happen under a given set of situations or circumstances. It is usually conducted by controlling certain conditions in which the independent variable and dependent variable operate.

Face validity   It refers to a kind of validity that is established on the basis of a subjective evaluation or intuition. For example, a measuring device or tool appears to be a good measure of whatever one is trying to measure.

Factor analysis   An analysis of the correlations among tests or test items to find out what elements or characteristics they have in common is referred to as factor analysis. There are several methods of analysing the intercorrelations among a set of test scores or test items. Factor analysis is a sophisticated statistical technique for sorting out the correlations between variables.

Frequency distribution   A frequency distribution is a quicker way of tabulating a lot of scores. It shows the number of times each score occurs in a total list of the possible scores. As a rule the largest score is placed at the top of the distribution.

Generalisation   This refers to the findings of research which can have applicability to other situations, contexts or settings. Generalisation is supposed to be a major aim of educational research.

Group test   A test that may be administered to several individuals at the same time, possibly by one administrator.

Halo effect   This refers to the tendency to be influenced by one's general evaluation of the other individual on one striking dimension (e.g. ability) and to attribute to him other characteristics arising from the evaluation of that dimension.

Histogram   A graphic representation of examination mark or score distribution in column form instead of curve form is called the histogram. The histogram is sometimes referred to as a 'frequency graph'.

Historical research   This type of research is concerned with a critical description and analysis of past events mainly for the purpose of gaining a better understanding of the present. It may include comparative and evaluative elements of research, or be partly philosophical in its approach.

Hypothesis An hypothesis is a tentative proposition which is subject to verification through subsequent investigation. It may also be seen as the guide to the researcher in that it depicts and describes the method to be followed in studying the problem. In many cases hypotheses are hunches that the researcher has about the existence of relationship between variables.

Independent variable The change or variable which the researcher systematically manipulates during the course of the experiment is called the independent variable. An educational treatment is a type of independent variable (e.g. teaching method).

Individual test A test that is designed for administration to a single person rather than to a group of individuals.

Inductive method of reasoning This method involves careful collection of elements or facts, and uses these as the basis for making generalisations.

Instrument Any technique or tool that the researcher uses to determine a value in terms of quality or quantity is called an instrument. For example, questionnaire, attitude scale, achievement test, etc.

Interview This is a method of obtaining data that involves face to face communication between the researcher and the respondent or subject.

Interview schedule A set of questions designed to elicit particular information. The questions may range from open-minded ones (e.g. semi-structured) which allow the repsondent to express himself/herself freely, to those which limit answers to predetermined categories (e.g. structured) as utilised in the public opinion survey.

Item analysis The procedures for selecting items to constitute psychological tests yielding scores which will satisfy prespecified conditions are called 'item analysis'. The term has been used loosely in the literature. However, it commonly refers to the determination of the difficulty index and discrimination index of a test item.

Lie scale A set of items, comprising part of a larger set on a questionnaire, intended to identify those respondents whose responses are unreliable because of their tendency to create a 'good' image of themselves, i.e. deliberate attempts to fake their responses to test items.

Longitudinal research   In this type of research data is directly collected on the same individuals at different points in time (e.g. longitudinal studies of children by J. Newson and E. Newson), at least on two occasions in the course of their development.

Mean (Arithmetic mean)   This usually refers to the arithmetic mean when it is used in psychology and education. It is obtained by summing all the scores in a group and by dividing the number of cases in the group. Thus, it indicates the average score obtained by a group.

Median   This term is referred to the score value in a distribution of scores which marks the midpoint of the set of data. Fifty per cent of the scores are above and fity per cent are below it.

Mode   The score or the measurement value that occurs most often in a distribution is called the mode. The mode is easy to locate in a frequency distribution because it is merely the score value that has the largest frequency.

Model   This term is used in both natural and social sciences. It indicates a close representation of certain aspects of complex phenomena designed by using objects or symbols which in some way resemble phenomena. A model is essentially an analogy which is useful in helping the researcher to think about phenomena.

N   The number of subjects in a particular study. Thus, when N equals one it is representative of a single case study.

NFER (National Foundation for Educational Research)   The NFER is an independent body which was set up in 1947. Its main function is to conduct large scale and long term educational research. It has established a journal, *Educational Research,* and a Test Service and Agency from which information about a wide variety of tests and the tests themselves can be obtained. It is supported by the DES (Department of Education and Science), LEA (Local Education Authorities) and teacher organisations.

Normal distribution   A distribution of test scores that in graphic form has a very specific bell-shaped appearance, called a normal distribution. The shape of the curve that can be drawn for these distributions is called a normal curve. The distribution has the same shape on either side of the centre point, the largest frequency of scores being located around the centre and the smaller frequencies of scores appearing at both tails of the distribution.

Norms   This refers to the levels of acceptable test performance based on response from a representative sample of a comparison group. Norms are descriptive of average, typical or mediocre performance, and should not be treated as desirable levels of attainment of specified groups.

Norm-referenced test   A type of test in which an individual's performance (cognitive or affective area) is compared with other individuals of similar age and background drawn from the same population. This is contrasted with criterion-referenced tests.

Null hypothesis   In research design it is quite common to formulate the hypothesis in a form known as the null hypothesis. This means that the researcher sets out by assuming that the 'hunch' he has is not true. In other words, there is no likelihood of the hypothesis being significant. In order to test this, he states the research hypothesis that no difference between two things is expected.

Objective test   A test in which the markers always agree on correctness or incorrectness of the responses. The correct answer to each question is predetermined and is given in the test manual, which has to be followed exactly.

Observation   A research technique which utilises direct contact between the researcher and the phenomena under investigation. The method is widely used in the study of child development (e.g. Piagetian studies). The major problem in observation is to assure that the behaviour is noted objectively and reliably.

Operational definition   In educational research many terms cannot readily be defined, and hence researchers attempt to define them according to their use which is called operational definition. An example of this way of defining is familiar to all educators, in the form of the term 'IQ'.

Parameters   The value of a particular measure (such as the mean or standard deviation) assigned to population is called a parameter.

In other words, if all scores of a defined population are available and the mean is calculated, the value obtained is a parameter of the population.

Personality assessment   A technique for the comprehensive appraisal of an individual's personality and the prediction of individual behaviour that utilises a number of standardised instruments and techniques.

Personality inventories   Methods for the measurement of personality traits or characteristics like those reflecting interests, attitudes, emotional and social adjustments. Such inventories usually consist of a large number of statements or questions, each to be answered by the subject in terms of specific categories. A total score is then obtained indicating a given trait.

Phenomenological theories   A diverse class of theories, all sharing the assumption that subjective experiences are meaningful and reliable data for understanding an individual's personality. Other approaches related to such a view are humanistic, existential and experiential.

Projective techniques   Methods intended for the measurement of personality characteristics or traits that involve the presentation of relatively unstructured stimuli to the respondent. The reason behind the use of such techniques is that deper lying tendencies in an individual are not readily ascertainable through direct methods. Projective techniques vary in the degree to which the stimuli are unstructured such as ink blots (the Rorschach test), pictures (TAT), sentence completion, etc.

Population   The term population has a specific meaning to the researcher. It refers to the larger group from which a sample is selected for study. The sample participates in research and then inferences or generalisations are made about population (also referred to as Universe). A population can be very small or very large. For example, all the people of a given class are referred to as the population of that class.

Quasi-experiment   Studies which involve non-manipulable independent variables are referred to as quasi-experiments (see Campbell and Stanley, 1966). In this type of experiment the conditions are taken as they are found in naturally occurring settings.

Random sample   A sample of the members of a given population is drawn in such a way that every member of that population has an equal chance of being selected, that is to say, the sampling technique eliminates the operation of bias in selection (c.f. biased sample).

Raw scores　　　　The original scores obtained from a test are called raw scores (c.f. converted scores).

Reliability　　　　The term is commonly used in connection with a test or examination. The procedure is also used when using observational methods in order to ascertain at least a minimum degree of confidence in the data. Reliability refers to the extent to which a test or technique functions consistently and accurately by yielding the same results.

Response sets　　　　Any tendency causing an individual to give different responses to test items than he/she would when the same content is present in a different form is known as a response set. This is part of attitudinal factors which tend to introduce bias into self-report personality inventories. One such factor is social desirability, in which a respondent tends to agree with a test item that is generally considered to express a 'good' characteristic, and tends to disagree with less desirable items or questions.

Sampling error　　　　An error which contributes to lack of representativeness of a sample. When a researcher obtains measurement results from a sample of subjects and attempts to generalise to the total population he/she may make wrong generalisations because the sample chosen for the investigation was not perfectly representative of the population.

Schools council　　　　It was founded in 1964 after an attempt by the Ministry of Education to take the initiative in curriculum reform through the formation of the Curriculum Study Group. Its aim has been the fostering of a 'new dynamic' in schools in the light of social and cultural changes.

Self　　　　The 'I' or 'me' of which the individual is aware in his/her thoughts, feelings, perceptions and actions. The self has a structure with various attributes and is subject to development and change as a result of interaction with others. The term 'self' should be distinguished from the terms 'identity', 'ego' and 'personality'. Briefly, the 'self' is just one element of the total personality of an individual.

Skewness　　　　It refers to deviation of the shape of a frequency curve from a normal curve. A skewed curve, therefore, is a frequency curve

188

that departs from the symmetrical shape either by having more cases on the right of the mean than on the left, or *vice versa*. In a skewed curve the values of the mean, median and mode are not identical.

Socialisation   The process by which socially determined factors become influential in controlling or modifying the patterns of an individual's behaviour (e.g. parental influence, schooling).

Sociogram   A diagrammatic representation of the study of the interrelation patterns existing between people is called a sociogram. Thus, the relationships between an individual child and his or her friends can be shown by the use of personal sociograms.

Sociometry   A method of investigation which allows the researcher to obtain a visual picture of the pattern of relationships between individuals in a group.

Standard deviation   In research studies the investigator also wishes to know something about how the test scores are spread out. The standard deviation is a measure of the dispersion of scores around the arithmetic mean. The more the scores cluster around the mean the smaller is the standard deviation.

Standardised test   A test that has been tried out on a representative sample before publication to ensure that there is a standard to which persons taking the test can be compared. Such a test is accompanied by a manual which contains the directions and other conditions of administration, time limits, scoring scheme, normative information, etc.

Stanford-Binet Intelligence Scale   The Stanford-Binet scale extends from the age of two years to the adult level. Most of the items are oral, but some require the subject to read, write, draw or carry out simple manipulative tasks. The latest revision of the test was done in 1960. The Stanford-Binet, like most intelligence tests, is an individual test.

Statistical significance   The term is used when researchers report 'findings' rather than opinions. It is common practice for them to use phrases like 'significant at the 1 per cent level'; 'significant at the 5 per cent level'; 'not significant' (NS). This shows the degree of certainty with which one can trust the findings. For example, the 5 per cent level of significance implies that there is a probability of 0.05 that the obtained result is due to sampling error. The best known types of significance tests which have been developed in the social sciences are the 't' tests, the chi-square tests and the F ratio tests.

Stereotype   The social perception of an individual in terms of his/her group membership rather than of his/her actual personal attributes is called stereotype. Such perceptions are often inaccurate for the person concerned, and may even be invalid for the group as a whole. However, once formed, stereotypes are difficult to change. They tend to be more rigid and less open to experience than the beliefs and attitudes one develops on his/her own.

Subjects   The individuals who are studied in an experiment are known as subjects.

Theory   In educational research the term usually implies a set of formal statements describing and explaining the relationship between human behaviour and the factors that affect or explain it. A theory can range from the simple to the complicated.

Test-retest coefficient   This type of reliability estimation is obtained by administering the same test a second time after a short interval (say, two weeks) and correlating the two sets of test scores. This method is preferred for the measurement of traits that are theoretically expected to be relatively stable and consistent over time (e.g. intellectual and aptitude characteristics).

Trait   An enduring characteristic of the individual that is manifested in a consistent way of behaving in a wide variety of situations. Traits are of many types; some are broad in scope, some narrow, some on the surface and others are deep-seated.

't' test   The 't' test provides a method by which the means of the samples can be compared when it is assumed that the samples have been randomly selected and the scores are obtained from normally distributed populations.

Treatment   The experimental condition introduced in an educational study is referred to as the treatment. A treatment is a type of independent variable, that is to say, all experimental treatments are independent variables.

True score   An individual's test score is affected by many floating variables that cannot be perfectly controlled. A true score is a hypothetical score, free of such influence.

Validity   In the field of educational measurement, validity refers to the degree to which a test, tool or technique measures what it is supposed to measure. No technique, tool or test possesses universal validity — it may be valid for use in one situation but invalid in another. Validity has different connotations for various kinds of tests, and accordingly, different kinds of validity (e.g. concurrent, predictive) are appropriate for each.

Variable   This refers to a measurable or non-measurable characteristic of a population which varies from one individual to another. Age, ability, personality characteristics are a few examples of human variables, and the researcher manipulates, controls or observes these characteristics.

Wechsler Adult Intelligence Scale (WAIS)   The 1955 scale consists of eleven sub-tests, six of which are grouped together to provide a verbal IQ, and the remaining five a non-verbal or performance IQ.

Wechsler Intelligence Scale for Children (WISC)   This scale was designed in 1949 for the 6½ to 16½ year age range. The scale provides scores on the verbal and performance tests. It consists of twelve sub-tests of which two are used as supplementary tests where time allows.

Bibliography

Ary, D., Jacobs, L.C. and Razavieh, A. (1972) *Introduction to Research in Education*, New York, Holt, Rinehart and Winston Inc.

Bagley, C. (1975) 'On the intellectual equality of races', in G.K. Verma and C. Bagley (eds) *Race and Education Across Cultures*, London, Heinemann.

Barker-Lunn, J. (1973) *Streaming in the Primary School*, Slough, England, National Foundation for Education Research.

Barnes, J.B. (1960) *Educational Research for Classroom Teachers*, New York, G.P. Putnam's Sons.

Barzun, J. and Graff, H.F. (1970) *Modern Researcher*, New York, Harcourt Brace.

Beard, R.M. (1969) *An Outline of Piaget's Developmental Psychology*, London, Routledge and Kegan Paul.

Bender, L. (1938) 'A visual motor gestalt test and its clinical use', *Research Monograph of the American Orthopsychiatric Association*, No.3.

Bennett, S.N. et al (1976) *Teaching Styles and Pupil Progress*, London, Open Books.

Best, J.W. (1970) *Research in Education*, Englewood Cliffs, New Jersey, Prentice Hall, Second Edition.

Bligh, D.A. (1974) Are varied teaching methods more effective? Unpublished PhD Thesis, University of London.

Bloom, B.S. (1966) 'Twenty-five years of educational research', *American Educational Research Journal*, No.3, 212.

Bogardus, E.S. (1970) 'Measuring social distance', in M. Fishbein (ed.) *Readings in Attitude Theory and Measurement*, New York, Wiley.

Brehaut, W. (1973) 'British research in education : some aspects of its development', in H.J. Butcher and H.B. Pont (eds) *Educational Research in Britain*, Part 3, London, University of London Press.

Bruner, J.S. (1960) *The Process of Education*, Cambridge, Mass., Harvard University Press (Vintage Books 1963).

Buckingham, B.R. (1926) *Research for Teachers*, New York, Silver, Burdette & Co.

Butcher, H.J. (1965) *Sampling in Educational Research*, Manchester University Press.

Campbell, D.T. (1957) 'Factors relevant to the validity of experiments in social settings', *Psychological Bulletin* LIV, 297–312.

Campbell, D.T. and Stanley, J.C. (1963) 'Experimental and quasi-experimental designs for research on teaching', in N.L. Gage (ed.) *Handbook of Research on Teaching*, Chicago, Rand McNally & Co.

Cattell, R.B. and Eber, H.W. (1962) *Manual for Forms A and B of the Sixteen Personality Factor Questionnaire*, Institute for Personality and Ability Testing, Champaign, Illinois.

Cattell, R.B. (1962) *Sixteen Personality Factor Questionnaire*, Champaign, Illinois, Institute of Personality and Ability Testing.

Chall, J. (1967) *Learning to Read : The Great Debate*, New York, McGraw Hill.

Chapanis, A. (1961) 'Men, machine and models', *American Psychologist,* 16, 113–31.

Child, D. (1970) *The Essentials of Factor Analysis*, London, Holt, Rinehart and Winston.

Clarke, P.A. (1972) *Action Research and Organisational Change*, London, Harper and Row.

Cohen, L., Reid, I. and Boothroyd, K. (1973) 'Validation of the Mehrabian Need for Achievement Scale with College of Education Students', *British Journal of Educational Psychology*, 43, 3, 269–77.

Corey, S.M. (1953) *Action Research to Improve School Practices*, New York, Bureau of Publications, Teachers' College, Columbia University.

Courtenay, G. (1978) 'Questionnaire construction', in G. Hoinville and R. Jowell (eds) *Survey Research Practice*, Chapter 3, London, Heinemann.

Cronbach, L.J. (1961) *Essentials of Psychological Testing*, New York, Harper and Row.

Cronbach, L.J. (1962) *Educational Psychology*, 2nd edition, New York, Harcourt Brace.

Cronbach, L.J. (1963) 'Evaluation for Course Improvement' in

R. Heath (ed.) *New Curricula*, New York, Harper and Row.

Cronbach, L.J. (1966) 'The role of the University in improving education', *Phi Delta Kappan*, 47.

Cronbach, L.J. and Suppes, P. (1969) *Research for Tomorrow's Schools: Disciplined Inquiry for Education*, New York, Macmillan.

Darley, J.G. and Haganah, T. (1955) *Vocational Interest Measurement: Theory and Practice*, Minneapolis, University of Minnesota Press.

Dennis, W. (1941) 'Infant development under conditions of restricted practice and of minimum social stimulation', *Genetic Psychology Monographs*, 23, 143–89.

Dewey, J. (1933) *How We Think*, Boston, Raytheon Education Co.

Doll, E.A. (1947) *The Vineland Social Maturity Scale*, Education Test Bureau, Princeton, New Jersey.

Douglas, J.W.B. (1967) *The Home and the School* : A study of ability and attainment in the primary school, England, Panther Books Ltd.

Douglas, J.W.B. et al (1968) *All Our Future*, London, Peter Davies.

Douglas-Savage, R. (1968) *Psychometric Assessment of the Individual Child*, Harmondsworth, Penguin Education.

Downie, N.M. and Heath, R.W. (1974) *Basic Statistical Methods*, London, Harper and Row.

Edinburgh Reading Tests – Edinburgh, Moray House College of Education, University of London Press.

Eggleston, J. (1979) 'The characteristics of educational research: mapping the domain', *British Educational Research Journal*, vol.5, No.1, 1–12.

Elliott, C. (1976) 'The measurement of development' in V.P. Varma and P. Williams (eds) *Psychology and Education*, London, Hodder and Stoughton.

Elliott, C.D., Murray, D.J. and Pearson, L.S. (1978) *British Ability Scales*, Slough, England, National Foundation for Educational Research.

Elliott, J. and Adelman, C. (1978) *Classroom Action Research*, Ford Teaching Project, Unit 2, Centre for Applied Research in Education, England, University of East Anglia.

Encyclopaedia of the Social Sciences (1934) New York, Macmillan, vol.13.

Ennis, R.H. (1975) 'Children's ability to handle Piaget's propositional logic: a conceptual critique', *Review of Educational Research*, 45, 1–14.

Esland, G. et al (1972) *The Social Organisation of Teaching and Learning*, Units 5–8 in Course E282, Bletchley, England, Open University Press.

Eysenck, H.J. and Eysenck, S.B.G. (1975) *Eysenck Personality Questionnaire (EPQ)*, Windsor, England, NFER Publishing Co.

Fisher, R.A. (1959) *Smoking: the Cancer Controversy*, Edinburgh, London, Oliver and Boyd.
Fisher, R.A. and Yates, F. (1963) *Statistical Tables for Biological, Agricultural and Medical Research*, ninth edition, London, Oliver and Boyd.
Fleishmann, E.A. (1954) 'Dimensional analysis of Psychomotor abilities', *Journal of Experimental Psychology*, 48, 437–54.
Fleishmann, E.A. (1956) 'Psychomotor selection tests: research and application in the US Air Force', *Personnel Psychology*, 9, 444–68.

Gage, N.L. (ed.) (1963) *Handbook of Research on Teaching*, Chicago, Rand McNally & Co.
Garfinkel, H. (1967) *Studies in Ethnomethodology*, Englewood Cliffs, New Jersey, Prentice Hall.
Giles, R. (1977) *The West Indian Experience in British Schools*, London, Heinemann.
Goodenough, F.L. and Harris, D.B. (1963) *Goodenough-Harris Drawing Test*, New York, Harcourt, Brace and World Inc.
Gottschaldt, K. (1926) Über den Einfluss der Erfahrung anf die Wahrnehmung von Figuren I. Über den Einfluss gehanfter Einpragung von Figuren anf ihre Sichtbarkeit in umfassenden Konfigurationen *Psychologische Forschung*, 8, 261–317.
Gowin, D.B. (1972) 'Is educational research distinctive?' in L.G. Thomas (ed.) *Philosophical Redirection of Educational Research*, Chicago, University of Chicago Press.
Gronlund, N.E. (1959) *Sociometry in the Classroom*, New York, Harper and Row.
Guga, E.G. (1969) 'Significant differences', *Educational Researcher*, 20, 3.
Guilford, J.P. (1956) *Fundamental Statistics in Psychology and Education*, New York, McGraw Hill.
Guilford, J.P. (1967) *The Nature of Human Intelligence*, New York, McGraw Hill.
Guttman, L. (1950) 'The basis for scalogram analysis', in S.A. Stouffer (ed.) *Measurement and Prediction*, Princeton, New Jersey, Princeton University Press.

Harre, R. and Secord, P.F. (1972) *The Explanation of Social Behaviour*, Oxford, Basil Blackwell.
Hartshorne, H. and May, M.A. (1929) *Studies in Service and Control*, New York, Shuttleworth.

Heath, S.R. (1942) 'Rail-walking performance as related to mental age and aetiological type among mentally retarded', *American Journal of Psychology*, 55, 240–47.

Hedges, B. (1978) 'Sampling', in G. Hoinville, R. Jowell et al *Survey Research Practice*, London, Heinemann.

Heim, A. (1970) *Manual of the AH4 Group Test of General Intelligence*, Revised Edition, Slough, England, National Foundation for Educational Research.

Helmstadter, G.C. (1970) *Research Concepts in Human Behaviour*, New York, Appleton-Century-Crofts.

Hilgard, E.R. (1954) 'A perspective on the relationship between learning theory and educational practices', in *Theories of Learning and Instruction*, E.R. Hilgard (ed.), Part I of the 63rd Yearbook of the National Society of the Study of Education. Chicago, University of Chicago Press.

Hodgkinson, H.L. (1957) 'Action Research: a critique', *The Journal of Educational Research*, 31, 137–54.

Husén, T. (1967) (ed.) *International Study of Achievement in Mathematics*, New York, John Wiley & Sons.

Jahoda, M., Deutsch, M. and Cook, S. (1951) *Research Methods in Social Relations*, New York, Holt, Rinehart and Winston.

Jones, R.M. (1972) *Fantasy and Feeling in Education*, Penguin.

Jensen, A.R. (1973) *Educability and Group Differences*, London, Methuen.

Karier, C. (1973) 'Ideology and evaluation: In quest of meritocracy', *Paper presented to the Wisconsin Conference on Education and Evaluation*, School of Education, University of Wisconsin, Madison, Wisconsin, April 26–27.

Kellmer-Pringle, L.M. (1966) *Social Learning and its Measurement*, London, Longman.

Kerlinger, F.N. (1973) *Foundations of Behavioural Research*, 2nd edition, New York, Holt, Rinehart and Winston.

Kerlinger, F.N. (1977) 'The influence of research on education practice', *Educational Researcher*, 6, 8, 5–11.

King, W.H. (1973) 'A prediction from A-level performance of University degree performance', *Physics Education*, 8(2), 106–7.

Kohlberg, L. (1964) 'Development of moral character and moral ideology', in H. Stevenson (ed.) *Child Psychology*, 62nd Yearbook, National Society for the Study of Education, University of Chicago Press.

Kohlberg, L. (1975) 'The cognitive developmental approach to moral education', *Phi Delta Kappan*, 56.

Koluchova, J. (1972) 'Severe deprivation in twins: a case study', *Journal of Child Psychology and Psychiatry*, 13, 107—14.

Koppitz, E.M. (1964) *The Bender Gestalt Test for Young Children*, New York, Grune and Stratton.

Kuder, G.F. (1956) *Kuder Preference Record* (6th edition), Illinois, Science Research Associates.

Kuder, G.F. (1956) *The Kuder Preference Record Forms C and D*, Science Research Associates.

Kuhn, T.S. (1970) *The Structure of Scientific Revolutions*, 2nd edition, International Encyclopaedia of Unified Science, enlarged, first published 1962. Chicago, The University of Chicago Press.

Lee, E.B. and Thorpe, L.P. (1956) *The Occupational Interest Inventory*, California Test Bureau.

Lehman, I.J. and Mehrens, W.A. (1971) *Educational Research: Readings in Focus*, New York, Holt, Rinehart and Winston.

Lieberman, M. (1956) *Education as a Profession*, Englewood Cliffs, New Jersey, Prentice Hall.

Likert, R.A. (1932) 'A technique for the measurement of attitudes', *Archives of Psychology*, 22, no. 140.

Lindquist, E.F. (1965) *Design and Analysis of Experiments in Psychology and Education*, Boston, Houghton-Miffin Co.

Lovegrove, M. and Poole, M. (1975) 'Groping towards tolerance: the Australian experience', in G.K. Verma and C. Bagley (eds) *Race and Education Across Cultures*, London, Heinemann.

Lovell, K. and Lawson, R.S. (1970) *Understanding Research in Education*, London, University of London Press.

Lynd, R.S. and Lynd, H.M. (1937) *Middletown in Transition*, New York, Harcourt, Brace and World Inc.

McNamara, D.R. (1979) 'Paradigm lost: Thomas Kuhn and educational research', *British Educational Research Journal*, vol.5, no.2.

Meyers, E.S., Ball, H.H. and Critchfield, M. (1973) *The Kindergarten Teachers' Handbook*, Los Angeles, Grammercy.

Moreno, J.L. (1953) *Who Shall Survive? Foundations of Sociometry, Group Psychotherapy and Sociodrama*, Beacon, New York, Beacon House.

Murray, H.A. (1943) *Thematic Apperception Test*, Cambridge, Mass., Harvard University Press (set of cards and manual).

Neale, M.D. (1966) *Analysis of Reading Ability*, 2nd edition, London, Macmillan.

Newson, J. and Newson, E. (1965) *Infant Care in an Urban Community*, Harmondsworth, Penguin Books.

Newson, J. and Newson, E. (1970) *Four Years Old in an Urban Community*, London, Allen and Unwin.

Newson, H. and Newson, E. (1978) *Seven Years Old in the Home Environment*, Harmondsworth, Penguin Books.

Nisbet, J.D. and Entwistle, N.J. (1970) *Educational Research Methods*, London, University of London Press.

Osgood, C.E. (1957) 'A behaviourist analysis', *Contemporary Approaches to Cognition*, Harvard University Press, Cambridge, Mass.

Osgood, C.E., Suci, G.J. and Tannenbaum, P.H. (1957) *The Measurement of Meaning*, Urbana, University of Illinois Press.

Page, E.B. (1975) 'Accentuate the negative', *Educational Researcher*, 5.

Parlett, M. and Hamilton, D. (1977) 'Evaluation as illumination: a new approach to the study of innovatory programmes', in Hamilton et al (eds) *Beyond the Numbers Game: A Reader in Educational Evaluation*, London, Macmillan.

Pemberton, C. (1952) 'The closure factors related to temperament', *Journal of Personality*, 21, 159–75.

Peters, R.S. and White, J.P. (1969) 'The Philosopher's contribution to educational research', *Educational Philosophy and Theory*, 1, 1–15.

Piaget, J. (1926) *The Language and Thought of the Child*, London, Routledge and Kegan Paul.

Piaget, J. (1932) *The Moral Judgement of the Child*, Glencoe, Free Press.

Pidgeon, D. and Yates, A. (1957) *Admission to Grammar Schools*, the third interim report on the allocation of primary school leavers to courses of secondary education, London, Newness.

Rasch, G. (1966) 'An individualistic approach to item analysis', in P.F. Lanarfield and N.W. Henry (eds) *Readings in Mathematical Social Science*, Chicago, Science Research Associates.

Raven, J.C. (1958) *Standard Progressive Matrices*, London, H.K. Lewis and Co. Ltd.

Remmers, H.H. (1949) 'The expanding role of research: *North Central Association Quarterly*, 23, 369–76.

Rice, J.M. (1897) 'The futility of the spelling grind', *Forum 23*, April and June 163–72, 409–19.

Rokeach, M. (1960) *The Open and Closed Mind*, New York, Basic Books Inc.

Rorschach, H. (1921-54) *The Rorschach Psychodiagnostic Plates*, New York, Grune and Stratton.

Rosenthal, R. and Jacobson, L. (1968) *Pygmalion in the Classroom*, New York, Holt, Rinehart and Winston.

Rowan, J. (1976) *Ordinary Ecstasy*, London, Routledge and Kegan Paul.

Rummel, J.F. (1964) *An Introduction to Research Procedures in Education*, 2nd edition, New York, Harper and Row.

Rusk, R.R. (1912) *Introduction to Experimental Education*, London, Longman.

Rutter, M. et al (1979) *Fifteen Thousand Hours*, London, Open Books.

Scates, D.E. (1947) 'Fifty years of objective measurement and research in education', *Journal of Education Research*, 41.

Schonell, F.J. (1942) *Backwardness in the Basic Subjects*, Edinburgh, Oliver and Boyd.

Schonell, F.J. (1955) *Analysis of Reading Ability*, 2nd edition, London, Oliver and Boyd.

Schools Council (1970) *The Humanities Curriculum Project: An Introduction*, London, Heinemann.

Schools Council (1973) *Science 5—13 Curriculum Project: With Objectives in Mind*, London, Macmillan. This project has been published as: Harlen, W. (1977) *Match and Mismatch*, Edinburgh, Oliver and Boyd.

Simon, B.S. (1978) 'Educational research: which way?' *Research Intelligence*, vol.4, no.1.

Skinner, B.F. (1959) 'A case history in scientific method', in S. Koch (ed.) *Psychology: A Study of a Science*, vol.2, New York, McGraw Hill.

Sloan, W. (1955) 'Manual for the Lincoln-Oseretsy motor development scale', *Genetic Psychology Monographs*, 51, 185—252.

Smith, I.M. (1973) A study of changes in attitudes of teaching of students attending a College of Education. (Technical) *Higher Education* 2, 361—76.

Snow, R.E. (1973) 'Theory construction for research on teaching', in R.M.W. Travers (ed.) *Second Handbook of Research on Teaching*, Chicago, Rand McNally & Co.

Solomon, R.L. (1949) 'Extension of control group design', *Psychological Bulletin*, XLVI, 137—50.

Stenhouse, L. (1975) *An Introduction to Curriculum Research and Development*, London, Heinemann.

Stott, D.H. (1963) *The Social Adjustment to Children*, Manual to the Bristol Social Adjustment Guides, London University Press, 2nd edition.

Strong, E.K. (1959) *Vocational Interest Blank for Men and Women*, California, Consulting Psychologists Press.

Taba, H. and Noel, E. (1957) *Action Research: A Case Study*, Washington DC, Association for Supervision and Curriculum

Development.

Taylor, P.H. 'Does initial training prepare teachers to understand and take part in educational research?', *Educational Research*, 166, vol.9, no.1.

Taylor, P.H. (1966) 'The role and function of educational research' – 3, *Educational Research*, 9, 11–15.

Taylor, W. (1973) 'Support for educational research and development', in Butcher, H.J. and Pont, H.B. (eds) *Educational Research in Britain*, Part 3, London, University of London Press.

Terman, L.M. (1931) 'The gifted child', in C. Murchison (ed.) *A Handbook of Child Psychology*, Worcester, Mass., Clark University Press.

Terman, L. and Merrill, M. (1960) *A Stanford-Binet Intelligence Scale*, Manual for Form L–M, 3rd revision, London, George G. Harrap & Co.

Terman, L. and Oden, M.H. (1959) *The Gifted Group at Mid-Life* Stanford, Stanford University Press.

Thigpen, C.H. and Cleckley, H. (1953) 'A case of multiple personality', *Journal of Abnormal and Social Psychology*, 49, 135–51.

Thorndike, E.L. (1914) An address at the First Annual Conference on 'Educational Measurement', Indiana University *Bulletin of Extension Division*, 12, Indiana University.

Thorndike, E.L. (1918) 'The nature, purpose and general methods of measurement of educational products', *Seventeenth Yearbook of the National Society for the Study of Education*, Part II. *The Measurement of Educational Products*, Bloomington, Illinois, Public School Publishing Company.

Thorndike, E.L. (1924) 'Mental discipline in high school subjects', *Journal of Educational Psychology*, 15, 1–22, 83–98.

Thorndike, R.L. (1968) 'Review of Rosenthal and Jacobson, Pygmalion in the classroom', *American Educational Research Journal*, 5, 708–11.

Thouless, R.H. (1969) *Map of Educational Research*, Slough, England, National Foundation for Educational Research.

Thurstone, L.L. and Chave, E.J. (1929) *The Measurement of Attitude*, Chicago, University of Chicago Press.

Townsend, H.E.R. (1971) *Immigrant Pupils in England*, Slough, England, National Foundation for Educational Research.

Travers, R.M.W. (1977) *Essentials of Learning*, New York, Macmillan, 4th edition.

Travers, R.M.W. (1978) *An Introduction to Educational Research*, New York, Macmillan Co. Inc., 4th edition.

Traxler, A.E. (1954) 'Some comments on educational research at mid-century', *The Journal of Educational Research*, 47, 359–66.

Tyler, R.W. (1949) *Basic Principles of Curriculum and Instruction*, Chicago, University of Chicago Press.

Tyler, R.W. (1978) 'How schools utilise educational research and development', in R. Glaser (ed.) *Research and Development and School Change*, New Jersey, Lawrence Erlbaum Associates.

Van Dalen, D.B. (1966) *Understanding Educational Research*, New York, McGraw Hill.

Verma, G.K. (1973) 'A use of Thematic Apperception to assess achievement motivation', *Japanese Psychological Research*, vol. 15, no.1.

Verma, G.K. (1977) 'Some effects of curriculum innovation on the racial attitudes of adolescents', *International Journal of Intercultural Relations*, vol. 1, no.3, 67–68.

Verma, G.K. (1979) 'Attitude measurement in a multi-ethnic society', *Bulletin of the British Psychological Society*, 32, 460–2.

Verma, G.K. (1980) *The Impact of Innovation*, Evaluation of humanities curriculum project, England, CARE, University of East Anglia Press.

Verma, G.K. and Humble, S. (1979) 'Sampling in curriculum evaluation: some problems in practice', *Indian Educational Review*, vol. XIV, no.2.

Verma, G.K. and Mallick, K. (1981) 'Tests and testing in a multi-ethnic society', in G.K. Verma and C. Bagley (eds) *Self-concept, Achievement and Multicultural Education*, London, Macmillan.

Vernon, P.E. (1961) *Intelligence and Attainment Tests*, London, University of London Press.

Vernon, P.E. (1964) *Personality Assessment*, London, Methuen.

Vernon, P.E. (1969) *Intelligence and Cultural Environment*, London, Methuen.

Walton, J. and Kuethe, J.L. (eds) (1963) *The Discipline of Education* Madison, The University of Wisconsin Press.

Ward, A.W., Hall, B.W. and Schramm, C.F. (1975) 'Evaluation of published educational research: A national survey', *American Educational Research Journal*, 12:2, 109–28.

Watson, F. (1953) *Research in the Physical Sciences*, Phi Delta Kappan.

Wechsler, D. (1974) *Wechsler Intelligence Scale for Children (WISC)*, New York, Psychological Corporation.

West, D.J. (1969) *Present Conduct and Future Delinquency*, London, Heinemann.

Wheeler, D.K. (1967) *Curriculum Press*, London, University of London Press.

Wise, J.E., Nordberg, R.B. and Reitz, D.J. (1967) *Methods of Research in Education*, Boston, D.C. Heath & Co.

Witkin, H.A. et al (1954) *Personality through Perception*, New York, Harper.

Wood, D. (1978) 'Interviewing', in G. Hoinville, R. Jowell et al (eds) *Survey Research Practice*, chapter 5, London, Heinemann.

Woodworth, R.S. (1917) *Personal Data Sheet*, Chicago, C.H. Stoelting.

Wrigley, J. (1976) Social Science Research Council Newsletter, October, quoted by B.S. Simon (1978) 'Educational research: which way?', *Research Intelligence*, vol.4, no.1.

Yates, A. (1971) (ed.) *The Role of Research in Educational Change*, Palo Alto, Pacific Books.

Young, P.V. (1966) *Scientific Social Surveys and Research*, Englewood Cliffs, New Jersey, Prentice Hall Inc.

Index

Action research 38
American Educational Research Assocation (AERA) 45
An Outline of Piaget's Developmental Psychology 52
Analysis 29
Analysis data 171
Anthropology, influence of 27
Applied research 19
Aristotle 4
Arithmetic 98
Ary, Jacobs and Razavieh (1972) 27
Attitude scales: enacted attitudes 110
Australia: attitudes to immigrants 112

Bacon, Francis 5
Bader Gestalt test 107
Bagley (1975) 32
Barker Lunn (1970) 165
Barnes (1960) 45, 54

Beard (1969) 52
Bennett et al. (1976) 170
Best (1970) 10, 17
Binet and Simon, intelligence scale 46, 95
Binomial distributions 117
Black Papers 170
Bligh (1974) 99
Bloom (1966) 24, 32, 153
Bogardus (1970) 112
Brehaut (1973) 47
British Ability Scales 96
British Educational Research Journal 158
British Journal of Teacher Education 158
British Psychological Society 46
'British Research in Education' 47
Bristol Social Adjustment Guide 104
Buckingham (1926) 46
Butcher (1965) 93

Campbell (1957) 76
Campbell and Stanley (1963) 70, 76
Carnegie Corporation 61
Cattell (1890) 46
Cause-effect relationships 4
Chall (1967) 60
Chapanis (1961) 13
Chi-square test 138
Child (1970) 151
Clarke (1972) 25
Classification of educational research 35
Coefficients of correlation 149
Cognitive ability tests 94-6
Cohen, Reid and Boothroyd (1973) 101
Computer assisted learning (CAL) 155
Computer technology 35
Construct 12-13
Consumer oriented research 38
Corey (1953) 20, 26, 39, 160
Correlations, Stanford University 102
Courtenay (1970) 113
Cronbach (1961) 101, 105; (1962) 22, 27; (1963) 38
Cronbach and Suppes (1969) 39
Curriculum: construction 23, 48; development 25; reform movement 153

Data collection 10, 11, 18, 29, 70; analysis 171; questioned 23; statistical methods 31; tools and techniques 86
Deductive reasoning 4, 5
Definitions 17, 26-7
Delinquency 64
Dennis (1941) 32
Department of Education and Science 60, 124, 157, 165

Design and Analysis of Experiments in Psychology and Education 136
Design research 70, 78
Developmental studies 61
Dewey (1933) 7
Differential Aptitude Test (USA) 97
Direct observation 5
Distribution 141
Doll (1947) 104
Douglas (1964, 1968) 24; (1967) 63
Douglas-Savage (1968) 107
Downie and Heath (1974) 151

Edinburgh Reading Tests 97
Educability and Group Differences 32
Educational psychologist 2, 5
Educational research 22-40, 43-6, 164-77; British contribution 27; classification 35-40; common element 27; curriculum development 25; defining objectives 23; definitions 26-7; disciplines involved 24; evaluation 33; examples 164-77; finance 24; gifted children 45; introduction of statistical methods 43; methodological advances 24; nature 23-6; operational strategies 28-30; organisational change 25; 'paradigm' 25; principles and methods 31; problems 30-3; teacher's role 152-6; use of tests 46
See also Research; Statistical concepts
Educator/researcher 159
Eggleston (1979) 25, 162
Elimination of Pupils from School 43

Elliot and Adelman (1978) 25, 96
Elliott (1976) 127
Empiricists 11
'Engineering Model' 48
Ennis (1975) 49
Esland (1972) 25
Essay on Population 6
Essentials of Psychological Testing (1961) 98
Evaluation 33-5
Evaluation research 38-9; defined 38; evaluation studies 38
Evidence, distortion of 4
Expected frequencies 116
Experimental methods 67-84; research 67
Experimental design types 78-84
Experimental Design 136
Extraneous variables 67
Eysenck Scale (1975) 99

F-distribution 133
Factorial design 81
Field dependence 108
Finance 24, 33
Fisher (1959) 149
Fisher and Yates (1963) 91
Fleishmann (1954), (1956) 109
Free Writing assessment 166
Freud 11

Gage (1963) 160
Galton (1886) 43
'Garfinkel' 110
General Aptitude Test (USA) 97
General Aptitude Test Battery (GATB) 109
Getzel (1978) 160
Gifted children studies 45
Giles (1977) 33
Goodenough Draw-a-Man Test 96
Gottschaldt tests (1926) 108

Gowin (1972) 22
Graff (1970) 55
Group interactions 106
Guildford (1956) 150, 151; (1967) 50
Guttman (1950) 110

Hartshorne and May (1929) 106
Heath (1942) 107
Hedges (1978) 93
Heim, A. 44; test 95
Helmstatder (1970) 39
Hereditary Genius 43
Hilgard (1954) 37
Historical developments 42-7; quantitative methods 42
Human behaviour: theoretical terms 11, 16
Human subject 32, 43
Husen (1967) 61
Hypothesis 9, 29; Kerlinger (1973) 9

I.Q. 94
Immigrants: attitudes to in Australia 112; pupils 60
Independent variable 67
Inductive method 5
Intelligence and Attainment Tests (1961) 98
Intelligence Quotient 121
Intelligence tests 44, 46, 88, 94, 121
Internal and external validity: internal instrumentation 77
International Study of Achievement in Mathematics 61
Interviews 113
Introduction to the Theory of Mental and Social Measurements 43
Inventories 101
Item analysis techniques 90

Jahoda, Deutsch and Cook (1951) 59
Jensen (1973) 32
Jones (1972) 49

Karier (1973) 45
Kellmer Pringle (1966) 104-5
Kerlinger (1973) 9; (1977) 37, 73
Khun (1970) 3, 25
Kinsey Report 114
Kohlberg (1964, 1975) 50
Koluchova (1972) 62
Kuder (1956) 102

Law of effect and reinforcement 44, 47
Lee and Thorpe (1956) 101
Libermann (1956) 159
Likert (1932) 110
Lincoln Oretsky, Motor Development Scale 107
Lindquist (1965) 73
Local Education Authorities (LEA) 157, 170
Logic 4
Longitudinal research 63, 176
Lovegrove and Poole (1975) 112
Lovell and Lawson (1970) 26
Lynd and Lynd (1937) 59

McNamara (1979) 25
Malthus, Thomas 6
Man: a course of study (MACOS) Curriculum Project 49
Map of Educational Research 27
Matching process 72
Mathematics, achievement in 61
Mathematics and Science 49
Median Test 143
Mehrabian Need for Achievement Scale 101
'Mental ages' 121

Mental Measurements Year Book 46
Mental Tests and Measurements 46
Merrill, Terence 121
Methods of educational research 2, 6, 53-84
    descriptive 57-66; case studies 61; comparative studies 65; developmental studies 61; ex post facto design 65; research workers' plans 58; types 59
    experimental 67-84; analysis of covariance (ANCOVA) 73; control groups 71; critics 67; essential steps 68; experimental design types 78-84; matching 72; randomisation 72; repeated measures 73; settings 68; terms 70; treatment 73; variables 67, 74, 75, 76-8
    historical 53-7; internal and external validity 75
Meyers, Ball and Critchfield (1973) 94
Middleton in Transition 59
Model 13
Moreno (1953) 106
Motor development scale 107
Motor and perceptual tests 106, 109
Multiple regression equation 151

National Association of Directors of Educational Research 45
National Foundation for Educational Research (NFER) 60, 124, 165
Natural science: social science, distinction between 14-16; theatrical ideas 11

Neale Analysis of Reading Ability 98
New Community 158
New Society 158
Newson and Newson (1965, 1970, 1978) 63
Nisbet and Entwistle (1970) 27
Non-parametric Statistics for Behavioural Sciences 143
Nuffield Projects 49

Observational techniques 104; halo effect 104
Operational strategies 28-30; choosing design 29; conclusions 29, 30; data collection and analysis 29; hypotheses 29; identifying problems 28
Orientation tests 108
Organisational change 25
Osgood et al. (1957) 112

Page (1975) 24
'Paradigm' 25
Pascal's triangle 118
Parlett and Hamilton (1977) 25
Pemberton (1952) 108
Perfect induction 6
Personal experience 3; Van Dalen (1966) 4
Personality traits scale 99
Peters and White (1969) 27
Phenomena: direct observation 5; educational 23
Pidgeon and Yates (1957) 24
Piaget (1926, 1932) 7, 48, 52
Plowden Report 165, 170
Primary school 165
Probabilities 117
Probability proportionate 93
Problems 30-3
Product moment correlation 149
Projective techniques 102
Proportional stratification 92

Psychological research 4
Psychological tests 46, 93-114; attitude scales 110; cognitive ability 94-6; criterion referenced 97; guess-who techniques 106; interviews 113; inventories 101; motor and perceptual tests 106; observational techniques 104; projective techniques 102; questionnaires 113; schedules 104; semantic difference 112; social distance scale 112; sociometric techniques 106; tests of achievement, aptitude and proficiency 96; time sampling 105
Psychology's influence 27
Psychometric measurement 45
Psychomotor abilities: major factors 109
Pupil Behaviour Inventory 172
Pupils 105, 168

Questionnaires 113

Race relations 75
Rasch (1966) 126; model 96
Rationalists 96
Raven's Matrices 96
Remmer (1949) 32
Research 16-18; action 20; applied or field 19; characteristics 18; evaluation 21; methods 7-11; modern 47-50; scope 18; types 18-21; unpure or basic 19
See also Educational research
Research findings: reporting on 30
Research programmes: exploration work 8
Researcher: principles and methods 31

Review of Educational Research
  46
Rice (1897) 43
Rokeach test 101
Rorschach test 103
Rowan (1976) 38
Rummel (1964) 7, 36
Rusk (1912) 46
Rutter (1979) 174

Sampling 91-3
Scates (1947) 42
Schonnell (1942) 98
Schools Council's Humanities
  Curriculum Project (Verma
  1980) 59
Science 5-13 Curriculum Project
  (Schools Council) (1973) 49
Scientific research measurement
  7
Scottish Council for Research in
  Eduction 46, 124
Secondary schools 174; selection
  24
Siegel, S. 143
Simon (1978) 22, 155
Skinner, F. 44, 47, 48 (1959) 11
Sloan (1955) 107
Snow (1973) 10
Social distance scale 112
Social science 2, 3, 14-16;
  theoretical ideas 11
Social surveys 31
Sociology's influence 27
Sociometric techniques 106
Spearman-Brown formula 86
Standardised tests 91
Stanford-Binet intelligence tests
  45, 88
Stanford University correlations
  for students 102

Statistical concepts 115-50;
  correlation regression: con-
    tingency table 146-51;
    correlation coefficients
    149-50; parallel forms
    148; scatter diagram 148;
  expected frequencies 116;
  item difficulty 126; item dis-
    crimination 126; Median Test
    143;
  normal distribution and the
    normal curve 117-124;
    Intelligence Quotient 121;
    mean and standard deri-
    vation 119; mental age
    121;
  other theoretical distributions
    133-40; F-distribution
    133; Later square 138;
    skewed 141
  probabilities 117;
  sample from a population 127
    best estimate of the popu-
    lation standard deviation
    129; degrees of freedom
    131; null hypothesis 131;
    standard error of the mean
    129
Signs Test 143
Statistical methods 36; intro-
  duction 43; race relations 75;
  statistical inference 43
Stenhouse (1975) 33
Stone Arithmetic Test 43
Stott (1963) 104
Strong's Vocational Interest
  Blank 101
Streaming in the Primary School
  165-9
Structure of Scientific Revolu-
  tions 3

Syllogism 5
Systematic sampling 92

Taylor (1966) 22; (1973) 46
Teacher and educational research 152-9; consumer and producer of research 159; effect on pupils 168; role conflict 161; role of researcher 159
Teaching Styles and Pupil Progress 170
Term evaluation research 38
Terman (1931) 45
Terman-Merrill revision 88
Terman and Oden (1959) 63
Tests of achievement, aptitude and proficiency 96
Thematic Apperception Test (TAT) 103
Theory: definitions 10; empiricists 11; Freud 11; rationalists 10; role of theory 10-12; why 11
Theory of Mental and Social Measurements 43
Thigpen and Cleckley (1953) 113
Thorndike (1914) 45; (1918) 7, 42; (1924) 67
Thorndike Handwriting Scale 43
Thouless (1966) 157; (1969) 25, 27
Thurstone (1929) 110
Times, The 132
Tools and techniques for collecting data 86-93; reliability 86; sampling 91; standardised tests 91; validity 88-9
Townsend (1971) 60
Travers (1978) 10, 26, 37, 44, 54, 154
Traxler (1954) 154; (1978) 26

Tyler (1949) 23; (1978) 158, 161

United States of America 23, 45, 48, 91; American Educational Research Association (AERA) 45; aptitude tests 97; psychological tests 94; US Air Force tests 109; US Employment Servicemen (USES) 109

Van Dalen (1966) 4, 9, 23, 37, 160
Variables 74-8
Verma (1969) 88; (1973) 103; (1977) 38; (1980) 20, 25, 29, 38, 59, 103
Verma and Humble (1979) 93
Verma and Mallick (1980) 96
Vernon (1964) 101
Vernon tests 98
Vineland Social Maturity Scale 104
Vocational Guidance Centres 101

Ward, Hall and Schramm (1975) 24, 152
Watson (1953) 26
Weschler Intelligence Scale for Children (WISC) 94
West (1969) 64
Wheeler (1967) 25
Wise, Nordberg and Reitz (1967) 16
Witkin (1954) 108
Wood (1978) 114
Woodworth Psychoneurotic Inventory 101
Wrigley (1976) 40, 158
Wundt, W. 42

Yates (1971) 154
Young (1966) 59, 62

WHAT IS EDUCATIONAL RESEARCH?

What is Educational Research?

Perspectives on Techniques of Research

GAJENDRA K. VERMA
RUTH M. BEARD

University of Bradford

Gower

Published by

Gower Publishing Company Limited,
Gower House,   Croft Road,
Aldershot, Hants, GU11 3HR

British Library Cataloguing in Publication Data

Verma, Gajendra K.
    What is educational research?
    1. Educational research
    I. Title   II. Beard, Ruth M.
    370'.7'8   LB1028
    ISBN 0-566-00323-6
    ISBN 0-566-00429-1 Pbk

Printed and bound in Great Britain by
Biddles Ltd, Guildford and King's Lynn